# Jewish Prince in Moslem Spain

# Jewish Prince in Moslem Spain:

# Selected Poems of Samuel Ibn Nagrela

Introduction, Translation,
and Notes by Leon J. Weinberger

THE UNIVERSITY OF ALABAMA PRESS

*Tuscaloosa*

Copyright © 1973
The University of Alabama Press
Tuscaloosa, Alabama 35487-0380
All rights reserved
Manufactured in the United States of America

∞
The paper on which this book is printed meets the minimum requirements of American National Standard for Information Science—Permanence of Paper for Printed Library Materials, ANSI Z39.48-1984.

Library of Congress Cataloging-in-Publication Data

Samuel, ha-Nagid, 993–1056.
Jewish prince in moslem Spain: selected poems of Samuel Ibn Nagrela / introduction,
translation, and notes by Leon J. Weinberger.
p. cm. — (Judaic studies series)
Includes bibliographical references.
Text of poems in English and vocalized Hebrew.
ISBN-13: 978-0-8173-5280-6 (pbk. : alk. paper)
ISBN-10: 0-8173-5280-5
I. Weinberger, Leon J. II. Title. III. Series

PJ5050.S3A28 2005
892.4'12—dc22

2005050620

In memory
of my loved ones
who perished
in the Holocaust 1941–3

Genia and Isaac Goldberg
and their son Simha
Chava and Monek Schiller
Miriam and Julek Birman

2 SAMUEL 1:23

לזכר
נשמות אהובי
שנספו
בשואת תשא-ג
גניה ויצחק גלדברג
ובנם שמחה
חוה ומונק שילר
מרים ויולק בירמן

הנאהבים
והנעימים בחייהם
ובמותם לא נפרדו

# Preface

In the 1920's H. Brody and I. Davidson edited collections of selected Hebrew poetic works with English translations from three of the leading figures of the Spanish "Golden Age"—Solomon Ibn Gabirol, Moses Ibn Ezra, and Judah ha-Levi. The Hebrew poetry of the other two luminaries of that period, Samuel Ibn Nagrela and Abraham Ibn Ezra, have as yet not been given a comparable introduction to the English reader, a task which this work intends, in part, to carry out. The Hebrew text of Ibn Nagrela's poetry accompanying the English translation is presented through the courtesy of the Bialik-Dvir Publishing Company.

In the translations I have relied on the Hebrew texts of Ibn Nagrela as presented by J. Schirmann, D. Yarden, and S. Abramson as well as in the Brody-Wiener collection. I am deeply grateful to Professor Schirmann for allowing me to reproduce the Hebrew text from his *Hebrew Poetry in Spain and the Provence* (in Hebrew) as well as for his kindness and encouragement over the years. My thanks are herein expressed to Professors Nahum Glatzer, A. M. Habermann, and Saul Lieberman for their help and advice and to Dr. Morgan Walters, Director of The University of Alabama Press, and his staff for their thoughtfulness and consideration.

To my good wife Estelle and patient children Gary, David, and Lisa, much love.

August 8, 1973 LEON J. WEINBERGER

# CONTENTS

# INTRODUCTION

Samuel ben Joseph ha-Levi Ibn Nagrela was one of the most versatile figures in all of Jewish history. For the influential 12th century historian Abraham Ibn Daud, Samuel not only earned, "four crowns: the crown of Torah, the crown of power, the crown of a Levite, and the crown of a good name" but was the model Jew and ideal leader.[1] At his death in 1056, he was mourned by almost the entire Jewish world from Spain to the Maghreb, from Egypt to Sicily to the Holy Land and as far as Babylonia. Even the Arab historian, Ibn Ḥayyan a younger contemporary, grudgingly admits that "this accursed Jew was in himself one of the most perfect men, although God had denied him his guidance. He excelled in learning, endurance, intelligence and wit, charm of character, perseverance, astuteness, cunning, self-control, and natural courtesy. He knew how to act according to the requirements of the moment, how to flatter his enemies and remove suspicion from their heart by his fine manners. What an uncommon man!"[2]

He was born in the Cordova of Al-Andalus in the year 993 and received from his early youth an exceptionally good education in the arts and sciences of his day. He had fond memories of his parents and happy childhood and is especially attached to his older brother Isaac at whose death he will write a series of moving elegies.[3] Samuel too would be a devoted father, taking time out even on the battlefield to send his son Joseph some choice books with which to improve his education[4] or relax in his company to drink wine and exchange pleasantries in the privacy of a quiet alcove.[5]

To understand the multi-faceted character of Samuel Ibn Nagrela it is important to remember that his parents lived originally in the ancient city of Merida. According to a tradition preserved by the historian Abraham Ibn Daud, the members of the Jewish community of Merida were exiled to Spain by Titus, at the request of one of his lieutenants in charge of the region who asked that he be sent "some of the nobles of Jerusalem."[6] Samuel saw himself as a direct descendant of this select group called to rule the Jewish community in Spain. "I am the David of my age," he writes;[7] while from his opponent the Arab theologian and historian Ibn Ḥazm we learn that Ibn Nagrela interprets the Messiah-announcing verse, "until Shiloh come" (Gen. 49:10), as applying to himself.[8]

Throughout his life Samuel will conduct himself with remarkable self-confidence and assurance, being as much at home in the Alhambra as in the synagogue. He is singularly free from fear and one would never imagine that he is after all living in exile in a predominantly

Moslem world. Who else would dare launch a frontal attack on the Qur'an and criticize its inconsistencies in a way hitherto unknown? [9] To be sure this was in line with Samuel's self-image as protector and defender of the Jewish people against all its enemies.

In this Samuel is thoroughly consistent. For not only does he challenge the pretensions of Islam and vigorously takes up the battle against the Qaraites, a Jewish sectarian group in Spain; [10] but he is equally vehement in denouncing those would-be-orthodox Jewish teachers who debase the words of the Rabbinic sages.[11] From his political base of power as vizier of King Badis of Granada he pictures himself as a latter-day Mordecai who in the battle of Alfuente defeats the Slav Zuhair, prince of Almeria, the modern "'Agag" whose desire is to eliminate "the Lord's congregation, remnant and offspring." [12] At other times as in the battle against Seville in the fall of 1039 he succeeds in saving the Jewish community in Granada, "a city and mother in Israel" which the enemy planned to annihilate.[13]

Moreover he directs that the victory at Alfuente be celebrated in Jewish congregations as a "second Purim" and the poem (Shira) which he composes for the occasion be recited as a part of the synagogue liturgy and "remembered from generation to generation." [14] Later he will write yet another song of praise (Tehilla) "for the redeemed" of Granada on the fall of Isma'il 'Ibn 'Abbad commander of the Sevillan armies and instruct that it too be set "in the mouths of old and young." [15]

From his early youth Samuel senses that he is under divine protection. In a revealing poem he recalls the promise made to him in a dream by the angels Michael and Gabriel:

"This is the word of God who pleads your cause:
Whenever you pass over dangerous waters, I will be with you.
Rivers will not drown you on the day that your foe approaches. . .
When you walk through fire you shall not be burned.
I shall speak to the flame that it never kindle upon you." [16]

It is this promise which sustains him throughout his life and he refers to it when beset by peril[17] or invokes the divine name YHWH in his plea for help as in the battle against 'Ibn 'Abbad,[18] probably the most dangerous campaign of his early military career.[19] From his writings it would appear that Samuel never doubted that he was designated by God for greatness. Although he lost his fortune after fleeing Cordova in 1013 when the city was over-run by the Berber invasion, he would recall more than thirty years later as the powerful vizier of Granada how far he had come since those early days:

"Do you remember the mountain pass of sand which I crossed
alone while fleeing from you and afraid?
Even today I am in transit,—but behind me are tens of
thousands who obey me like their fathers." [20]

After settling in Granada, he moves from one success to another. First he is appointed vizier and *katib* (secretary) to King Ḥabbus of Granada[21] and upon the latter's death he wisely chooses to side with Badis, the king's older son, who emerges victorious in his struggle for the throne against the younger brother Buluggin. After being rewarded by Badis and retained in his high post, he manages to survive the numerous intrigues of the Granada court designed to depose both him and his ruler. One such event Samuel recounts with particular vividness. It is the revolt of Yadair, cousin of Badis and his attempt to seize the throne of Granada in 1041 some three or four years after the latter was installed as king: [22]

"This foe was kin to my king and the treachery of a stranger
Is less painful than that of a friend." [23]

At best, life at the Granada court was charged with an almost continuous vying for power and influence among the king's subordinates. As the lone Jew in high position standing above Moslems, Berbers, and Slavs, Samuel was particularly vulnerable and his writings reflect the tensions which he must have endured in the service of the king:

"A monarch will not favor you unless he hopes to be
At ease while you labor and exert yourself in his service.
You are caught in his tongs: With one hand he brings you into
The flames,—while protecting you from the fire which with both hands he sets against you." [24]

However Samuel continues to live dangerously in this way, motivated in part by personal ambition:

"Can one restrain himself whose soul is pure and who like the moon labors to rise?
Can one remain still until with her wings he girds his loins like a man strengthening a tent-cloth;
Until he achieves and his feats are made known, and he continues to increase in reputation like the sea?" [25]

as well as from a sense of mission and responsibility to his people:

"He contends with me for my consorting with kings.
I reply to him: This is a portion of my inheritance and my lot." [26]

There is also in Samuel's character what J. Schirmann calls "the temperament of a gambler and adventurer." [27] This, and a fatalism that was typical of the contemporary culture,[28] would account for the kind of life he led.

## A. THE ANDALUSIAN WORLD OF SAMUEL IBN NAGRELA

It was a period of transition between the decline and eventual disappearance from al-Andalus of the Ummayad dynasty after the death of al-Mansur in August 1002 and the ultimate reconquest of Spain by the Christian monarchs with the fall of Seville to Ferdinand III in November 1248. In the interim the historian is able to discern three stages. In the first there is the division of al-Andalus into a number of small states dominated by Arab, Berber, and Slav factions. Of the five dynasties that vied for control of the region—including the Aftasids of Badajoz, the Ḥudids of Saragossa, the Dhu-'l-Nunids of Toledo, the Abbadids of Seville and the Zirids of Granada—the struggle was fiercest among the latter two particularly during the reigns of 'Abbad b. Abu'l-Qasim Muhammad al-Mu'tadid of Seville (1042–1069) and Badis b. Ḥabbus of Granada (1038–1073). The second and third stages were marked by the invasion and occupation of the area by the Berber Almoravids and Almohads respectively.[29] Our concern will be mainly with the first stage since therein falls the life and activity of Samuel Ibn Nagrela.

At this time the population of Moslem Spain comprised the three factions mentioned above as well as considerable numbers of Jews and Christians in addition to Negroes brought in from the Sudan in the slave trade. The former two minority groups were under the protection and control of the Moslem central authorities to whom they paid taxes, being in fact known as the "tributaries" (mu'ahidun). Their status was that of the *dhimmi*, which although never clearly defined in Moslem law allowed them to enjoy a measure of toleration and protection as "people of the book" and placed them somewhere between the dar-al-Islam—the community of true believers—and the dar-al-ḥarb, the world of unbelievers who were to be converted to Islam by force if need be.[30] As *dhimmis*, they were autonomous to the extent that one of their own served as administrative head of the institutions in the community and collected its taxes for the Moslem state. This was apparently Samuel Ibn Nagrela's responsibility in Granada, in consequence of which he is known as the *Nagid*—a term comparable to the Arabic "Ra'is al-yahud" and used to designate the leader of the Jewish community.[30]

The Jewish population which at this time was concentrated in the cities of Granada, Lucena, Seville, and Tarragona included some with-holdings of large estates and in some cases of entire villages. In his studies from the Geniza documents S. D. Goitein suggests that there were five different social levels in the Jewish community of this period. These included (a) the upper class, (b) the upper middle class comprising the business men and professionals, (c) the lower middle class consisting of the above two groupings plus the master artisans, (d) urban craftsmen and laborers, and (e) the peasants called "beggars."[32] From the Geniza materials it appears that the Mediterranean area at this time was a flourishing free-trade community with almost unrestricted freedom of movement. Jewish merchants in Spain actively participated in the commercial life of the region, dealing in such items as silk, sugar, olives, pottery, and corkwood. However, the largest percentage of the Jewish population at this time was engaged in agriculture of various forms, in manufacture, and handicraft.[33]

In 11th-century Andalusia the upper class comprised men with the following qualifications:

- descent from an old and distinguished family preferably that of Merida; [34]
- thorough familiarity with classical Hebrew, Aramaic, and Arabic literature, Rabbinic studies, and "Greek wisdom"; [35]
- influence at the court of the ruling monarch; and
- philanthropic activity and patronage of the arts, service to the Jewish community and proper piety and humility. The company also included the distinguished poets, philosophers, and scientists of the day who were called upon to enliven the frequent parties held in the courtly homes of its members and—in the case of the poets—to properly flatter their patrons.[36]

Samuel Ibn Nagrela was a member of the highest standing in the upper class. One might even say that he set the standards for the class as a whole. He had, as mentioned above,[37] the best of pedigree, and his family ranked alongside that of the Ibn Albalia, Ibn Megash, Ibn Ezra, Ibn Muhajir, and Ibn Falija as the most prominent in Moslem Spain.[38] Frequently we hear him boast of his Levitic ancestry:

"Mine is the heritage from Merari . . .
From my forbear Yedutun the musician of praises
I learned to glorify (God) and I am worthy of him." [39]

The Nagid's mastery of classical Hebrew is abundantly evident in those of his poetic writings wherein he pioneers the use of the new Arabic meters that he, more than anyone else, is responsible for introducing into Hebrew poetry. In fact he is credited with using a greater variety of metric forms in his verses than any of his illustrious contemporaries, even including Solomon Ibn Gabirol, Judah ha Levi, and Moses Ibn Ezra.[40] His full competence in the language is further seen in the way he extends the range of poetic themes and moods to include for the first time the description of military campaigns as well as his unique treatment of narrative and epic forms.[41] It is likely that his skill in composing in Aramaic and Arabic was at least equal to that of his Hebrew works judging even from the little material that survives. He was equally at home in the intricacies of Hebrew grammar—a lively topic for discussion and debate in his time—and his writings on the subject were called "second to none in excellence" by as astute a critic as Abraham Ibn Ezra.[42]

In Rabbinic studies the Nagid is considered as one of the three leading authorities of his age. The other two who are well-known to us through their commentaries on the Talmud were R. Ḥananel b. Ḥushiel and R. Nissim b. Jacob Ibn Shahin of Qairawan.[43] He is the outstanding disciple of R. Ḥanok b. Moses and is the father of Talmudic studies in Spain. Thanks to the efforts of M. Margalioth, the Nagid's monumental achievement in this field—the *Hilkḥata Gibrata*—has been in part reconstructed. The work is an attempt to codify Jewish law as it relates to contemporary life, utilizing the existing Rabbinic and Gaonic sources. This was the first such attempt in Spain and was to serve as the basis for the influential codes of Isaac al-Fasi and Moses b. Maimon that followed.[44] In line with his attempts at juridical codification, the Nagid appears to have made an effort to synthesize into six principles the essentials of Jewish belief reminiscent of the thirteen articles of faith later enunciated by Maimonides and probably an influence thereon:

I am thankful that my Rock has no beginning like things created
and there is no end to him.
I am grateful that the resurrection is a certainty and that the dead
will be awakened from the earth,
And that Moses and his Torah which is in our hands is truthful
and with perfection written,
And that the words of our sages are just and their lore and the
study thereof is pleasant,
And that there is reward in the world to come for the pure and
the dead are recompensed for their hidden sins,
And that God is ruler on dry land and on the seas, in the heavens
and over 'Ayish and Kimah.[45]

It is likely that he was equally well-versed in the Jewish mysticism of his day as evidenced by his observations on the *Ma'ase Merkabah*, the description of the chariot throne in Ezekiel 1:1–28.[46]

As regards his familiarity with "Greek wisdom," we have the Nagid's own words in which he gives thanks to God for making him know "the lore of the Greeks" which helped him "open eloquently among the famous the doors of wisdom that were heretofore not penetrated."[47] Needless to say a Jewish courtier needed all his wits about him to survive in the palace of a dissolute monarch like Badis of Granada. Undoubtedly the unlettered Berber was impressed with the wide range of learning exhibited by the Nagid.[48]

The Nagid's power at the court of Granada must have been considerable. He demonstrated his usefulness to Badis, saving his life on one occasion during the rebellion of Yadair and generally proving himself trustworthy in the sensitive post of *hajib,* chief minister of the state, to which, as Dozy tells us, "neither an Arab nor a Berber could be suitably entrusted." [49] Thus even as he had no illusions about the precarious nature of his status in the service of a monarch like Badis he nevertheless exerted sufficient influence to get rid of his enemies and promote his friends if only from a desire for sheer self-preservation.[50] Moreover as a Jew he knows that in addition to the normal hazards of his high office there are added burdens that he alone must bear:

"When 'Agag (Zuhair of Almeria) who dwells by the shore of the sea, and his vizier called the son of 'Abbas saw
How I was esteemed by the king and that all royal matters and counsels were confirmed by me,
And all plans of which I did not approve were not put into effect.
They envied my glory and sought by force speedily to drive me away,
As they said: 'How is it that power and dominion over this people is given to this foreign folk?' " [51]

Although his luck held out during his own lifetime, his son, Joseph, successor to the vizierate of Granada, was less fortunate. Although highly successful and efficient in the discharge of his office according to the recently published memoirs of Abdallah, grandson of Badis, Joseph is an almost constant target for defamatory attacks directed both against his person and the Jewish community of Granada as a whole. In 1066 Joseph together with more than 3,000 of the leading Jews in the city are set upon and killed by an enraged mob.[52]

Rounding out the portrait of the Nagid as the ideal of Jewish Andalusia is his widely acclaimed philanthropic activity and patronage of learning which apparently extended to all parts of the then freely accessible Mediterranean world.[53] He supports impoverished scholars, retains scribes who copy for him the leading classics of the age, and sends them as gifts—together with regular contributions to the academies in Babylonia and the synagogues of Jerusalem.

In his penetrating study of Abraham Ibn Daud's *Sefer Ha-Qabbalah*, Gerson Cohen observes that the historian goes to great lengths to stress "the almost exclusive dominion of the Andalusian rabbinate" over the other Jewish centers of learning at that time. This, and the remarkable achievements of Samuel Ibn Nagrela, the "model courtier-Rabbi and ideal Jew," led to considerable messianic speculation among Andalusian Jews in the 11th and 12th centuries.[54] It is not unlikely that the Nagid took himself seriously on this point. From Ibn Ḥazm we learn that he applies to himself the verse, "until Shiloh come," even as he sends notices of his military victories to the sages in Qairawan, Egypt, Babylonia, and Baghdad, and to the Exilarch Hezekiah in Jerusalem. In informing the latter of his victory over Seville in 1055 he acknowledges him as a kindred spirit who as a descendant of the house of David will one day restore the monarchy to Israel. "To you royalty and to me prophecy are vouchsafed; you and I alone are the divine sign on this earth," he writes.[55] When the Nagid dies the most gifted Hebrew poets of the age like Ibn Chalfon, Ibn Ḥisdai, Ibn Gabirol, and Ibn Gayyat eulogize him and here too he sets a standard in what has become the "quasi-official formulae of praise" when referring to his person.[56] One hundred years after his death Judah Ibn Tibbon in a last testament to his son will quote almost exclusively from the Nagid's *Ben Mishle* in illustrating the ideal way to live.[57]

## B. THE POETRY OF THE NAGID

In order to put into perspective the Nagid's contribution to Hebrew poetry, it is necessary to see it in relation to post-Biblical Hebrew poetry in its earlier development from the Talmudic period through the era of the anonymous poets and the later Palestinian and Babylonian schools.[58]

Hebrew poetry in the Talmudic age arose out of individual and collective needs in giving expression to worship. This developed spontaneously in the course of public gatherings and showed a wide variety of forms. Among these was the *Beracha*, a standard form of required synagogue prayer, and the forms associated with the Temple services. The latter included the *Hoshanot*—probably the earliest series of hymns designed to accompany the procession around the Temple altar during the fall harvest festival of Sukkot. Other forms of prayer such as the "confession of sins" grew out of Rabbinic law-court practices in that man viewed himself as being judged by God. The study of Scripture by individuals and in groups served as the setting for prayers of the 'Bet-Midrash' (House of Study) type. Some of the value concepts coming out of Scripture study, such as the nature of God and his relationship to man and to Israel, were incorporated in this way into liturgical forms.[59] In this category also belong the prayers that grew out of the hermeneutic rules (*middot*) of Rabbinic exegesis.[60] For example the rule that a general principle as contained in one or two Biblical laws applies to all related laws (*binyan 'av*) is in its short form framed by the two terms *ma* and *af*. The terms were then put to use in the development of legends (*'agadot*) and from there found their way into the liturgy. Thus one of the early forms of poetry in the Talmudic age consists of a series of strophes with the recurring terms *ma* and *af* as in the following from an anonymous poet writing on the verse from Canticles 4:5 "Thy two breasts are like two fawns":

"These two breasts are Moses and Aaron
Even as (*ma*) these breasts are the pride of a woman
So (*af*) are Moses and Aaron the pride of Israel . . .
Even as (*ma*) these breasts are filled with milk
So (*af*) do Moses and Aaron fill Israel with Torah . . .
Even as (*ma*) these breasts, one is not larger than the other
So (*af*) were Moses and Aaron" [61]

The anonymous poets flourished for about a century between the time of the completion of the Talmud and the poet Jose b. Jose. They did use the alphabetic acrostic but not for name signatures as was the practice of the later poets. Moreover they are noted for their ability to develop themes independently without the excessive reliance upon Midrashic and Talmudic materials that the later poets were to show. The Talmud upon its completion became among other things a major literary source for synagogue poets. The transitional figures in the movement from independent theme development to reliance upon Rabbinic literature were the anonymous poets. The further back one goes in the poetry of the Talmudic age, the less one finds a dependence upon its materials.

The first poet of the new age, Jose b. Jose, shows some traces of the earlier creativity. He is for the most part, however, given to the versification of written Rabbinic sources. The two best known poets of this time were the Palestinians Yannai and Qalir, who probably flourished in the Byzantine period just prior to the Moslem invasion. The poets now sign their names and occasionally even their place of origin in the acrostic and begin to follow consistent rhyme patterns. Moreover the structure of the poetry takes on new forms like the *Qerovah* (near) and *Yoẓer* (creator) designed to embellish the two main elements in the synagogue worship service the *Sh'ma* (Deut. 6:4–10; 11:13–22 and Num. 15:37–41) and the *'Amidah* (lit. standing). The following description of a nine part *Qedushta* (holy) (a *Qerovah* preceding the recitation of the *trishagion* (Is. 6:3) in the *'Amidah*) by Yannai may be compared to links in a bracelet wound around the standing devotion.

1. After stating the first verse of the *Seder* (the pericope from the Pentateuch) there follows a poem of three stanzas in hemistichs with acrostic from *'Aleph* to *Lamed* for the first blessing of the *'Amidah*. The unity of the poem is seen in its ending, which refers back to the first verse of the *Seder*. There then follow several Scrip-

tural verses designed to reinforce the theme of the poem. The section continues with another poem (called *Ḥatimah,* lit. seal) consisting of a strophe in either hemi or tristichs, and closes with a reference to the following *'Amidah* blessing, the *Magen 'Avraham* (shield of Abraham).

2. This section is like the first, except that the alphabetic acrostic in its poem continues to its conclusion and the reference is to the second verse of the *Seder.* There then follows the reinforcement of the theme with corresponding Scriptural verses as in section one. The section then concludes with a *Ḥatimah* as above but with a reference here to the *Meḥaye ha-Maytim* (resurrection of the dead)—the next blessing of the *'Amidah.*

3. A poem of four stanzas bearing the name of Yannai in the acrostic. It ends with a reference to the first verse of the pericope from the Prophets which in turn is reinforced with corresponding Scriptural verses.

4. This is at most a three stanza poem in rhymed hemistichs. It has no acrostic and is similar in form and structure to the *Silluk* (lit. ascent)[62] in section eight of the Qerovah. It ends with the word Qadośh (holy).

5. In the Geniza collection of Hebrew manuscripts this section is called *'Asiriya* (ten) because it consists of ten stanzas with acrostic from *'Aleph* to *Yod.*

6. Eleven stanzas in rhymed hemistichs as well as a full alphabetic acrostic. The poem is usually an introduction (Petiha) to those that follow in sections seven and eight.

7. From one to three poems in which the author is not bound by any one form and hence is free to fully exercise his creative powers. Yannai's well known work "'Az rov nissim" is found in this section.

8. The *Silluk* is the preface to the Qedusha (trishagion). Its language is comparatively uncomplicated, frequently in rhyme and as a rule without acrostic. It always ends with the words, 'as it is written' followed by Isaiah 6:3.

9. The Qedusha.

Qalir, one of the most prolific poets in the post-Biblical period, was already incomprehensible to Andalusians like Abraham Ibn Ezra.[63] This was probably because Qalir's language reflected a contemporary popular usage which was not preserved in written sources and therefore unknown to later generations.[64] Elements of mysticism and myth make their appearance in Qalir's poetry. A good example of the latter is his account of the great battle between the two mythical monsters Behemot and Leviathan which God arranges at the 'end of days' for the entertainment of the righteous.

"The giant creatures confront each other, with no space left between them. Each one uses his weapons: Behemoth gores his opponent with his horns, and Leviathan fights back with his fins, which stab like knives. As they fight, the struggle takes a strange and amazing turn: the fire issuing from the nostrils of Leviathan suddenly takes hold of the fleece on the loins of Behemoth and sets it alight. The pain he suffers as a result of the burns causes Behemoth to leave the battle and flee among the trees of the Garden. Here, unwittingly, he sets fire to the spicewood, and these give forth the fragrance of incense which rises to the very heart of the Heavens. The Garden becomes entirely filled with sweet smoke, and at that instant a heavenly voice is heard from on high, addressing the winds in the words of the verse 'Blow upon My garden, let its fragrance be wafted abroad!' (Cant. iv:16). Forthwith the winds of the north and the south awaken, and they waft the fragrance of the spices in all directions. In the meantime Behemoth recovers somewhat from his defeat, and he is able to take his stand for the second round. The two renew the fight: Behemoth gores with his horns, and Leviathan hits back with stabs from his fins. The length of the battle is not stated this time, and the decision is slow in coming. Then God Himself enters the battle. He makes peace between the contestants, slaying both of them together. After they have been slaughtered in accordance with ritual law, it is permissible to offer them as excellent fare to the assembly of the Righteous. Behemoth and Leviathan embellish the great banquet that is prepared in honour of the Garden Dwellers, and with this the epic draws to a close."[65]

With the appearance of the Babylonian Saadia Gaon (882–942) themes in philosophy and theology become the subject matter of Hebrew poetry. Saadia is the father of medieval Jewish philosophy and his influence is seen in the works of the later Andalusians like Maimonides and Judah ha-Levi.[66] In his Qerovah for the Day of Atonement *Dorchi Nafshi*, we discover a penetrating discussion of such topics as the soul and its creator, the contrast between the nature of God and the nature of man, the heavenly fire, the heavenly light and wisdom, the dimensions of the heavens, the upper waters, the clouds, winds, and two classes of angels. Saadia's treatment of the contrast between God and man is seen in the following excerpt from his work:

"Greater are You than all the builders
For they build from the bottom up
Whereas You established first the heavens and beneath them
the earth.
O Lord my God You are exceedingly great

Greater are You than all the artificers

For they create with the help of light
Whereas You create all life in the womb and in secret inner
    chambers
O Lord my God You are exceedingly great

Greater are You than all the monarchs
For they are protected by their servants from foe and rebel
Whereas You protect your servants and do exalt them
O Lord my God You are exceedingly great

Greater are you than all the heroes
For they are moved to action by their anger
Whereas You contain your anger and forgive your people's sins
O Lord my God You are exceedingly great"[67]

In Andalusia Hebrew poetry reaches new horizons both with regard to rhyme and meter as well as new themes and poetic forms. Beginning with rhyme the Andalusians advanced far beyond the unisorous verse endings found in Qumran or the chain of suffix rhymes in the Talmudic literature. Now the rhyme in the second half verse is the same as for the entire poem regardless of its length. The *muwashahat* or 'girdle poem' which Ibn Nagrela introduced into Hebrew letters became very popular with the Andalusians after the 11th century. A typical *muwashahat* would consist of a two line opening 'girdle' ('ezor) rhyming aa. This to be followed by the first strophe comprising three lines rhyming bbb. The second strophe of similar length rhyming ccc would then be encircled by the second and third 'girdles' rhyming aa as the first. There were many variations of this basic form as well as new uses of internal rhyme combined with rhyme of the final word in which all three consonants agree (ḥaruz meshubaḥ). Sometimes the more skillful poets would use words with the same sounds but with different meanings (tigris).

The new metrics which the Hebrew Andalusians employed differed from the syllabic and tonal forms of the ancient Greeks and Romans. The Andalusian prosody was based on a quantitative principle in which two elements forming a Hebrew syllable the *t'nua* (movement) = (–) and *yated* (peg) = (v) or *sh'va mobile* and its *ḥataf* derivations were used in a rich variety of metric combinations. Moreover as many as 14 types of Arabic metric structures were fitted for use in Hebrew poetry including the Tawil, Madid, Basit, Kamil, Sari', Wafir, Hajaz, Khafif, Mutaqarib, Ramal, Munsarih, Mujtath, Mutadarik and Rajaz.[68]

Samuel Ibn Nagrela is the first important Hebrew poet in Andalusia. He pioneers in the development of "secular" themes in what S. Spiegel calls "the knightly and courtly taste and tradition."[69] To be sure he has left us only a few "sacred" poems designed specifically to adorn the synagogue worship service after the manner of Yannai and his followers. Here he differs from the other Hebraic masters of Spanish poetry, Ibn Gabirol, Judah Halevi, and Moses Ibn Ezra, who did write extensively in the traditional genres. The Nagid prefers to chart new directions in Hebrew poetry. He uses as many as fifty-seven different meters in his poems, exceeding any of his rivals, and is the first to employ the *muwashahat*.[70] This led to a demand for new Hebrew forms and usages and helped to enrich the language.[71] He is the first to set into Hebrew verse the colorful and warmly human episodes of a personal life having few parallels in Jewish history. In his literary capabilities as in other aspects of his career, the Nagid exhibits the temperament of an "adventurer."[72]

To be sure the Nagid's most appealing quality as a poet is when he talks about himself. The poetry then becomes the writing of a personal memoir in which he tells about his early life and his ambitious dreams, the divine promises made to him, the hardships he endures, and the wonders he observes. In a poem in which he describes his miraculous rescue at sea from the giant sea monster Al Tina he combines dramatic skill with a sense of awe and mystery at having survived where others perished:

"All who knew the sea were amazed saying: 'By what merit
 were these spared and why?
For never before has a ship been delivered from the hands
 of Qorha, the angry one!' "[73]

He carries these skills into his descriptions of the war scenes in which he was personally engaged as commander of Granada's armies. The carnage of battle which he draws in the sharpest images is both a source of disgust and amazement to him:

"The day was obscure and misty and the sun like
 my heart was dark,
And the voice of the multitudes was like the voice of the
 Almighty, like the sound of the sea and its breakers
 at the time of its raging tempest.
When the sun came out, the earth was dissolving at its
 pillars as if drunk,
And the horses sped and then turned back like vipers drawn
 from their caves.
The flying spears like lightning filled the air with light
And the arrows were like drops of rain and the bucklers
 as sieves.

The bows were used like serpents and each spit out a bee
with his mouth.
The sword upon their heads was like a torch whose light
was dimmed as it fell
And the blood of men upon the earth ran like the blood of
rams at the side of the Temple court."[74]

However, the Nagid has no illusions about war:

"War at the outset is like a beautiful maid
With whom every one wishes to flirt.
At the end it is like a despised hag
Bringing tears and sadness to whomever she meets."[75]

The Nagid's love and drinking poems comprise a considerable part of his total output. One can imagine these works being recited in the salons of the Andalusian aristocracy accompanied by such musical instruments as the *ḥalil* (flute) and the *kinnor* or *'ud* (an Arabic forerunner of the West-European lute) in the hands of comely lads and maidens and set to a given melody (*laḥan*). Here the tensions and cares of the day were eased as the wine and the choice foods were served to the company of select and illustrious guests by young and handsome cup-bearers of both sexes. These young people, called by the endearing names of *ẓ'vi* (gazelle) and *'ofer* (doe) or *ẓ'viyah* and *'ofrah* when referring to the female are the objects of much of the Nagid's love poems. Although, the love of young boys was not unusual in the European High Middle Ages, it is not likely that the Nagid is here to be taken literally not only because this would not be in keeping with his precise observance of Jewish law[76] which prohibits such practices[77] but for the even more plausible reason that the love poems themselves follow a stylized pattern after the Arabic models known to us from this period.[78]

The gazelle is never called by name and often it is difficult to tell whether the reference is to a male or female. The features of the beloved conform to a set pattern. Their faces radiate light like the sun or are pale like the lily and framed in hair of pitch-black as the night. Their eyes are dark, their cheeks crimson, and their lips like threads of scarlet. Their mouths give off the fragrance of spices and their teeth sparkle like bdellium. They stand tall like the palm tree or like the branch of the myrtle. Equally standardized is the relationship of the poet to the object of his desire. His ardent love is usually unrequited as he describes the suffering he endures from the fierce arrows which the beloved emits from her eyes. Even her nails are red from the blood of the victims that have been slain by her charms. She revels in the pain she brings to her love-sick suitors who plead for her mercy and favors which she consistently refuses to grant.[79]

Like his contemporaries the Nagid wrote numerous poems in praise of friendship although, unlike the professional poetry of his age, his was not the fawning flattery of prospective patrons.[80] Here too, however, the *laudes* follow familiar patterns known to us from Hebrew and Arabic models. He is bound to his friend by a faithful covenant never to be severed, which he reaffirms repeatedly with vows and pledges. He is prepared to give his life as a "ransom" for his friend and he awaits his presence like grass eager for the rains. The friendship does not always function smoothly. Occasionally there are quarrels or the pain of separation. At times like these the friends are sick from lack of sleep and long to be reunited. There is envy of the enemy if only because he has the privilege of seeing the now separated friend. Even the letters the friend receives and handles are more fortunate than the poet who must remain at a distance.[81]

Yet another theme in the Nagid's poetry deals with the ravages of time, which with an unrelenting pace leads man from birth to old age and death:

"For from the beginning you are consigned to death;
Even every branch to its root returns." [82]

The irrevocable presence of death brings terror and induces a mood of uncertainty and resignation. It is, however, also man's great teacher. This is forcefully brought out in the Nagid's description of a Granada street scene with its butcher shops, fish peddlers, and bakeries. There is much activity on the busy street as animals are slaughtered and the catches of fish are "dragged" to the homes of their buyers. As in a flash, the poet then understands "their mystery:"

"Even as you they breathe and have a heart which makes them
function upon the earth.
There is never a time when one among them does not die or
is in the process of giving birth.
Think about this, you who are pure and you princes who take
pride in your honor:
If you would understand the mystery of the world know that
this is all there is to man." [83]

From the universality of death the Nagid derives the unity of all life. Moreover, in spite of the uncertainties of his existence man will find within himself the resources to prevail:

"When you are depressed, make strong your heart
Even while standing at death's door.
There is light in the candle before 'tis put out
And in the gored lion a roar."[84]

In his description of the drinking parties which formed a part of the social life of his circle, the Nagid is at his lyrical best. The poems exude a healthy love of life and the pleasures of the senses. The parties themselves combining music, poetry, and the dance were part of a larger aesthetic experience particularly when, as frequently happened, they were held in the stillness of the dawn in order to greet the rising sun, or at the beginning of the autumn rains to the accompaniment of its thunder and lightning. In this way did one gain a heightened awareness of the universe in which he lived:

"Come at dawn and see the curtain
Of sky dotted with silver and fine gold
While the face of darkness flees like a black man
Before a light-skinned maiden,
And to the voices of high-flying birds drink,
From the hand of a young maid in splendid attire,
The wine which reflects in the cup the light of sun
And whose fragrance is like myrrh and cassia." [85]

In 1041 the death of his older brother, Isaac, whom he looked upon almost like a father, made a deep impression upon the Nagid. He composed no less than ninety elegies on this occasion covering the sequence of events from the time he first heard of his brother's illness through the moments of his death and burial as well as the subsequent periods of mourning which he observed. The Nagid, who was 48 at the time and, being at the height of his career, was himself almost daily exposed to the dangers of the court and the battlefield, reveals in the elegies the fears for his own life:

"In a ripe old age He has made you sip the deadly cup
And in a little while I too will drink from it!" [86]

Here too his faith in God sustains him:

"O first-born of my father, I have left you,
As security in the hands of my Creator
Whose assurance I trust
That you will go in peace." [87]

The skilled Andalusian poet was usually a master at satire and the Nagid is no exception. Although only a few samples have survived, they are sufficient to show that the Nagid was as capable as an Ibn Gabirol or a Judah Halevi[88] of demolishing with barbs of wit and sarcasm an offending subject. Notable among these is the description of a synagogue which he passes on his way where he thinks he hears "an ass braying and the shrieks of oxen." On entering the building however, he finds "a teacher and his students, their heads swaying like lonely trees in the desert." But, "with their mouths they insulted Hillel and Shammai and slapped the face of Rabbi 'Aqiva." [89]

As we have seen, the Nagid was not only a versatile but a complex figure as well. From his poetry one is given a glimpse of the many facets of his character. Like all great men he is given to contradictions. He is at one time a fatalist and a man of abiding faith in God. He is deeply devoted to the Biblical-Rabbinic tradition even as he is capable of writing odes to handsome young men that border on the erotic.[90] Perhaps, we should not "judge the courtiers of Andalus by the standards of Troyes, Mainz, and Cracow," [91] or, as the Nagid himself tells us, we ought not to take the poet too seriously:

"He will incite you to evil with dream-like talk
And with words of poetry he will urge you to deception.
My son not every dream comes true
Neither are all the words of the poet veritable!" [92]

# THE POEMS

# A.
# The Early Years

## 1. The Poet Leaves Cordova

The soul is far from its desire and the spirit is refused its requests.
The body is fat and satisfied and vigorous but its precious spirit is left unfulfilled.
And a humble man walks upon the earth but his thoughts are spread upon the heavens.
For what help is his flesh to the voluptuary even his goods when his soul is afflicted!
I have friends who cause me distress; they do not do good; they are great of body but their minds are lacking.
They think that I have departed and turned from rest to wandering in order to increase my wealth
Seeing that my head grows with hair disheveled and my eyes are encircled with the paint of night.
Yet my friends do not know the secret of my heart, moreover my companions do not speak with wisdom,
And like an animal of cloven hoof their souls do not know or understand!
Can one restrain himself whose soul is pure and who like the moon labors to rise?
Can one remain still until with her wings, he girds her loins like a man strengthening a tent-cloth;
Until he achieves and his feats are made known, and he continues to increase in reputation like the sea?
As God lives and as the servants of the Lord flourish,—even I will keep the promise,
I will climb the rock with my feet and descend into the pit that is stuck in the depths

And I will sew together one rim of the desert with another and I will split the sea with every swimming sail.
I will roam until I ascend and reach the heights that are known unto eternity!
And my enemies will be in terror of me but my friends I will save;
Free men will be faithful to me even as I to them
My spirit holds fast to friends even as it avoids my accusers.
And for you whose essence is a garden bed planted by a river of love from full affection is
A friendship, nurtured from youth like a seal set in a signet ring
Graven like the carvings of gold upon the windowpane that was cut into the threshold of the Temple!
May God be with you according to your love and may your devoted soul be delivered from distress,
And may the redeeming Lord send you salvation until the sun and moon are no more.

[בצאתו מקורדובה]

נְשָׁמָה מֵאֲשֶׁר תִּתְאַו גְּדוּעָה, / וְנֶפֶשׁ מֵאֲשֶׁר תִּשְׁאַל מְנוּעָה,
וְגוּף שָׁמֵן וְשָׂבֵעַ וְדָשֵׁן – / וְנַפְשׁוֹ הַכְּבוּדָּה לֹא שְׂבֵעָה,
וְאִישׁ עָנָו מְהַלֵּךְ עַל אֲדָמָה – / וּמַחְשַׁבְתּוֹ עֲלֵי שַׁחַק שְׂרוּעָה,
וּמַה יּוֹעִיל לְאִישׁ בָּשָׂר בְּשָׂרוֹ / וְטוּבָתוֹ – וְהַנֶּפֶשׁ בְּרָעָה?
וְיֵשׁ רֵעִים מְרֵעִים לֹא מְטִיבִים, / גְּדוֹלֵי גוּף וְזִמָּתָם גְּרוּעָה,
יְדַמּוּ כִּי לְהוֹסִיף הוֹן אֲנִי סָר / וְנֶעְתָּק מֵחֲנִיָּה אֶל נְסִיעָה,
וְאִם רֹאשִׁי בְּצִיצִית רֹאשׁ פְּרוּעָה, / וּבַת־עַיִן בְּפוּךְ לַיִל קְרוּעָה –
וְלֹא יֵדְעוּ מְרֵעַי סוֹד לְבָבִי, / אֲבָל לֹא דִבְּרוּ רֵעַי בְּדֵעָה,
וְנַפְשָׁם מִבְּלִי הַכֵּר וְהָבִין / כְּנֶפֶשׁ הַבְּהֵמָה הַשְּׁסוּעָה!
הֲיִתְאַפַּק אֲשֶׁר נַפְשׁוֹ לְבָנָה / וְכִלְבָנָה לְהִתְנַשֵּׂא יְגֵעָה?
וְיִשְׁקֹט, עַד אֲשֶׁר יֶאְזֹר בְּמָתְנָיו / כְּנָפֶיהָ, כְּאִישׁ אוֹזֵר יְרִיעָה,
וְעַד יִפְעַל וְיִשָּׁמְעוּ פְעָלָיו, / וְיוֹסִיף עוֹד כְּיָם עַל הַשְּׁמוּעָה?
בְּחֵי הָאֵל וְחֵי עַבְדֵי אֱלֹהִים / – וְכָמוֹנִי יְהִי שׁוֹמֵר שְׁבוּעָה –
בְּרַגְלַי אֶעֱלֶה סֶלַע, וְאֵרֵד / אֱלֵי פַחַת בְּמַעְמַקִּים תְּקוּעָה,
וְאֶתְפֹּר אֶת שְׂפַת מִדְבָּר בְּמִדְבָּר, / וְאֶקְרַע יָם וְכָל שׁוֹחָה קְלוּעָה,
וְאָשׁוּט עַד אֲשֶׁר אֵרוֹם וְאַעַל / אֱלֵי שִׂיאָה, תְּהִי לָעַד יְדוּעָה!
וְתִמָּצֵא לְצָרַי בִּי חֲרָדָה, / וְתִמָּצֵא לְדוֹדַי בִּי תְּשׁוּעָה,

וְאֶרְצַע אֶת בְּנֵי חֹרִים בְּאֹזֶן, / וְלִי אֹזֶן לְמוֹדַעַי רְצוּעָה,
וְלִי נֶפֶשׁ לְרֵעִים מַחֲזֶקֶת, / וְלִי נֶפֶשׁ לְמַשְׂטִינַי מְנוּעָה!
וְלָךְ תּוֹכָהּ עֲרוּגָה מִן יְדִידוּת / מְלֵאָה, עַל נְהַר אַהַב נְטוּעָה,
יְדִידוּת הַשְּׁמוּרָה מִנְּעוּרִים, / כְּחֹתֶמֶת בְּטַבַּעַת קְבוּעָה,
מְפֻתַּחַת כְּפִתּוּחֵי יְרַקְרַק / עֲלֵי שִׁמְשָׁה בְּסַף הֵיכָל קְרוּעָה!
יְהִי לָךְ יָהּ כְּאַהֲבָתֵךְ, וְנַפְשֵׁךְ / אֲשֶׁר אָהֵב תְּהִי מִצַּר פְּדוּעָה
וְיִשְׁלַח אֵל לְמוֹשָׁעוֹת לָךְ עַד / בְּלִי שֶׁמֶשׁ וְיָרֵחַ יְשׁוּעָה!

## 2. The Wanderer

My thoughts hurl my heart like a boat by a flying sail on a stormy day.
I am destined to wander, by the book of God, and to roam over every land.
For all who are fated to exile move about like Cain and flee as Jonah.

[קללת הנדודים]

מְזִמּוֹתַי תְּקַלַּעְנָה לְבָבִי / כְּנֵס יָנִיס בְּיוֹם סַעַר סְפִינָה,
וְעוֹד נִכְתַּב בְּסֵפֶר הָאֱלֹהִים / עֲלֵי נַפְשִׁי וְשׁוּט עַל כָּל מְדִינָה.
וְכֹל נִכְתַּב נְדוֹד עָלָיו יְהִי נָע / כְּמוֹ קַיִן וּבוֹרֵחַ כְּיוֹנָה.

# B.
# The Wars

## 3. The Battle of Alfuente

O mighty God and Lord, jealous and fearful.
You are raised above all hymn and song.
For great are your deeds and the day whereon You redeem; your salvation is certain.
And upon all that are haughty and boast of evil and oppress the poor, by You the net is spread.
And all who cry calling your name have cried and called in the name of him who answers in distress.
Yours are the miracles both small and great and wonders both easy and difficult.

And the favor which You, O Lord have done to me is greater than any of which I have heard.
On the day of distress He said to me: 'Hide until the indignation passes! '
I replied to him: 'The Rock for the distress.'
And He said to me: 'Do you not fear?' I replied in amazement: 'The Lord is with me and I should fear? '
For there exists a redeemer and there is One who avenges the blood of the poor and One who rewards and there is a recompense for Torah.

There are those who make a covenant against me, but I too have the patriarchs covenant to protect me!
Why then should I not relate the works of the Lord, since I am eloquent and a man of words!
When 'Agag, who dwells by the shore of the sea, and his vizier called the son of 'Abbas, saw
How I was esteemed by the king and that all royal matters and counsels were confirmed by me,
And all plans of which I did not approve were not put into effect,
They envied my glory and sought by force speedily to drive me away,
As they said: 'How is it that power and dominion over this people is given to this foreign folk?
Thus speaks the vizier against me with boasting and evil without dread or fear.
He wove his mighty and numerous lies in a scandalous letter,
But far be it for me to imitate his intentions,
And he spread abroad in the provinces his letters to make them well known among his people,
And to set them against me with lies like the gossip of those who bore a branch upon a pole.
Not me alone did he wish to destroy with his slander which he invented and created,
But also intended to cut off the Lord's congregation, remnant and offspring, the woman giving birth and the one with child.
Yet my master did not hearken to his words nor give heed to his defective opinion.
However, he died a short while thereafter on a day of wrath for my sinful soul.
And I said: 'Woe! How will I survive since my shade is removed and my doom is come.

For God found my sin and judged me and his punishment was properly measured.
Thereupon this enemy who rejoiced at my misfortune sent a message to his friends:
'The day whose coming I have long awaited is here for the fear is removed
And Samuel is lost since his king has perished and his hope is gone and parted.'
I was indignant and God was angry and his face like a fire was kindled in rage against him.
Then there arose a young lion of the nations and succeeding his father governed his people as sovereign.
And my enemy in haste wrote a fierce and haughty letter to him without entreaty,
And sent to him (saying:) 'Do you know that according to our faith it is a sin to allow Samuel to live.
For there is no peace or quiet so long as the soul of this Jew is in his body preserved.
Send him away and strife and contention will be removed and take a settlement in his place.
For if not, know then that kings have conspired to plot a war against you.'
Thus answered he in his letter: 'If I grant your request a curse will come upon me!
And if I deliver my servant into the hands of his enemies may my life be given over to my foes!'
At this my enemy was wroth and he persevered in his accusations and it did not suit him and he was enraged
He did not rest until he had gathered his armies: 'Amalek and 'Edom and the Sons of Q'turah.
But from the beginning God decreed their fall in the city of Alfuente, in a dug out pit.
He multiplied his movements and hurried like a bird seen riding the wings of the wind.
Both he and God deliberated, and God's counsel for which there is no annulment, prevailed.
And the month of 'Av left with the ancient evil tidings and 'Elul entered with the good that was not to be delayed.

He pitched his tent on the mountain on one side and we pitched ours on the way of the crossing.
We were not concerned about his troops; we considered them a caravan.

Yet he continued to speak as he approached and set men upon me to incite them.
But when our foes saw that our company agreed with me,
Then did he draw the spear, the lance, the sword and the javelin in order to do battle.
Even as the foe arose the Rock stood up against him, and how can a creature survive when the Rock is his opponent?
The armies stood in battle array facing the lined-up positions of the enemy.
On the day of anger and fury and revenge men think that the angel of death is a prize,
And each seeks to purchase fame for himself though he sell his life in the bargain.
The earth was moved from its foundation and was overturned as in the destruction of ‘Amorah.
And the faces whereon beauty and splendor were gathered turned into the blackness of pot bottoms.
The day was obscure and misty, and the sun like my heart was dark.
And the voice of the multitudes was like the voice of the Almighty like the sound of the sea and its breakers at the time of its raging tempest.
When the sun came out, the earth was dissolving at its pillars as if drunk,
And the horses sped and then turned back like vipers drawn from their caves.
The flying spears like lightning filled the air with light.
And the arrows were like drops of rain and the bucklers as sieves,
The bows were used like serpents and each spit out a bee with his mouth.
The sword upon their heads was like a torch whose light was dimmed as it fell.
And the blood of men upon the earth ran like the blood of rams at the side of the Temple court.
Mighty men were weary of life and chose death instead.
Young lions saw a festering sore upon their heads as a crown.
To die was right, they believed and to live was forbidden.

What am I to do? There is no escape or stay or staff and hope is sterile!
Enemies spill blood like water on the day of distress while I pour forth prayer
To the God who brings low and fells all evildoers into his pit which He did surely dig.

On the day of battle He turns back into the heart of the enemy the sword and arrows which he prepared and threw.
I did not say: 'Give me victory Lord because I walk in a straight path
Or because of my learning which travailed and gave birth at a time when the knowledge of the "learned" is barren
Or for the sake of my logic in resolving difficulties in the nights when I awoke before the watches.'
Rather, I said: 'For your sake be unto me a sheltering rock and a fortified wall of fire.
As for the enemy,—dispatch your anger upon him that he may be consumed like stubble on the day of the whirlwind.
Do to them as to Sisera and for me as you did for Baraq and Deborah.
Flash lightning O God and scatter them; rebuke them that they may perish from the reproach!
Redeem me from bitterly destructive hands and make my pursuers atone for me on this day.
Do not recall my sins: remember in my behalf the merit of Isaac and Abraham and Sarah!
O my father Jacob, pray and son of 'Amram, stand by me in distress.
And those who are interred in the Machpelah, will ye rest on a day like this? Arise from the cave
And take hold of the throne of God and call to the merciful Lord and speak to him with bitterness!
And if He says: "What is this about, my beloved?" Answer him: "Stand, rise up and bestir yourself"
For if it does not please You to have mercy upon Joseph your young one, when will salvation be revealed?
And if today in this You do not vindicate me—is this how Torah is rewarded?
Will the man who was made happy by, 'If thou passest through the waters' drown? For your hand is not waxed short!
And will the man who was notified that, 'If you walk into fire' be consumed in the flaming battle?
Say to him: "God, rise up in anger, consume them that they may be destroyed in the flame!
Open a door in the straits and save your servant since all portals are closed.
Turn back their swords upon their hearts and rise up against them; be not with them and set their bows to breaking.
Ye angels! Draw near and make war upon them even stars and shining sun,

That the choruses of mighty nations may say: "There is One who looks after the humble scattered lamb!" '
And the Lord heard my prayer when I called like a woman in labor, like one who brings forth her first child in anguish.
And He blew upon them as on the day of the Sea of Reeds and they were destroyed by his storm and He showed them the power.
And the fire of death consumed them and they were annihilated like wood in a hot stove and cooking oven;
As flaming chaff in the midst of the bonfire were my enemies all of them in the dust.
And the heads of the lords were on the ground, like figs selling a thousand for a Gerah.
And the officers in their downfall were puffed up like skin bottles, like a pregnant woman.
There they lay, slaves upon masters and paupers with kings with no choice in the matter.
There they were with 'Agag their king as dung in the midst of the field and no burial was given them.
And one of ten thousand survived among them as gleanings in the vineyard on the day the vintage is done.

Now the traces of 'Amalek were wiped out from Spain and the armies were destroyed and their dominion uprooted
As once before when 'Agag perished at the hands of Samuel and Haman by the Logician,
And as earlier when 'Amalek came to evil, indeed he has since not returned!
We abandoned them in the plain for the hyenas, the serpents, the leopard and the sow
And we left them reclining on rocks and leaning on brier and thorn.
We gave their flesh as a gift to the vulture and offered them a present to the lion and wolf
And we satisfied them with blood, but not the blood of a torn animal, and much meat albeit not from a dish.
They were amazed at the pampered heads of households which they found, but not in the shade of house and roof,
Who, in the middle of a day burning with heat no longer entered a palace of marble or a cool upper chamber.
The offspring of ostriches will weep for them and the daughter of the young she-goat shall dance
And the young lions will make a banquet over their flesh and the lioness will have enough to leave for her young.

We conquered their cities and their lands and we razed with vengeance wall and castle.

And we took possession of villages and towns and we vanquished with power city and fortress.

Then we returned, and there was not missing even one of our company and no one failed in his task!

The sixth day of the week on the first of 'Elul was to me like the ninth of 'Av or the tenth.

But its end was one of redemption, a day of rejoicing, as when the poor delight in the harvest.

The day when we divided the spoil of my enemies, even a day of gladness, was like the giving birth by a withholding, barren woman.

And prior to the advent of the year nine and ninety, salvation was sent to me and light!

For the vizier who counselled and ordered to slay me even issuing a decree,

And who came to the shore of rivers to do me harm, was there shaved by the razor that is hired!

I seized him and brought him in chains to the prison house and put him under saws.

And I realized my desire for my enemy and my revenge for his accursed soul

Even as I took hold of the Testimony,—for its value to me is greater than all others,

Then did he die the death of a churl on the night of rejoicing with the precious Torah.

And God fulfilled the word of my father to his tribe, the children of song and the offerers of incense

For wisely did Zeresh speak to the Buyer with his Kikars about the Men bringing Gifts of an 'Agorah.

Then I was at ease and rested from my foes and was honored and added to my power.

And among the nations no one thinks to do me ill and all jealousy and hatred is held back.

Do not pay heed to the foolish adversary since the deeds of the ignorant pour destruction out upon him.

Do not fret when the idiot rises in stature, the raising of the fool's head removes it also from him.

For if you make entreaties unto him (God) and the former persists in his wickedness, then his fall is imminent.

The judgment on all vessels retaining impurity in themselves regarding immersion, is to break them,

And concerning a goring ox which cannot be guarded they have already said that to slaughter him is to guard him.
To the Lord who has done great things I will expand in song that it be as a minister to all others.
With words like sapphire I will weave and with speeches of bdellium I will stich
Like the Tummin, but filled with rhyme and like the songs of Tehillim in number.
With them mourners will make a festival and every Nazarite will drink a cup of salvation.
Every tongue will be filled with jubilation and with rejoicing in song about my redemption,
And the mouth of each person will be given leave to be filled with laughter in this world for the saving of my life.
Therefore my brethren give forth with hymns to the eternal God and increase the songs and praise in the assembly.
Say to him: 'May You continue to support me as well as those who hold on to the Torah true.'
Now make a second Purim for the God who arose and cut off from 'Amalek flower and fruit.
And make it heard in Africa and Egypt and notify the children of the Chosen House,
And tell it to the elders of Pumbeditha and to the sages of the academy at Sura,
And call its name: 'Sister to the Happening of Ahaswerosh and Lady Esther!'
And write it in your books that it may abide forever and be remembered from generation to generation!

[הקרב על יד אלפואֶנְטֶה]

אֱלוֹהַּ עֹז וְאֵל קַנּוֹא וְנוֹרָא, / מְרוֹמָם אַתְּ עֲלֵי כָל שִׁיר וְשִׁירָה,
לְמַעַן כִּי פְעָלֶיךָ מְרוֹמִים / וְיוֹם תִּגְאַל – גְּאֻלָּתְךָ בְהִירָה,
וְעַל כָּל רָם וּמִתְהַלֵּל בְּרָעָה / וְעֹשֶׁק רָשׁ לְךָ רֶשֶׁת מְזֹרָה
וְכָל צוֹעֵק אֲשֶׁר יִקְרָא בְשִׁמְךָ – / בְּשֵׁם עוֹנֶה בְּצַר צָעַק וְקָרָא.
לְךָ נִסִּים קְטַנִּים וַעֲצוּמִים / וְנִפְלָאָה נְקַלָּה וַחֲמוּרָה,
וְהַטּוֹבָה אֲשֶׁר לִי, אֵל, עֲשִׂיתָהּ / עֲלֵי כָל טוֹב שְׁמַעְתִּיהוּ יְתֵרָה.
וְאוֹמֵר לִי בְיוֹם צָרָה "חֲבֵה עַד / עֲבָר זַעַם!" עֲנִיתִיו "צוּר לְצָרָה!"
וְאוֹמֵר לִי "הֲלֹא תִירָא?" עֲנִיתִיו / בְּתִמָּהוֹן "יְיָ לִי – וְאִירָא?"
וְיֵשׁ פּוֹצֶה וְיֵשׁ דּוֹרֵשׁ דְּמֵי דַל / וְיֵשׁ גּוֹמֵל וְיֵשׁ שָׂכָר לְתוֹרָה,

וְיֵשׁ כּוֹרְתִים עֲלֵי נַפְשִׁי בְּרִיתָם – / וְיֵשׁ גַּם לִי בְּרִית אָבוֹת שְׁמוּרָה!
וְאֵיכָה לֹא אֲסַפֵּר מַעֲשֵׂי אֵל / וְלִי פֶּה וַאֲנִי בַּעַל אֲמִירָה!
בְּעֵת רָאָה אֲגַג שׁוֹכֵן לְחוֹף יָם / וּמִשְׁנֵהוּ בְּנוֹ עַבָּאס מְקָרָא
כְּבוֹדִי אֶת פְּנֵי מַלְכִּי וְכִי כָל / דְּבַר מַלְכוּת וְעֵצָה בִּי גְזוּרָה
וְכָל מִלָּה גְמוּרָה, כַּאֲשֶׁר לֹא / גְּמַרְתִּיהָ אֲנִי, אֵינָהּ גְּמוּרָה –
חֲמָדוּנִי עֲלֵי הוֹדִי וּבִקְשׁוּ / לְהָדְפֵנִי בְּיָדַיִם מְהֵרָה.
וְאָמְרוּ: אֵיךְ תְּהִי מַעְלָה לְעַם זָר / עֲלֵי עַם זֶה וּמֶמְשָׁלָה אֲשׁוּרָה?
וּמִשְׁנֶה זֶה יְדַבֶּר בִּי גְדוֹלוֹת / וְרָעוֹת מִבְּלִי חִתִּית וּמוֹרָא,
וְחִבַּר אֶת כְּזָבָיו הָעֲצוּמִים / וְהָרַבִּים בְּאִגֶּרֶת חֲקוּרָה.
וְחָלִילָה לְכָמוֹנִי לְדַבֵּר / בְּפִי מִלָּה תְּהִי עָלָיו נְטוּרָה!
וּפִזַּר בַּמְּדִינוֹת אִגְּרוֹתָיו / לְשַׁוּוֹת זֹאת בְּפִי עַמּוֹ סְדוּרָה
וְלַהֲקִימָם עֲלֵי נַפְשִׁי בְּדִבָּה / כְּדִבַּת נוֹשְׂאִים בַּמּוֹט זְמוֹרָה.
וְלֹא אוֹתִי לְבַד בִּקֵּשׁ לְהַשְׁמִיד / בְּדִבָּתוֹ אֲשֶׁר בָּדָא וּבָרָא,
אֲבָל בִּקֵּשׁ לְהַכְרִית לַעֲדַת אֵל / שְׁאָר וָנִין וְיוֹלֶדֶת וְהָרָה.
וְלֹא הֶאֱזִין אֲדוֹנִי אֶל דְּבָרָיו / וְלֹא שָׁת לֵב לְדַעְתּוֹ הַחֲסֵרָה –
וְאוּלָם מֵת אֱלֵי יָמִים מְעַטִּים / בְּיוֹם עֶבְרָה לְנַפְשִׁי הָעֲכוּרָה.
וְאָמַרְתִּי: אֲהָהּ, אֵיךְ אֶחְיֶה עוֹד – / וְסָר צִלִּי וּבָאָה הַצְּפִירָה,
וּמָצָא הָאֱלֹהִים אֶת עֲוֹנִי / וְדָנַנִי וְדִינוֹ בַּמְּשׂוּרָה!
וְאָז שָׁלַח מְשַׂנְאִי זֶה אֲשֶׁר שָׂשׂ / לְאֵידִי אֶל מְיֻדָּעָיו בְּשׂוֹרָה:
כְּבָר בָּא יוֹם אֲשֶׁר מֵאָז אֲקַוֶּה / תְּבוֹאָתוֹ, וְסָרָה הַמְּגוֹרָה,
וְאָבַד בַּאֲבֹד מַלְכּוֹ שְׁמוּאֵל / וְתוֹחַלְתּוֹ כְּבָר אָזְלָה וְסָרָה.
וְחָרָה לִי – וְחָרָה לָאֱלֹהִים / וְאַפּוֹ בוֹ כְּאֵשׁ נִשַּׂק וְחָרָה.
אֲזַי עָמַד כְּפִיר עַמִּים וְעָצַר / בְּעַמּוֹ אַחֲרֵי אָבִיו עֲצָרָה,
וְכָתַב צוֹרְרֵי אֵלָיו בְּנַחַץ / כְּתָב חָזָק וְרָם מֵאֵין פְּצִירָה
וְשָׁלַח לוֹ: הֲתֵדַע כִּי שְׁמוּאֵל / לְחַיּוּתוֹ בְּדָתֵנוּ עֲבֵרָה?
וְאֵין שָׁלוֹם וְאֵין הַשְׁקֵט – וְנֶפֶשׁ / יְהוּדִי זֶה בְּתוֹךְ גּוּפוֹ נְצוּרָה!
שְׁלַח אוֹתוֹ – וְיִסּוּרוּ מְדָנִים / וּמִדְיָנִים, וְקַח עָלָיו פְּשָׁרָה.
וְאִם אַיִן, דְּעֵה כִּי הַמְּלָכִים / עֲלֵי מִלְחַמְתְּךָ קָשְׁרוּ קְשִׁירָה.
וְכֹה הֵשִׁיב בְּסִפְרוֹ: אִם אֲמַלֵּא / שְׁאֵלָתְךָ, תְּבוֹאֵנִי מְאֵרָה!
וְאִם אֶמְסֹר בְּיַד צָרָיו מְשָׁרְתִי, / תְּהִי נַפְשִׁי בְּיַד צָרַי מְסוּרָה!
לְזֹאת קָצַף מְשַׂנְאִי זֶה וְאָחַז / בְּשִׂטְנָתוֹ וְהוּרַע לוֹ וְחָרָה

וְלֹא נָח עַד אֲשֶׁר אָסַף חֲיָלָיו, / עֲמָלֵק וֶאֱדוֹם וּבְנֵי קְטוּרָה,
וְאֵל שָׁת מִן יְמֵי רֵאשִׁית לְנִפְלָם / בְּקִרְיַת מַעְיָן שׁוּחָה חֲפוּרָה.
וְכָפַל אֶת נְסִיעוֹתָיו וּמִהַר / כְּעוֹף יִרְכַּב כְּנַף רוּחַ וְיֵרָא.
וְיָעַץ הוּא – וְיָעַץ אֵל, וְקָמָה / עֲצַת הָאֵל אֲשֶׁר אֵין לָהּ הֲפָרָה!
וְיָצָא אָב בְּרָעָה הַקְּדוּמָה, / וּבָא אֱלוּל בְּטוֹבָה לֹא אֲחוּרָה,
וְתָקַע אָהֳלוֹ בָּהָר בְּעֵבֶר / וְתָקַעְנוּ בְּדֶרֶךְ הָעֲבָרָה,
וְלֹא שַׁתְנוּ לְבָבֵינוּ לְחֵילוֹ / חֲשַׁבְנוּהוּ כְּאִלּוּ הוּא שְׂיָרָה.
וְהִרְבָּה, כַּאֲשֶׁר בָּא, הַדְּבָרִים / וְשִׂסָּה בִי אֲנָשֵׁינוּ וְגֵרָה.
וּבִרְאוֹת צוֹרְרַי כִּי עַל לְשׁוֹנִי / בְּפֶה אֶחָד תְּדַבֵּר הַחֲבוּרָה,
אֲזַי הֵרִיק חֲנִית רֹמַח וְחֶרֶב / וְגַם סָגַר לְהִלָּחֵם סְגִירָה.
וְקָם הַצַּר – וְקָם הַצּוּר לְנֶגְדּוֹ, / וְאֵיךְ תָּקוּם, בְּקוּם צוּר, הַיְצִירָה?
וְעָמְדוּ הַחֲיָלוֹת מַעֲרָכָה / לְעֻמַּת מַעֲרֶכֶת צַר בְּשׁוּרָה,
אֲנָשִׁים יַחְשְׁבוּ יוֹם אַף וְחֵמָה / וְקִנְאָה אֶת בְּכוֹר מָוֶת בְּכוֹרָה,
וְכָל אֶחָד מְבַקֵּשׁ לוֹ קְנוֹת שֵׁם / וְנַפְשׁוֹ בַּאֲשֶׁר יִקְנֶה מְכוּרָה.
וְנָעָה הָאֲדָמָה מִיְּסוֹדָהּ / וְנֶהֶפְכָה כְּמַהְפֵּכַת עֲמֹרָה
וּפָנִים קִבְּצוּ פָּארוּר וְהָדָר / וְנֶהֶפְכוּ אֱלֵי שׁוּלֵי קְדֵרָה.
וְהַיּוֹם – יוֹם עֲרָפֶל וַחֲשֵׁכָה, / וְהַשֶּׁמֶשׁ כְּמוֹ לִבִּי שְׁחוֹרָה,
וְקוֹל הָמוֹן – כְּקוֹל שַׁדַּי, כְּקוֹל יָם / וּמִשְׁבָּרָיו בְּעֵת יִסְעַר סְעִירָה,
וְהָאָרֶץ בְּצֵאת שֶׁמֶשׁ נְמוֹגָה / בְּעָמְדֶהָ כְּאִלּוּ הִיא שְׁכוּרָה,
וְהַסּוּסִים יְרוּצוּן גַּם יְשׁוּבוּן / כִּצְפְעוֹנִים נְטוּשִׁים מִמְּאוּרָה.
כְּאִלּוּ הָרְמָחִים הַשְּׁלוּחִים – / בְּרָקִים מִלְאוּ אֲוִיר בְּאוֹרָה,
וְהַחִצִּים כְּמוֹ נִטְפֵי גְשָׁמִים / וְהַגַּבּוֹת כְּאִלּוּ הֵם כְּבָרָה,
וְקַשְׁתּוֹתָם בְּכַפָּם כַּנְּחָשִׁים / וְכָל נָחָשׁ בְּפִיו יָקִיא דְבוֹרָה
וְהַחֶרֶב עֲלֵי רֹאשָׁם כְּלַפִּיד / בְּנָפְלוֹ דָּהֲתָה בוֹ הַנְּהָרָה,
וְדַם אִישִׁים עֲלֵי אֶרֶץ מְהַלֵּךְ / כְּדַם אֵילִים בְּצִדֵּי הָעֲזָרָה.
וְקָצוּ הַגְּבָרִים הַגְּבִירִים / בְּחַיֵּיהֶם, וְהַמִּיתָה בְּחוּרָה,
כְּפִירִים יֶחֱזוּ מַכָּה טְרִיָּה / עֲלֵי רֹאשָׁם כְּאִלּוּ הִיא עֲטָרָה
וְהַמִּיתָה בְּדָתֵיהֶם יְשָׁרָה / וְחַיָּתָם בְּעֵינֵיהֶם אֲסוּרָה.
וּמָה אֶעֱשֶׂה? וְאֵין מָנוֹס וּמַשְׁעֵן / וּמַשְׁעֵנָה וְהַתִּקְוָה עֲקוּרָה!
מְשַׂנְאִים יִשְׁפְּכוּ דָמִים כְּמַיִם / בְּיוֹם צַר – וַאֲנִי אֶשְׁפֹּךְ עֲתָרָה
לְאֵל מַשְׁפִּיל וּמַפִּיל כָּל מְעַוֵּל / בְּגוּמָצוֹ אֲשֶׁר חָפַר וְכָרָה

וּמֵשִׁיב יוֹם קְרָב חֶרֶב וְחִצִּים / בְּלֵב אוֹיֵב אֲשֶׁר הֵכִין וְיָרָה.
וְלֹא אֹמַר: תְּנָה לִי אֵל תְּשׁוּעָה, / לְמַעַן כִּי הֲלִיכָתִי יְשָׁרָה
וְתוֹרָתִי אֲשֶׁר תָּחִיל וְתֵלֵד / בְּעֵת תּוֹרַת בְּנֵי תוֹרָה עֲקָרָה,
וְהֶגְיוֹנִי לְפַתֵּחַ סְגוּרוֹת / בְּלֵילוֹת קִדְּמוּ עֵינַי שְׁמוּרָה,
אֲבָל אֹמַר: לְמַעַנְךָ הֱיֵה לִי / לְצוּר מָעוֹז וְחוֹמַת אֵשׁ בְּצוּרָה,
וְהָאוֹיֵב תְּשַׁלַּח בּוֹ חֲרוֹנְךָ / וְיֹאכְלֵמוֹ כְּמוֹ קַשׁ יוֹם סְעָרָה.
עֲשֵׂה לָהֶם כְּסִיסְרָא, וַעֲשֵׂה לִי / כְּמַעֲשֶׂיךָ לְבָרָק עִם דְּבוֹרָה.
בְּרֹק בָּרָק, אֱלֹהַי, וַהֲפִיצֵם, / גְּעַר בָּהֶם וְיֹאבְדוּ מִגְּעָרָה!
פְּדֵנִי מִן יְדֵי קֶטֶב מְרִירִי / וְשִׁית רוֹדְפַי בְּיוֹם זֶה לִי תְמוּרָה,
וְאַל תִּזְכֹּר עֲוֹנוֹתַי – זְכָר־לִי / זְכוּת יִצְחָק וְאַבְרָהָם וְשָׂרָה!
וְאָבִי יַעֲקֹב, הַפֵּל תְּחִנָּה / וּבֶן עַמְרָם, עֲמָד־לִי בַמְּדוּרָה,
וְכָל שׁוֹכֵב בְּמַכְפֵּלָה, הֲתִשְׁכַּב / בְּיוֹם כָּזֶה? עֲלוּ מִן הַמְּעָרָה
וְהִתָּלוּ בְּכִסֵּא אֵל, וְקִרְאוּ / לְאֵל רַחוּם וְאִמְרוּ לוֹ בְּמָרָה!
וְאִם יֹאמַר "עֲלֵי מַה זֶּה, יְדִידַי?" / עֲנוּהוּ "קוּם וְהָקִיצָה וְעוּרָה!"
וְאִם נָא לֹא תְרַחֵם אֶת יְהוֹסֵף / צְעִירְךָ, אָן יְשׁוּעָתָה בְרוּרָה?
וְאִם הַיּוֹם בְּזֹאת לִי לֹא תְקַנֵּא – / הֲזוֹ תוֹרָה וְאִם זֶה הוּא שְׂכָרָהּ?
וְאִישׁ שָׂמַח בְּ"כִי תַעֲבֹר בַּמַּיִם" / הֲיִשָּׁטֵף? וִידִידְךָ לֹא קְצָרָה!
וְאִישׁ בָּשַׂר בְּ"כִי תֵלֵךְ בְּמוֹ אֵשׁ" / הֲיִשָּׂרֵף בְּמִלְחָמָה בְעוּרָה?
וְאִמְרוּ לוֹ: אֱלֹהִים, קוּם בְּחֵמָה, / בְּעַר בָּהֶם וִיכְלוּ בַבְּעֵרָה,
פְּתַח דֶּלֶת בְּמָקוֹם צַר וְהוֹשַׁע / לְעַבְדֶּךָ, וְכָל דֶּלֶת סְגוּרָה,
הֲפֹךְ חַרְבָּם אֱלֵי לִבָּם, וְקוּם בָּם / וְאַל אִתָּם, וְשִׁית קַשְׁתָּם שְׁבוּרָה,
וּמַלְאָכִים, גְּשׁוּ הִלָּחֲמוּ בָם, / וְכוֹכָבִים וְשֶׁמֶשׁ הַמְּאִירָה,
וְיֹאמְרוּ מַקְהֲלוֹת עַמִּים עֲצוּמִים: / "מְבַקֵּשׁ יֵשׁ לְעַנְוֵי שֶׂה פְזוּרָה".
וְאֵל שָׁמַע תְּפִלָּתִי, בְּקָרְאִי / כְּמוֹ חוֹלָה כְּמַבְכִּירָה מְצֵרָה,
וְנָשַׁף בָּם כְּיוֹם יַם־סוּף – וְסָפוּ / בְּסוּפָתוֹ וְהֶרְאָם הַגְּבוּרָה,
וְאֵשׁ מָוֶת אֲכָלָתַם וְתַמּוּ / כְּמוֹ עֵצִים בְּתַנּוּר חַם וְכִירָה,
כְּאִלּוּ צוֹרְרַי כֻּלָּם בְּעָפָר / חֲשַׁשׁ לַהַב בְּקֶרֶב הַמְּדוּרָה,
וְרָאשֵׁי הַגְּבִירִים בָּאֲדָמָה – / תְּאֵנִים נִמְכְּרוּ אֶלֶף בְּגֵרָה,
וְהַשָּׂרִים בְּמַפַּלְתָּם נְפוּחִים / כְּמוֹ נֹאדוֹת, כְּמוֹ אִשָּׁה עֲבָרָה,
וְשָׁכְבוּ שָׁם עֲבָדִים עַל אֲדוֹנִים / וּמָכִים עִם מְלָכִים, אֵין בְּרֵרָה,
וְהָיוּ עִם אֲגַג מַלְכָּם כְּדֹמֶן / בְּתוֹךְ שָׂדֶה וְאֵין לָהֶם קְבוּרָה,

וְאֶחָד מִן רְבָבָה נִשְׁאֲרוּ בָם / כְּעוֹלֵלוֹת בְּכֶרֶם יוֹם בְּצִירָה.
וְתַם זֵכֶר עֲמָלֵק מִסְפָּרַד / וְסָף חֵילָם וּמַמְלַכְתָּם גְּזוּרָה,
לְפָנִים מֵת אֲגַג עַל יַד שְׁמוּאֵל / וְהָמָן עַל יְדֵי בַעַל סְבָרָה
וּמִקֶּדֶם עֲמָלֵק בָּא בְרָעָה – / וְאוּלָם אֵין לְבִיאָתוֹ חֲזָרָה!
עֲזַבְנוּם בָּעֲרָבָה לַצְּבֹעִים / וְתַנִּינִים וְנָמֵר וַחֲזִירָה,
וְהִנַּחְנוּם מְסֻבִּים עַל אֲבָנִים / וְנִשְׁעָנִים עֲלֵי סִלּוֹן וְסִירָה,
וְנָתַנּוּ בְשָׂרָם שַׁי לְעַיִט / וְשַׂמְנוּם לַאֲרִי וּזְאֵב תְּשׁוּרָה,
וְהִשְׂבַּעְנוּם בְּדָם – לֹא דַם טְרֵפָה, / וּבָשָׂר רַב – וְלֹא מִתּוֹךְ קְעָרָה,
וְתָמְהוּ עַל בְּנֵי בָתִּים סְרוּחִים / מְצָאוּם לֹא בְצֵל בַּיִת וְקוֹרָה,
וְלֹא בָאוּ בְּיוֹם שָׁרָב וְחֹם יוֹם / בְּבֵית שַׁיִשׁ וּבַעֲלִיַּת מְקֵרָה.
עֲלֵיהֶם יִבְכְּיוּן נִינֵי יְעֵנִים / וְתִרְקֹד בַּת שְׂעִירָה הַצְּעִירָה
וְיִבְרוּ עַל לְחוּמֵימוֹ כְּפִירִים / וְתַנִּיחַ לְגוּרֶיהָ כְּפִירָה.
וְלָכַדְנוּ מְדִינוֹתָם וְאַרְצָם / וְקִרְקַרְנוּ בְנָקָם קִיר וְטִירָה,
וְיָרַשְׁנוּ פְרָזִים עִם כְּפָרִים / וְכָבַשְׁנוּ בְכֹחַ עִיר וּבִירָה,
וְשַׁבְנוּ מִבְּלִי מִפְקַד אֱנוֹשׁ מִן / חֲבֵרֵינוּ וְלֹא נִבְצַר בְּצִירָה.
וְיוֹם שִׁשִּׁי בְּרֹאשׁ אֱלוּל בְּעֵינַי / כְּיוֹם תִּשְׁעָה בְאָב אוֹ הָעֲשָׂרָה,
וְסוֹפוֹ יוֹם גְּאֻלָּה, יוֹם שְׂמָחוֹת, / כְּיוֹם שִׂמְחַת עֲנִיִּים בַּקְּצִירָה,
וְיוֹם חַלֵּק שְׁלַל צָרַי וְיוֹם גִּיל, / כְּיוֹם לֶדֶת עֲקָרָה הָעֲצוּרָה,
וְלִפְנֵי בוֹא שְׁנַת תִּשְׁעִים וְתֵשַׁע / תְּשׁוּעָה שָׁלְחָה אֵלַי וְאוֹרָה.
וְהַמִּשְׁנֶה אֲשֶׁר יָעַץ וְחָתַךְ / לְהָרְגֵנִי וְגָזַר הַגְּזֵרָה
וְאֶל עֵבֶר נְהָרוֹת בָּא לְרַע לִי / וּבוֹ גִלַּח בְּתַעַר הַשְּׂכִירָה –
תְּפַשְׂתִּיו וַהֲבִיאוֹתִיו בְּחַבְלִי / לְבֵית סֹהַר וְשַׂמְתִּיו בַּמְּגוּרָה,
וְרָאִיתִי בְאוֹיְבִי תַּאֲוָתִי / וְנִקַּמְתִּי בְּנַפְשׁוֹ הָאֲרוּרָה.
וְכַאֲשֶׁר בַּתְּעוּדָה הֶחֱזַקְתִּי / וְטוֹב לִי סַחֲרָהּ מִכָּל סְחוֹרָה –
כְּמוֹ כֵן נֶהֱרַג הֶרֶג נְבָלִים / בְּלֵיל שִׂמְחַת תְּעוּדָה הַיְקָרָה,
וּמִלֵּא אֵל דְּבַר אָבִי לְשִׁבְטוֹ, / בְּנֵי הַשִּׁיר וּמַקְרִיבֵי קְטוֹרָה,
וְדָבָר דִּבְּרָה זֶרֶשׁ לְקוֹנֶה / בְּכִכָּרָיו מְתֵי שַׁי בַּאֲגוֹרָה.
וְשָׁקַטְתִּי וְנַחְתִּי מִמְּשַׂנְאַי / וְנִכְבַּדְתִּי וְהוֹסַפְתִּי שְׂרָרָה,
וְאֵין זוֹכְרִי לְרָעָה בַּלְאֻמִּים / וְכָל קִנְאָה וְשִׂנְאָה נֶעֱצָרָה.
שְׁעֵה מִצַּר כְּסִיל, יַעַן פְּעֻלַּת / כְּסִיל עָלָיו מְחִתָּתוֹ מְעִירָה,
וְאַל תִּדְאַג בְּעֵת יָרִים אֱוִיל רֹאשׁ – / תְּרוּמִיַּת אֱוִיל רֹאשׁוֹ מְסִירָה,

וְאִם תַּפִּיל תְּחִנָּה לוֹ וְיַחְזִיק / בְּרִשְׁעָתוֹ – נְפִילָתוֹ מְהֵרָה,
וּמִשְׁפַּט כָּל כְּלִי מַחְזִיק טֻמְאוֹת / בְּגוּפוֹ, כִּי טְבִילָתוֹ שְׁבִירָה,
וְשׁוֹר נַגָּח אֲשֶׁר אֵין לוֹ שְׁמִירָה / כְּבָר אָמְרוּ: שְׁחִיטָתוֹ – שְׁמִירָה!
לְאֵל הִגְדִּיל עֲשֵׂה שִׁירָה אֲגַדֵּל, / תְּהִי עַל כָּל בְּנוֹת הַשִּׁיר לְשָׂרָה,
בְּמִדְבָּרִים כְּסַפִּירִים אֲרוּגָה / וְשִׂיחִים מִן בְּדֹלָחִים תְּפוּרָה,
מְמֻלָּאִים כְּתָמִים בַּחֲרִיזָה / וְכִזְמִירוֹת תְּהִלִּים בַּסְּפִירָה.
עֲלֵיהֶם יַעֲשׂוּ יוֹם טוֹב אֲבֵלִים, / וְתִשְׁתֶּה כּוֹס יְשׁוּעוֹת כָּל נְזִירָה,
וְכָל לָשׁוֹן תְּמַלֵּא מְרַנְּנָה / וְגִילָה עַל גְּאֻלָּתִי בְּשִׁירָה,
וְכָל נֶפֶשׁ תְּמַלֵּא פֶּה שְׂחוֹק עַל / פְּדוּת נַפְשִׁי בְּעוֹלָם זֶה – פְּטוּרָה.
לְכֵן, אַחַי, תְּנוּ זִמְרָה לְאֵל חַי / וְהַרְבּוּ שִׁיר וְתוֹדָה בַּעֲצָרָה
וְאִמְרוּ לוֹ: יְהִי לִי עוֹד לְסוֹמֵךְ / וְלַתּוֹמְכִים בְּתוֹרָה הַיְשָׁרָה.
וּפוּר מִשְׁנֶה עֲשׂוּ לְאֵל אֲשֶׁר קָם / וְסִעֵף בַּעֲמָלֵק צִיץ וּפֻאָרָה,
וְהַשְׁמִיעוּ בְּאַפְרִיקִי וְצֹעַן / וְהוֹדִיעוּ בְּנֵי בֵית הַבְּחִירָה,
וְהַגִּידוּ לְזִקְנֵי פּוּם בְּדִיתָא / וְלִישִׁישֵׁי בְּנֵי בֵי רַב בְּסוּרָא,
וְקִרְאוּ אֶת שְׁמָהּ אָחוֹת לְמִקְרֵה / אֲחַשְׁוֵרוֹשׁ וְאֶסְתֵּר הַגְּבִירָה
וְכִתְבוּהָ בְּסִפְרֵיכֶם, לְמַעַן / תְּהִי לָעַד וּמִדּוֹר דּוֹר זְכוּרָה.

### 4. Prayer Before a Battle

Behold my distress this day, hear and be entreated by my prayer.
Remember the promise to your servant and let me not be ashamed of my hope.
Can any hand reach out to do me ill when You are my power and protection?
You appointed me and were gracious; by the hands of angels You brought me glad tidings.
I am passing through the waters, draw me out of my fears;
I am walking in a conflagration, set me free from my flames.
And if there are bitter decrees against me,—what am I or my miserable deeds?
I am in dire straits and I cannot say more.
Do to me that which my heart desires and hasten to my aid.
And if in your judgment I am not worthy, then do it for my son and my Torah!

[תפילה בשדה הקרב]

רְאֵה הַיּוֹם בְּצָרָתִי, / שְׁמַע וּשְׁעֵה עֲתָרָתִי,
זְכָר־דָּבָר לְעַבְדֶּךָ / וְאַל אֵבוֹשׁ בְּשִׂבְרָתִי.
הֲתַגִּיעַ לְרַע לִי יָד – / וְאַתְּ יָדִי וְסִתְרָתִי?
יְעַדְתַּנִי וְהֵיטַבְתָּ / בְּיַד צִירִים בְּשׂוֹרָתִי.
אֲנִי עוֹבֵר בְּתוֹךְ מַיִם – / דְּלֵנִי מִמְּגוּרָתִי,
אֲנִי הוֹלֵךְ בְּמוֹקִד אֵשׁ – / פְּצֵנִי מִבְּעֵרָתִי.
וְאִם יֶשׁ לִי מְרוֹרוֹת – מָה / אֲנִי אוֹ מַה מְּרוֹרָתִי?
אֲנִי בַצַּר וְלֹא אוּכַל / לְהַרְבּוֹת אֶת אֲמִירָתִי.
עֲשֵׂה לִי תַּאֲוַת לִבִּי / וְחוּשָׁה נָא לְעֶזְרָתִי,
וְאִם אֵינִי כְדַאי אֶצְלָךְ, / עֲשֵׂה לִבְנִי וְתוֹרָתִי!

## 5. Victory Over Seville

Will You do wonders for me each year
As You have done for the patriarchs and saints?
Will You slay lions for me like he-goats
Sacrifice them in my behalf like ewes?
Will the depths of the sea that I cross each year
Be turned into paved highways?
Each year into fire I enter,—
Will its flames be transformed into dew?
To You O Rock praise is fitting,
For You are God and might is from your hand.
You entice those who run away,—for their end has come,
And on the day of vengeance You remove the impure.
I will speak of your glory in the gates
And give thanks to You among the multitudes.
I will tell of your wondrous deeds in the assembly of the saints
And of your miracles among those clothed with fringes.

About a year ago, on a fearful day
You redeemed me, making the foe my ransom.
Now after the death of Ben ‘Abbas,
I am filled with fear as Ben ‘Abbad approaches.
They both pursued me, though upon the latter's head
Sits the crown of royalty, while the former was a commoner.

By his decree nobles are raised up to rule over their
Dominions and by his command they are removed.
By his leave the mighty are given lands
To control and at his wish they are put to death.
The Berber captains heed his words
And he is acclaimed by the princes of the Arabs.
They wait for his command as for the early showers
And anticipate his murmurings like the rain.

Now there were quarrels and jealousy between him and my king.
And they remained apart in their own lands.
Both were like cedars among royalty
And all the earth's monarchs were like saplings.
Both learned how to ravage kings
While the mighty were consumed by their swords.
For a long time they slew kings like paupers
And slaughtered the powerful like rams.
There was no one in Spain to stand up to them
To defy them or rise in revolt.

At that time he (Ben 'Abbad) set out to engage in war
And stood with his armies on the borders.
He seized in his march cities and their rulers
And none could restrain him or harm him at all.
Before his hosts, masters became as slaves
While the robust became feeble from fear of him.
The generals in his army were thousands in number
And rulers came to him bearing their banners.

In their land wicked men stoned with the rocks
Of their tongues the children of the living God.
They conspired against them and took
Weapons and purchased shackles for their feet
In order to destroy the Jewish community and lay waste
Both high and low, the suckling infant and he that is weaned!
And when the king grew arrogant and spoke
With a disdainful mouth, we looked upon him with derision
And crossed over to his land with a mighty force
To take revenge for the leaders that were ravaged.
With us were men like young lions
And a host as numerous as a swarm of locust.
They were not heavy with excess flesh
Nor with fat upon their flanks
Each was dressed for war on that day of wrath.

And each removed his cloak for the battle.
Each one hastened to his sword and ran to his
Death with a willing heart and joyfully
In coats of armor that gleamed like the waves,
And shields crimson like dyed parchment
With rounded helmets and brow-plates
Upon horses like fleet and darting clouds.
They were not weighed down by the daggers and spears
In their hands as (light as) tamarisks.
Only the flashes of their swords were visible
Only their animated shouts were heard.

We returned after the carnage and the burning
And our hands were filled with spoils.
His spies hastened to him with words
Like silver become dross and wine mixed with water.
They deceived him with their wantonness and lies
As if they were conspiring against him,
Since God put to naught the counsel of his princes
And made their discernment the equal of infants.
Upon our return they said to him: "Will you remain
In the fortified city and not pursue those that stagger away?
Will you not go forth to despoil the feeble ones
Nor hasten to smite them from the rear?"
Thereupon he left in a hurry to give chase as they had counselled
With his hundreds upon thousands of hosts.
They were stationed by the river's bank, while he stood
Facing them like the rock on the day when the brooks flowed over.
They stood prepared for battle
And like pipes gave voice to mighty shouts.
It would not do to liken them to the warriors
Of the dead 'Agag, nor compare their weapons.
Though the previously mentioned were known to be like women in the eyes
Of their beholders, these however were men
Who, when they rode, were fleet like wild asses,
And on foot were swift like gazelles or antelopes.
They wore royal garb of fine workmanship
And magnificence, while wreaths were upon their heads.
With their might and armed hosts and power
They inspire the makers of parables.

When I beheld this army, so unlike the hosts

Of the despised and slain Amalekites,
And saw the fear of our brave men
And the mighty and powerful tremble,
The commanders reluctant to enter the fray
The chieftans refusing to do battle,
When I remembered the designs of the enemy
Against my people, degraded and unfortunate
Whose property the wicked had already divided as spoils
And upon whose lands, they cast lots;
When I beheld death's first born before me
And men perishing and slain in the battle,
I raised my voice with the name of God, glorified
And feared by the chorus of the seventy angels.
For times of danger I prepared it in my heart
To entreat therewith the Dweller in the Heavens
To prevail over the hosts of the foe with the power of the Rock
Who takes armies in a handful.
In times like these, the Patriarchs in my behalf pray
To the mighty God with cries and supplications.
Together from their graves they draw up
And raise salvation with cords of prayer.
With their charity and perfection they urge
That justice be done even as they hold back in restraint his anger.

Mine is the Lord that said: "Trust me
And I will make your steps to fall in pleasant places
For you I will break the teeth of the young lions
And cause the giants to fall before you."
He then put on the garb of anger and went forth
As on the day when Pharoah and his hosts were sunk in the sea.
He was revealed,—not through a window or in secret,
And looked in,—and not from behind a wall.
And He raised himself above his foes and they were
Like chaff from the threshing floor, and they withered there like leaves.
He terrorized them and made them dance
Like young oxen, like a kid and like a calf.
He made them forget their strength and they were
Like women and children in battle.
He sent an angel who deflected their swords
And turned their right hands into left hands.
Another angel he sent to confuse their counsel
And made his strategists the equal of fools.

He put lies in the mouths of his scouts and spies
Even his commanders, in order to make them die the death of vile men.

When they saw those whom they thought to have driven off, close by
They fled in seven different directions.
Surely this is the act of God, who turned
Their efforts into the work of fools,
And tied their hands with thick ropes
While binding their hearts with a covering.
They stumbled over their own chariots
Their own horses enchained them.
With the breath of his mouth He cut them off
Like cords in the hands of a weaver; He severed them like threads.
Men of renown I saw as prisoners bound
And brought in dragged by their fetters
To the king. By his order some were spared
While others were slain by his permission.
I grew weary of seeing the smiting and the smitten
Reeling in blood immersed.
The soles of feet that had never been set
On the ground were punished with thorns,
While mighty men were fallen, stabbed to death
And thrown aside as corpses of the vile.

On the night of the sixth day we pursued them
Like hunters for partridge, even as do the swarm of bees.
We felled their nobles and king
Their princes and their servants were killed
They were like filth upon the face of the earth;
Their heads in the dust were like dung.
All together they exchanged their rooms
And spacious chambers and wide halls.
Our would be captors we captured and those
Who sought to consume us were consumed.
They thought that we would be their possession
And they were by us possessed.
They relied upon their bows and spears
But I was helped by the name of the mightiest among the mighty.
They are put to shame who took for pledges
The shoes and garments of God's people.
For they have seen performed the works of the awesome One
Who renders to designers of evil their desert,

Who decided to destroy
Their giants in his wrath as in a premature birth;
Their nobles were as worms to him
In his anger, and their armies like ants!

I have seen You and like a lion You roar.
You destroy lions with your roar.
I have looked upon You and You prevail and cry out
And sound the trumpet and scatter the armies!
You were revealed and the bowels of my enemies
Moaned like the sound of lutes.
You were angry and I saw monarchs
Unable to abide your wrath and indignation!
They were anxious to fight before they saw us
And when they saw us, You turned them into laggards.
You made their bows seem like straw
And their arrows into broken pebbles.

On the second day their judgment was declared
And you brought the death of their judges on the fifth day in my behalf.
To do justice for your servant You stretched forth
Your hand upon Berber and Arab as the day's shadows lengthened,
And redeemed Abraham's son from the worshippers of idols.

In the month of the Mighty Ones.
After the passage of ninety-nine years
Salvation blossomed for me like a plant.
For You were a sanctuary to me and from the foe
You preserved me even from the hosts of the uncircumcised.
You extended your right hand to me in help
And against my enemies with hurting blows.
The angels of harm and destruction who make
The heaven and earth to shudder, were given orders.
For they hurled upon them vessels of wrath
Like the rains and anger like the issue of a storm-cloud.
You gave your servant to drink of the cup of salvation
And to his adversaries, the poisonous cup.
There was light for me on the eve of the festival of the Harvest Gathering
And it brightened all my darkened paths,
As it did on the night of Abram and the night of Moses,
As on Joshua's afternoon, as on the night when the burden of siege was removed!

**I observed properly the Lord's festivals**
**As was the practice among the Dwellers in Tents,**
**Even the Sabbath days and the day of the Shofar and Atonement**
**The days of the Booth until the exit of the pilgrims.**
**The dread of profaning them was like a fire**
**In my heart, though there were some less scrupulous.**
**God granted that the armies were freed from their labors**
**On the days that work was forbidden!**

**I will multiply my songs to God**
**For the wonders which He did increase.**
**He makes a laughing stock out of the scoffers**
**And fulfills the desires of the humble workers.**
**I will relate his praises abroad and tell them**
**To the generations to come, the children of wanderers and exiles.**
**Though the dwellers of heaven and earth**
**Be unable to laud his name for this cause.**

**At the time that the people brought into their booths**
**Myrtle from the rock and branches of the palm tree,**
**The Rock exalted me with the palm of his hand and his booth**
**Was my shelter like a sealed up fortress.**
**When they brought their willow, He made the steppes**
**Into a city of walls and ramparts for his servant's son.**
**He plucked out the glory of my enemies as they harvested**
**The yield from the splendid trees they planted.**
**And the leaves of the myrtle made atonement for**
**Me like the burnt offerings or the half-shekel.**
**He magnified himself by the waters while the people were occupied**
**With the four kinds that grow upon the waters.**

**As my enemies drew near to eat my flesh**
**I rose up while they fell down enfeebled.**
**They brought pain to my heart but God**
**Sent healing balm at the time of suffering and anguish.**
**He commanded the ministering angels and they were**
**My help from the heavens, descending and ascending;**
**Even to the nation which thought to divide**
**The booty of his people, He allotted ruin in his wrath.**
**We will build the** *succot* **with joy**
**While they lament in their shame.**
**We will recite the** *Hallel* **with gladness**
**While they chant the dirge and bewail.**

Is this done for me? For I am a worm and not a man
Despised among people, lowliest among the low.
Who am I and what is my life, my Lord?
I am great with sin, evil in deeds;
I am puny and unworthy of these triumphs,
And all your gracious gifts.
If You reward me for my merits in this world
And requite me according to my righteousness
How shall I fare on the day of judgment,
And how shall my guilt and sins be forgiven?
To the God of strength who appears in the storm
And in the whirlwind against the idol-worshippers,
Who has not given his glory to another
Nor bequeathed his praise to statues,
To him I have heretofore composed a *Shira*
And now a *Tehilla* which is bright as the stars.
Its form is similar to that of its sister.
In number of lines it is like the Psalmist's praises.
Its subject matter is more precious than pearls
With stanzas balanced in measures of verse.
The creators of verse are barren unable to bear its like.
Even the fathers of poetry are bereaved.
Both of them all the days of my life shall be
Bracelets upon my arm and rings in my ears.
On the judgment day they shall speak in my behalf
With words dripping myrrh and aloes.

Children of my people, join me in this praise.
Put it at the head of all laudations.
Set its words in proper order
In the mouths of old and young.
For when in future times yours sons will ask:
"What is this?" You will then to the questioner reply:
"A song of praise it is to God who redeemed his beloved,
Who composed it for the redeemed to recite.
It is a song of praise, great and glorious
To the glory of God and his mighty works."

[תבוסת גדודי סביליה]

הֲלִי תַעַשׂ בְּכָל שָׁנָה פְּעָלִים / כְּפָעָלְךָ לְאָבוֹת וַאֲצִילִים,
וְלִי תִשְׁחַט כְּפִירִים כַּצְּפִירִים, / וְלִי תִזְבַּח שְׁחָלִים כָּרְחֵלִים!
הֲכָל שָׁנָה אֲנִי עוֹבֵר בְּלֶב יָם – / וְיֵהָפֵךְ לְמַסְלוּלִים סְלוּלִים,
וְכָל שָׁנָה אֲנִי הוֹלֵךְ בְּמוֹ אֵשׁ – / וְתַחְלִיף לַהֲבוֹ לִי בַּטְּלָלִים!

לְךָ, הַצּוּר, לְךָ נָאוָה תְהִלָּה, / וְאַתָּה אֵל וּמִיָּדְךָ אֱיָלִים,
וְאַתְּ מֵסִית – בְּבוֹא קִצָּם – נְסוּגִים, / וְאַתְּ מֵסִיר בְּיוֹם נָקָם בְּדִילִים.
אֲסַפֵּר אֶת כְּבוֹדְךָ בַּשְּׁעָרִים, / וְאוֹדֶה אֶת שְׁמָךְ בֵּינוֹת קְהָלִים,
וְאַגִּיד פִּלְאֲךָ בַּעֲדַת חֲסִידִים, / וְנִסֶּיךָ בְּתוֹךְ עוֹטֵי גְדִילִים.
גְּאַלְתַּנִי וְשַׂמְתָּ לִי לְכֹפֶר, / בְּיוֹם אֵיד זֶה כְּמוֹ שָׁנָה, אֱוִילִים,
וְאַחֲרֵי מוֹת בְּנוֹ עַבָּאס, לְבִיאַת / בְּנוֹ עַבַּאד אֲחָזוּנִי חֲבָלִים.
שְׁנֵיהֶם רְדָפוּנִי, אַךְ בְּרֹאשׁ זֶה / כְּלִיל מַלְכוּת, וְזֶה מִן הַטְּפֵלִים,
וְעַל פִּי זֶה אֲצִילִים יַעֲלוּ אֶל / מְלוּכָתָם, וְעַל פִּיו נֶאֱצָלִים,
וְאַדִּירִים נְתוּנִים עַל אֲרָצוֹת / בְּרִשְׁיוֹנוֹ, וּבִרְצוֹנוֹ קְטוּלִים,
וְאֵלָיו יִשְׁמְעוּ סַרְנֵי פְלֶשֶׁת / וְלוֹ יוֹדוּ נְשִׂיאֵי יִשְׁמְעֵאלִים,
וְלִדְבָרוֹ כְּמוֹ יוֹרֶה מְצַפִּים / וְהֶגְיוֹנוֹ כְּמוֹ מָטָר יְחֵלִים.
וּבֵין מַלְכִּי וּבֵינוֹ רִיב וְקִנְאָה, / וְזֶה מִזֶּה בְּאַרְצוֹתָם בְּדֵלִים:
שְׁנֵיהֶם בֵּין מְלָכִים כָּאֲרָזִים, / וְכָל מַלְכֵי אֲדָמָה כַּשְּׁתִילִים,
שְׁנֵיהֶם לָמְדוּ לִטְרֹף מְלָכִים, / וְכַבִּירִים בְּחַרְבָּם נֶאֱכָלִים,
וּמֵאָז חִלְּלוּ רָאשִׁים כְּרָשִׁים, / וְקֶדֶם זִבְּחוּ אֵלִים כְּאֵילִים,
וְאֵין עוֹמֵד בְּאִסְפַּמְיָא לְנֶגְדָּם / לְהַמְרוֹתָם, וְאֵין מוֹעֵל מְעָלִים.
אֲזַי יָצָא וְהִתְקָרֵב לְמָדוֹן, / וְעָמַד בַּחֲיָלָיו עַל גְּבוּלִים,
וְלָכַד עִיר וּמַמְלָכָה בְּדַרְכּוֹ, / וְאֵין עוֹצֵר וְאֵין מַכְלִים בְּמִלִּים,
לְצִבְאוֹתָיו אֲדוֹנִים כַּעֲבָדִים, / וּמֵאֵימָיו בְּרִיאֵי גוּף כְּחוֹלִים,
וְאַלּוּפִים בְּחֵילוֹ לַאֲלָפִים, / וְלוֹ רָאשִׁים וְעַל רֹאשָׁם דְּגָלִים.
בְּאַרְצוֹתָם בְּנֵי עַוְלָה, בְּאַבְנֵי / לְשׁוֹנוֹתָם בְּנֵי אֵל חַי סְקוּלִים,
עֲלֵיהֶם הֶעֱרִימוּ סוֹד וְלָקְחוּ / כְּלֵי זַיִן וְקָנוּ הַנְּעָלִים –
לְהַכְרִית אֵם בְּיִשְׂרָאֵל, וְלַשְׁמִיד / גְּבִיר וָדַל וְיוֹנֵק עִם גְּמוּלִים!
וְכַאֲשֶׁר רָם לְבַב מַלְכָּם וְדִבֶּר / בְּפִיו עָתָק – חֲשַׁבְנוּהוּ הֲתָלִים,
וְעָבַרְנוּ אֱלֵי אַרְצוֹ בְּכֹחַ, / לְהִנָּקֵם לְאַדִּירִים גְּזוּלִים,
וְעִמָּנוּ גְּבָרִים כַּכְּפִירִים, / וְעַם הַרְבֵּה כְּאַרְבֶּה אוֹ חֲסִילִים,
וְאִישִׁים – לֹא בְרֹב בָּשָׂר כְּבֵדִים, / וְלֹא חֵלֶב אֲשֶׁר עַל הַכְּסָלִים,
וְכֹל חוֹגֵר בְּיוֹם חֵמָה חֲגוֹרָה, / וְכֹל פּוֹשֵׁט לְמִלְחָמָה מְעִילִים,
וְכֹל מָהִיר אֱלֵי חֶרֶב, וְכֹל רָץ / אֱלֵי הֶרֶג בְּטוּב לֵבָב וְגִילִים,
בְּשִׁרְיוֹנִים מְשֻׁבָּצִים כְּגַלִּים, / וּמָגִנִּים אֲדֻמִּים כַּגְּוִילִים,
עֲלֵי סוּסִים כְּעָב סוֹעִים וְטָשִׁים, / וּבִמְצָחוֹת וְכוֹבָעִים עֲגֻלִים.

יְדֵיהֶם לֹא מְלֵאוֹת בַּחֲנִיתוֹת / וּבִרְמָחִים – כְּאִלּוּ הֵם אֲשָׁלִים,
וְלֹא תִרְאֶה לְבַד לַהַט שְׁלָחִים, / וְלֹא תִשְׁמַע לְבַד רֶגֶשׁ צְהָלִים!
וְשַׁבְנוּ אַחֲרֵי הַכּוֹת וְשָׂרוֹף / וְיָדֵינוּ מְלֵאוֹת בַּשְּׁלָלִים,
וְתָרָיו מִהֲרוּ אֵלָיו בְּמִלִּים / כְּמוֹ סִיגִים וְכִסְבָאִים מְהוּלִים,
וּפִתּוּהוּ בְּפַחְזוּתָם וְשִׁקְרָם, / כְּאִלּוּ הֵם עֲלֵי נַפְשׁוֹ רְכִילִים.
וּבִלַּע אֵל עֲצַת שָׂרָיו, וְשִׁוָּה / תְּבוּנָתָם תְּבוּנַת תַּעֲלוּלִים,
וְאָמְרוּ לוֹ בְּשׁוּבֵנוּ: הֲתֵשֵׁב / בְּעִיר מִבְצָר וְלֹא תִרְדֹּף כְּשֵׁלִים?
הֲלֹא תֵצֵא לְצוֹדֵד הָעֲיֵפִים, / הֲלֹא תָאִיץ לְזַנֵּב נֶחֱשָׁלִים?
וְחָשׁ לָצֵאת וְלִרְדֹּף כַּעֲצָתָם / בְּמוֹ מֵאוֹת וְרִבּוֹאוֹת רְגָלִים,
וְעָמְדוּ עַל שְׂפַת נַחַל וְעָמַד / לְנֶגְדָּם צַר כְּיוֹם אֶשֶׁד נְחָלִים.
וְעָמְדוּ חוֹצֲצִים לָרִיב, וּבַעְנוֹת / גְּבוּרָה יִתְּנוּ קוֹל כַּחֲלִילִים,
וְלֹא יִכּוֹן לְדַמּוֹתָם לְאַנְשֵׁי / אֲגַג הַמֵּת, וְלֹא כֵלִים לְכֵלִים –
אֲשֶׁר הָיוּ בְּעֵין יוֹדְעָם לְפָנִים / כְּמוֹ נָשִׁים – וְאֵלּוּ הַבְּעָלִים.
בְּעֵת רָכְבָם – יְרוּצוּן כַּפְּרָאִים, / וְרַגְלִים – כַּצְּבָאִים אוֹ יְעֵלִים,
וּמַלְבּוּשָׁם לְבוּשׁ מַלְכוּת וְרִקְמָה / וּמַכְלוּלִים, וְעַל רֹאשָׁם כְּלִילִים,
בְּעָצְמָתָם וְצִבְאוֹתָם וְכֹחָם / וּבָהֶם יִמְשְׁלוּ מוֹשְׁלִים מְשָׁלִים.
וּבִרְאוֹתִי צְבָאוֹת לֹא כְצִבְאוֹת / עֲמָלֵק הַהֲרוּגִים הַגְּעוּלִים,
וְרָאִיתִי בְּנֵי חַיִל יְרֵאִים, / וְגִבּוֹרִים וְכַבִּירִים זְחֵלִים,
וְרָאשִׁים הָלְכוּ לַקְּרָב בְּכֹבֶד, / וְשָׂרִים מִלְּהִלָּחֵם חֲדֵלִים,
וְחָכַרְתִּי אֲשֶׁר בִּלְבַב עֲדָתָם / לְעַמִּי הַנְּמוּכִים הָאֲמֻלִים,
מְרֵעִים חִלְּקוּ מֵאָז שְׁלָלָם, / וְגוֹרָלוֹת עֲלֵי אַרְצָם מְטִילִים,
וְרָאִיתִי בְּכוֹר מָוֶת בְּעֵינַי, / וְאִישִׁים בַּקְּרָב סָפִים וְכָלִים –
הֲרִימוֹתִי בְּשֵׁם אֵל, הַמְּכֻבָּד / וְהַנּוֹרָא בְּקוֹל שִׁבְעִים דְּגָלִים,
לְעֵת צָרָה הֲכִינוֹתִיו בְּלִבִּי, / לְחַלּוֹת בּוֹ פְּנֵי שׁוֹכֵן זְבוּלִים,
לְהִתְגַּבֵּר עֲלֵי חֵיל צָר בְּחֵיל צוּר, / אֲשֶׁר יַקְּח חֲיָלִים בַּשְּׁעָלִים!
וְלִי אָבוֹת – בְּעֵת כָּזֹאת בְּשֶׁוַע / וְתַחְנוּנִים פְּנֵי אֵל עָז מְחַלִּים,
וּמֵעָפָר – בְּחֶבֶל הַתְּפִלָּה – / תְּשׁוּעָה שׁוֹאֲבִים יַחַד וְדוֹלִים,
בְּצִדְקָתָם וְתֻמָּתָם מְלִיצִים / דְּבַר צֶדֶק, וְאַף מוֹנְעִים וְכוֹלִים,
וְלִי אָדוֹן, אֲשֶׁר אָמַר: בְּטַח בִּי / וְאַפִּיל בַּנְּעִימִים לְךָ חֲבָלִים,
אֲנִי אֶשְׁבֹּר לְךָ שִׁנֵּי כְפִירִים, / אֲנִי אַפִּיל לְפָנֶיךָ נְפִילִים!
אֲזַי לָבַשׁ לְבוּשׁ חֵמָה וְיָצָא / כְּיוֹם פַּרְעֹה וְחֵילוֹ הַצְּלוּלִים,

וְנִגְלָה – לֹא בְעַד חַלּוֹן וְסֵתֶר, / וְהִשְׁגִּיחַ – וְלֹא אַחַר כְּתָלִים,
וְהִתְעַלָּה עֲלֵי צָרַי, וְהָיוּ / כְּמֹץ גֹּרֶן וְנָבְלוּ שָׁם כְּעָלִים,
וְהִבְהִילָם, וְהִרְקִידָם כְּמוֹ בֶן־ / רְאֵם וּכְמוֹ גְדִי וּכְמוֹ עֲגָלִים,
וְהִשָּׁם אֶת גְּבוּרָתָם, וְהָיוּ / בְּמִלְחַמְתָּם לְנָשִׁים וַעֲוִילִים,
וְשָׁלַח צִיר וְהִטָּה הַשְּׁלָחִים, / וְהָפַךְ אֶת יְמִינֵיהֶם שְׂמֹאלִים,
וְשָׁלַח צִיר וְעִוָּה אֶת עֲצָתָם, / וְשִׁוָּה יוֹעֲצָיו יַחַד סְכָלִים,
וְשָׂם שֶׁקֶר בְּפִי צִירָיו וְתָרָיו / וְשָׂרָיו – לַהֲמִיתָם מוֹת נְבָלִים,
וְעֵת רָאוּ אֲשֶׁר רָדְפוּ לְנֶגְדָּם – / אֲזַי נָסוּ עֲלֵי שִׁבְעָה שְׁבִילִים!
הֲלֹא זֹאת הִיא פְּעֻלַּת אֵל אֲשֶׁר שָׁת / פְּעֻלָּתָם פְּעֻלַּת הַכְּסִילִים,
וְשָׁת לָהֶם עֲבוֹתִים עַל יְדֵיהֶם / וְעַל לִבָּם צְמוּדִים הַפְּתִילִים,
וְהָיוּ מַרְכְּבוֹתֵיהֶם לְנַפְשָׁם / לְמִכְשׁוֹלִים, וְסוּסֵיהֶם כְּבָלִים,
וְהִכְרִיתָם בְּרוּחַ פִּיו, כְּמוֹ חוּט / בְּיַד אוֹרֵג, וְקִצֵּץ כַּפְּתִילִים,
וְרָאִיתִי מְכֻבָּדִים אֲסוּרִים / וּמוּבָאִים סְחוּבִים בַּחֲבָלִים
אֱלֵי מֶלֶךְ, בְּפִיו חָיוּ קְצָתָם, / וּמִקְצָתָם בִּרְצוֹנוֹ קְטוּלִים!
וְנִלְאֵיתִי רְאוֹת מַכִּים וּמֻכִּים / מְגוֹלָלִים בְּדַם נֶפֶשׁ טְבוּלִים,
וְכַף רֶגֶל אֲשֶׁר לֹא הֻצְּגָה עַל / אֲדָמָה – הֻכְּתָה בַּנַּהֲלֹלִים,
וְגִבּוֹרִים מְחוֹלָלִים, נְחוּרִים, / וּמֻשְׁלָכִים פְּגָרִים כַּנְּבָלִים;
וְלֵיל שִׁשִּׁי כְּמוֹ קוֹרֵא רְדַפְנוּם, / וְכַאֲשֶׁר תַּעֲשֶׂינָה הַנְּחִילִים,
וְהִפַּלְנוּ גְּבִירֵיהֶם וּמַלְכָּם / וְשָׂרֵיהֶם וְעַבְדֵיהֶם חֲלָלִים,
וְהָיוּ עַל פְּנֵי אֶרֶץ כְּדֹמֶן, / וְרָאשֵׁיהֶם בְּעָפָר כַּגְּלָלִים,
וְיַחַד חָלְפוּ מִן הַחֲדָרִים, / וּמִתָּאִים מְרֻוָּחִים וְאֵילִים,
וְשָׁבִינוּ לְשׁוֹבֵינוּ, וְהָיוּ / אֲשֶׁר חָשְׁבוּ לְאָכְלֵנוּ – אֲכוּלִים,
וְיָזְמוּ כִּי אֲנַחְנוּ נַחֲלָתָם – / וְהָיוּ הֵם בְּיָדֵינוּ נְחוּלִים,
וּבָטְחוּ עַל קְשָׁתוֹת וַחֲנִיתוֹת / וְנוֹשַׁעְתִּי בְּשֵׁם אַדִּיר בְּאֵלִים,
וּבוֹשׁוּ כֹּל אֲשֶׁר לָקְחוּ נְעָלִים / עֲלֵי עַם אֵל, וּמַלְבּוּשִׁים חֲבוּלִים,
וְרָאוּ נִפְלְאוֹת נוֹרָא עֲלִילָה, / אֲשֶׁר יָשִׁיב לְחוֹשְׁבֵי רָע גְּמוּלִים,
אֲשֶׁר עָלָה בְּמַחְשַׁבְתּוֹ לְהַפִּיל / נְפִילֵיהֶם בְּאַפּוֹ כַּנְּפָלִים,
וְהַשּׁוֹעִים כְּתוֹלָעִים חֲשָׁבָם / בְּקִצְפּוֹ, וַחֲיָלִים כַּנְּמָלִים!
רְאִיתִיךָ – וְאַתְּ תִּשְׁאַג כְּשַׁחַל, / וְהִצְמַתְּ בְּשַׁאֲגָתְךָ שְׁחָלִים,
וְשַׁרְתִּיךָ – וְאַתְּ תִּגְאֶה וְתִצְרַח / וְתָרִיעַ וְתָפִיץ הַחֲיָלִים!
וְנִגְלֵיתָ – וְהָמוּ כָל קְרָבִים / בְּתוֹךְ צָרַי, כְּמוֹ הֶמְיַת נְבָלִים,

וְזָעַמְתָּ – וְרָאִיתִי מְלָכִים / חֲרוֹן אַפְּךָ וְזַעְמְךָ לֹא מְכִילִים!
וְנִמְהָרִים בְּטֶרֶם יֶחֱזוּנוּ – / וְשַׂמְתָּם עֵת רְאוֹתֵנוּ עֲצֵלִים,
וְשַׁתָּ קַשְׁתוֹתֵיהֶם כְּמוֹ קַשׁ, / וְחִצֵּיהֶם כְּמוֹ חָצָץ פְּסוּלִים!
וְגָזַר דִּין בְּיוֹם שֵׁנִי, וְשַׂמְתָּ / לְדִינִי בַּחֲמִישִׁי בָּם פְּלִילִים,
וְנָטִיתָ בְּמִשְׁפַּט עַבְדְּךָ עַל / פְּלֶשֶׁת וַעֲרָב – בִּנְטוֹת צְלָלִים,
וְהוֹשַׁעְתָּ לְבֶן־אֵיתָן בְּיֶרַח / לְאֵיתָנִים – עֲלֵי עוֹבְדֵי בְעָלִים,
וְאַחַר צֵאת שְׁנַת תֵּשַׁע וְתִשְׁעִים – / תְּשׁוּעָה צָמְחָה לוֹ כַּיְבוּלִים.
וְהָיִיתָ לְסֵתֶר לִי וּמִצָּר / נְצַרְתַּנִי וּמִצִּבְאוֹת עֲרֵלִים,
וּמָשַׁכְתָּ יְמִינְךָ לִי בְּיֶשַׁע, / וְעַל צָרַי בְּמַכּוֹת וַחֲבָלִים,
וְצִוּוּ מַלְאֲכֵי רָעִים מְפִיצִים, / אֲשֶׁר אֶרֶץ וְשָׁמַיִם מְחִילִים,
וְהִשְׁלִיכוּ עֲלֵיהֶם כַּגְּשָׁמִים / כְּלֵי זַעַם, וְעֶבְרָה כָּאֲגָלִים,
וְהִשְׁקִיתָ לְעַבְדְּךָ כּוֹס יְשׁוּעוֹת, / וְהִשְׁקִיתָ לְצָרָיו כּוֹס רְעָלִים.
וְאוֹר לִי לֵיל עֲרוּבַת חַג אֲסִיפָה, / וְאוֹרוּ כָל שְׁבִילֵי הָאֲפֵלִים,
כְּלֵיל אַבְרָם, כְּלֵיל מֹשֶׁה, כְּמִנְחַת / יְהוֹשֻׁעַ, כְּלֵיל הָסֵר סְבָלִים!
וְשָׁמַרְתִּי בְּיֹשֶׁר מוֹעֲדֵי אֵל, / כְּהִלְכָתָם לְיוֹשְׁבֵי הָאֳהָלִים,
יְמֵי שַׁבָּת וְיוֹם שׁוֹפָר וְכִפּוּר / יְמֵי סֻכָּה וְעַד צֵאת הָרְגָלִים,
וְהָיָה מִמְּגוּר חִלּוּל כְּמוֹ אֵשׁ / בְּתוֹךְ לִבִּי, וְאִם תִּמְצָא מְקִלִּים,
וְאֵל שָׁת כָּל יְמֵי בִטּוּל מְלָאכָה / חֲיָלִים מֵעֲבוֹדָתָם בְּטֵלִים!
אֲנִי אַעַשׂ לְאֵל שִׁירִים כְּפוּלִים / עֲלֵי נִסִּים אֲשֶׁר עָשָׂה כְּפוּלִים,
אֲשֶׁר יָלִיץ לְכָל לֵצִים, וְיִתֵּן / כְּלִבָּם לָעֲנָוִים הָעֲמֵלִים,
וְאַשְׁמִיעַ שְׁבָחָיו, וַאֲסַפֵּר / לְעַם נִבְרָא בְּנֵי סוֹרִים וְגוֹלִים,
וְאִם אֵין כָּל בְּנֵי שַׁחַק וָאָרֶץ / לְשַׁבֵּחַ שְׁמוֹ עַל זֹאת יְכוֹלִים!
בְּעֵת הָעָם לְסֻכּוֹתָם יְבִיאוּן / הֲדַס מִצּוּר וְכַפּוֹת הַדְּקָלִים –
בְּכַפּוֹ רוֹמְמַנִי צוּר, וְסֻכּוֹ / צְפָנַנִי כְּמִבְצָרִים נְעוּלִים;
וּבַהֲבִיאָם עֲרָבָה – שָׁת עֲרֵבָה / לְבֶן עַבְדּוֹ כְּעִיר חוֹמוֹת וְחֵילִים,
וְהַדּוֹר צוֹרְרַי קָטַף – בְּקָטְפָם / תְּבוּאָה מֵעֲצֵי הָדָר שְׁתוּלִים,
וְהָיוּ לִי עֲלֵי עֹבֶת לְכַפֵּר / עֲלֵי נַפְשִׁי כְּעוֹלָה אוֹ שְׁקָלִים,
וְהִתְגַּדֵּל עֲלֵי מַיִם בְּעַם קָם / בְּאַרְבָּעָה עֲלֵי מַיִם גְּדֵלִים,
וּבִקְרֹב צוֹרְרַי לֶאֱכֹל בְּשָׂרִי – / אֲנִי קַמְתִּי וְהֵם נָפְלוּ אֲמֵלִים!
וְהִכְאִיבוּ לְבָבִי – אַךְ אֱלֹהִים / צָרַי שָׁלַח בְּעֵת מַכְאוֹב וְחִילִים,
וְצִוָּה מַלְאֲכֵי שָׁרֵת, וְהָיוּ / בְּעֶזְרִי מִזְּבוּל יוֹרְדִים וְעוֹלִים,

וְאַף עַל עָם, אֲשֶׁר אָמְרוּ לְחַלֵּק / שְׁלַל עַמּוֹ, בְּאַף חִלֵּק חֲבָלִים;
אֲנַחְנוּ נַעֲשֶׂה סֻכּוֹת בְּשִׂמְחָה, / וְהֵמָּה מִכְּלִמָּתָם אֲבֵלִים,
וַנַּחְנוּ נַעֲנֶה הַלֵּל בְּחֶדְוָה, / וְהֵם עוֹנִים דְּבַר קִנִּים וְאוּלִים!
הֲלִי זֹאת? וַאֲנִי תוֹלַע וְלֹא אִישׁ, / בְּזוּי עַמִּים וְנָקֵל בַּשְּׁפָלִים!
וּמָה אָנִי וּמֶה חַיַּי, אֲדֹנָי? / אֲנִי רַב מַעֲוֶה, רַע מַעֲלָלִים!
אֲנִי קָטֹן וְצָעִיר מִיְּשׁוּעוֹת / וּמִכָּל הַחֲסָדִים הַפְּעוּלִים,
וְאִם תַּשְׁלִים בְּעוֹלָם זֶה זְכוּתִי / וְתָשִׁיב לִי כְּפִי צִדְקִי גְּמוּלִים —
בְּמַה זֶּה אֶעֱמֹד יוֹם דִּין, וּבַמָּה / יְהִי חוֹבִי וְחַטָּאתִי מְחוּלִים?
לְאֵל עִזּוּז, אֲשֶׁר נִרְאָה בְסוּפָה / וּבִשְׂעָרָה עֲלֵי שׁוֹעֲרֵי אֱלִילִים.
וְלֹא נָתַן כְּבוֹדוֹ לַאֲחֵרִים, / וְלֹא הוֹרִישׁ תְּהִלָּתוֹ פְּסִילִים,
הֲכִינוֹתִי כְּבָר שִׁירָה, וְעַתָּה / תְּהִלָּה הַמְּאִירָה כַּכְּסִילִים,
מְמֻלָּאָה, עֲלֵי חֶשְׁבּוֹן רְעוּתָהּ, / בְּטוּרֵי שִׁיר כְּמַהֲלָלֵי תְהִלִּים,
וְעִנְיָנִים יְקָרִים מִפְּנִינִים / וּבִבְנֵי שִׁיר בְּמֹאזְנֵי שִׁיר שְׁקוּלִים,
וְאֵם הַשִּׁיר עֲקָרָה מִלְּהוֹלִיד / כְּמוֹתָן, וַאֲבוֹת הַשִּׁיר שְׁכוּלִים.
שְׁתֵּיהֶם כָּל יְמֵי חַיַּי צְמִידִים / בְּאֶזְרוֹעִי וְעַל אָזְנַי עֲגִילִים,
וְיוֹם מִשְׁפָּט תְּלִיצֶינָה לְפָנַי / בְּמִלּוֹת נוֹטְפוֹת מֹר וַאֲהָלִים!
בְּנֵי עַמִּי, עֲנוּ עִמִּי תְהִלָּה, / תְּהִי שׂוּמָה לְרֹאשׁ כָּל מַהֲלָלִים,
וְשִׁיתוּ אֶת אֲמָרֶיהָ נְכוֹנִים, / מְסֻדָּרִים בְּפִי עֻבִּים וְעוּלִים!
וְכַאֲשֶׁר יִשְׁאָלוּ "מַה־זֹּאת?" בְּנֵיכֶם / לְמָחָר, יַעֲנוּמוֹ הַשְּׁאוּלִים:
תְּהִלָּה הִיא לְאֵל גָּאַל יְדִידוֹ, / חֲקָרָהּ לַעֲנוֹת אוֹתָהּ גְּאוּלִים,
תְּהִלָּה הִיא, גְּדוֹלָה וַהֲדוּרָה, / לְאֵל הָדוּר וּמִפְעָלָיו גְּדוֹלִים!

## 6. The Poem in a Dream

Ben ‘Abbas has already perished as well as his friends and familiars,—to God praise be renewed!
And the ruler who counselled in his company was quickly beaten like dill and threshed (easily).
Where are all their murmurings and their evil deeds and their power? May the name of the Lord be sanctified!

[שיר שראה המשורר בחלום לילה]

כְּבָר אָבַד בְּנוֹ עַבַּאס וְרֵעָיו / וּמוֹדָעָיו — לְאֵל הַלֵּל יְחֻדַּשׁ! —
וְהָרוֹזֵן אֲשֶׁר נוֹסַד בְּסוֹדוֹ / יְחֻבַּט חִישׁ כְּמוֹ קֶצַח וְיוּדַשׁ.
וְאַיֵּה כָל תְּלֻנּוֹתָם וְרִשְׁעָם / וְשִׁלְטוֹנָם? יְהִי שֵׁם אֵל מְקֻדָּשׁ!

## 7. On the Fall of 'Ibn 'Abi Musa

Yours is wealth and sovereignty and power is before You.
And You are monarch, ruling over all and their souls are in your hands!
I do see it and will recount your deeds to humankind.
A blind man is he who has not observed the splendor of your glory
And a dumb one who will be silent and not tell of your works.
Yours is the majesty and the glory upon your earth and your heavens.
Often You elevated a man though he despised You,
And You honored him, and he sought to harm your loved ones,
And like Haman he denied You and said: "I have not seen You!"

O bringer of good tidings, inform me, and raise your voice with your favor
Chirp it to me like a swallow or a crane and be not stingy with your words:
"Is it true what I have heard, and how then did it come about?"
Tell me "Has the body of Ben 'Abi Musa been stabbed?
And his corpse,–is it dragged about in the streets and cast away?"
He answered me: "Rejoice and be happy and let your heart be glad,
And rise and stamp with your feet and keep on clapping your hands.
Refresh yourself with apples and be sustained with your wine,
Magnify the name of your God and let your mouth be filled with laughter.
Rise up and read the Canticles and draw not near to Lamentations.
In return for these tidings give me your spoils and your uniform.
For Ben 'Abi Musa is fallen in a pit
He longed for Ben 'Abbas, who sought to slay you.
In the darkness and in the shadows he went to see him
While the city rejoiced from its enemies happy like yourself;
It was excited and perplexed at the ruin of his house."
I replied: "Sweet honey and milk are upon your tongue
And know at once that a similar fate awaits your foes!
Take my regalia and my garments and place my crown upon your head
And go to all my friends and make them happy with your words,
That they may know that his soul is being dragged into hell
For a king has slain him, his desire for him has been realized."
Rejoice Ben 'Abbas for your companion has come to visit you.
Dwell together and take turns beating each other in the darkness.
And if you wish, tie ropes upon your heads

And let him bemoan his past and be you a chorus to him in lament.
He will be an idol to you and you to him, Micah (the priest).
And on the rim of the pit, you two may conspire to do evil and to destroy.
Like you may Ben 'Abi Musa rot in his grave.
And be forgotten, even as your miserable name and memory have been obliterated.
You had already reached the limit with snares of the fowler and with the net,
Relief came to the kingdom from your desolation and it was calmed.
There is none among you who will succeed in acquiring power in the councils or gaining dominion.
You, the digger who will scoop out his grave with your hands.
Dig for him as he has dug (for others), by your faith and your God.
Deepen it until the abyss and I will pay your reward
And smite with the spade each eye which will weep for him.
For this occasion I will dress up and cover myself with adornments and perfume and ointments.
And I will conduct myself with a cheerful heart then will I return and go.
I will be compared to doves that stand by water-filled pools
And like Samson I will buttress myself against the pin of the beam and the web.
I rejoiced at the death of my foes whether in their homes or on the battlefield.
And he said: "Who is it that accomplished your desire for you?"
I replied: "Do you not know. God has done it!"
Be silent now and write you the lines in your book for a memorial.
Read them as you do the Sabbath lesson according to your tradition
And may they be upon your heart and make them known to your children.

[בבוא הידיעה על מות אויבו אבן־אבי־מוסא]

לְךָ עֹשֶׁר וּמַמְלָכָה / וְהָעֹז מִלְּפָנֶיךָ,
וְאַתְּ מוֹשֵׁל בְּכָל מוֹשֵׁל / וְנַפְשׁוֹתָם בְּיָדֶיךָ!
אֲנִי אֶרְאֶה וְאַגִּיד לַ־ / אֲנָשִׁים מַלְאֲכוֹתֶיךָ,
וְהָעִוֵּר – אֲשֶׁר לֹא יֶ־ / חֱזֶה הַדְרַת כְּבוֹדֶךָ,
וְהָאִלֵּם – אֲשֶׁר יִדֹּם / וְלֹא יַגִּיד פְּעָלֶיךָ.

לְךָ הַהוֹד וְהַכָּבוֹד / בְּאַדְמָתְךָ וְשָׁמֶיךָ,
וְכַמָּה הֶעֱלֵיתָ אִישׁ / וְהָיָה מִמְּשַׂנְאֶיךָ,
וְכִבַּדְתּוֹ – וְהוּא בִקֵּשׁ / לְהָרַע אֶל יְדִידֶיךָ
וְכִחֵשׁ בָּךְ כְּמוֹ הָמָן / וְאָמַר "לֹא רְאִיתִיךָ!"
מְבַשֵּׂר טוֹב, הֲבִינֵנִי / וְהָרִים קוֹל בְּחַסְדֶּךָ
וְצַפְצֵף לִי כְּסוּס עָגוּר / וְאַל תַּמְעִיט אֲמָרֶיךָ:
הֲצֶדֶק הוּא אֲשֶׁר אֶשְׁמַע / וְאֵיךְ הָיָה וְאֵיכָכָה?
הֲבִינֵנִי, הֲגוִיַּת בֶּן־/ אֲבִי־מוּסִי מְחֻתָּכָה?
וְנִבְלָתוֹ הֲנִסְחָבָה / עֲלֵי חוּצוֹת וְהָשְׁלָכָה?
הֱשִׁיבַנִי "חֲדֵה וּשְׂמַח / וְיַעֲלֹץ לְבָבֶךָ,
וְקוּם וּרְקֹד עֲלֵי רֶגֶל / וְשׁוּב וּמְחֵה בְכַפֶּךָ,
וְהֵרָפֵד בְּתַפּוּחִים / וְהִסָּמֵךְ בְּיֵינֶךָ,
וְגַדֵּל שֵׁם אֱלֹהֶיךָ / וּמַלֵּא מִשְּׂחוֹק פִּיךָ,
וְקוּם וּקְרָא בְ"שִׁיר שִׁירִים" / וְאַל תִּקְרַב אֱלֵי "אֵיכָה".
וְתֵן לִי בַבְּשׂוֹרָה אֶת / חֲלִיצָתְךָ וּמַדֶּיךָ,
לְמַעַן בֶּן־אֲבִי־מוּסִי / כְּבָר נָפַל בְּמַהְפֵּכָה,
כְּבָר נִכְסַף לְבֶן־עַבַּאס / אֲשֶׁר בִּקֵּשׁ לְהָרְגֶךָ,
וְהָלַךְ לַחֲזוֹת פָּנָיו / בְּצַלְמָוֶת וּבַחֲשֵׁכָה.
וְהָעִיר מִמְּשׂוֹשׂ קָמָיו / מְשַׂמַּחַת כְּמוֹתֶךָ
וּמִשּׁוֹאַת בְּנֵי בֵיתוֹ / מְבֹהָלָה וְנָבוֹכָה".
הֲשִׁיבוֹתִיו "דְּבַשׁ מָתוֹק / וְחָלָב עַל לְשׁוֹנֶךָ,
וְתִתְבַּשֵּׂר מְהֵרָה כִּי / כְּמוֹ זֹאת בָּא לְצָרֶיךָ!
קְחָה מַדַּי וּמַלְבּוּשַׁי / וְשִׂים נִזְרִי בְרֹאשֶׁךָ,
וְלֵךְ אֶל כָּל מְיֻדָּעַי / וְהַשְׂמִיחֵם בְּמִלֶּיךָ –
וְיֵדְעוּ כִּי יְחִידָתוֹ / לְגֵיהִנֹּם מְמֻשָּׁכָה
וְכִי מֶלֶךְ הֲרָגָהוּ / וְרָאָה בוֹ אֲשֶׁר חִכָּה".
בְּנוֹ עַבַּאס, שְׂמַח כִּי בָא / לְשַׁחֶרְךָ חֲבֵרֶךָ!
שְׁבוּ יַחַד, וְהַכֵּהוּ / בְּצַלְמָוֶת וְיַכֶּךָּ.
וְאִם תַּחְפֹּץ, קְשֹׁר חֶבֶל / עֲלֵי רֹאשׁוֹ וְרֹאשֶׁךָ,
וְיָנוּד עַל אֲשֶׁר הָיָה – / וְתָשִׁיב לוֹ בְקִינֶיךָ,
וִיהְיֶה לָךְ כְּמוֹ פֶסֶל – / וְתִהְיֶה לוֹ כְּמוֹ מִיכָה,

וְחִרְשׁוּ עַל פְּנֵי שַׁחַת / שְׁנֵיכֶם רַע וְתַהְפּוּכָה.
וְיִרְקַב בֶּן־אֲבִי־מוּסַי / כְּמוֹתְךָ בְּקִבְרֶךָ,
וְיִשָּׁכַח כְּמוֹ נִשְׁכַּח / שִׁמְךָ הָרַע וְזִכְרֶךָ.
כְּבָר בָּאתֶם אֱלֵי צַוָּאר / בְּפַח יָקוּשׁ וּבִשְׂבָכָה,
וְנָחָה הַמְּלוּכָה מִן / מְשׂוֹאַתְכֶם וְשָׁכָכָה,
וְאֵין בָּכֶם אֲשֶׁר יִצְלַח / לְמוֹעֵצוֹת וְלִמְלָאכָה.
וְאַתְּ, חוֹפֵר, אֲשֶׁר תַּחְפֹּר / קְבוּרָתוֹ בְּיָדֶיךָ –
כְּרֵה לוֹ כַּאֲשֶׁר כָּרָה, / בְּדִינְךָ וֶאֱלֹהֶיךָ,
וְהַעְמִיק עַד תְּהוֹם לוֹ – וַ־ / אֲנִי אֶתֵּן שְׂכָרֶךָ,
וְהַךְ בָּאֵת לְכָל עַיִן / אֲשֶׁר עָלָיו תְּהִי בוֹכָה.
לְזֹאת אֶלְבַּשׁ וְאֶתְעַטֵּף / וְאֶתְבַּשֵּׂם וְאָסוּכָה
וְאֶתְנַהֵג בְּטוּב לֵבָב / וְאָשׁוּבָה וְאֵלֵכָה
וְאֲדַמֶּה אֱלֵי יוֹנִים / עֲלֵי מִלֵּאת וּבִבְרֵכָה,
וְאֶתְאַמֵּץ כְּשִׁמְשׁוֹן עַל / יְתַד אֹהֶל וּמַסֵּכָה,
וְאָגִילָה בְּמוֹת צָרַי / בְּבֵיתָם אוֹ בְּמַעֲרָכָה.
וְאוֹמֵר: מִי אֲשֶׁר עָשָׂה / לְךָ אֶת זֹאת כְּנַפְשֶׁךָ?
עֲנִיתִיהוּ: הֲלֹא תֵדַע, / אֱלֹהִים יַעֲשֶׂה כָּכָה!
שְׁתֹק וּכְתֹב לְךָ טוּרִים / לְזִכָּרוֹן בְּסִפְרֶךָ,
וְתִקְרָאֵם קְרִיאָתְךָ / בְּיוֹם שַׁבָּת בְּדָתֶךָ,
וְיִהְיוּ עַל לְבָבֶךָ / וְהוֹדַעְתָּם לְבָנֶיךָ.

## 8. The War with Yadair I

Give me leave my companion and friend and attend to my discourse.
Will you intimidate me with words that are not true?
For why should I fear, since the Lord is my salvation and my light!
You are still my friend, though if you continue to make accusations you will be in my estimation like the cruel ones and the heathens.
It does not go well for him who exalts himself over my house and there is no respite for the trouble maker in my city.
And if you will not abandon your evil words and persist in your sedition like a company of rebels
Then face and hear me my companions and judge between our words.

He contends with me for my consorting with kings. I reply to him: 'This is a portion of my inheritance and my lot.'
He is frightened by their rage and anger.
I answer him: 'The Lord is my protection and my hope.'
Whereupon he said: 'What have you to do with wars? I reply: 'My death and my grave have already been determined
And the Lord who informs by his seraphs in a dream, will be my help.
If I am consumed by my iniquities,—do I have a choice in the matter? All that is written in my book will (surely) come upon me!
There are some who saw no pleasure in life, like Tivni dying before his time or Zimri.
Others who never argued or entered combat yet were buried like the Egyptian.
Some were taken away unjustly and some were hungry and childless while yet alive.
Leave me be, perchance I will happily spend my days with my turban upon my head,
Drinking the still waters from my well with a helping cup and a running brook from my canal.
Will it benefit me if I despise my portion and am not content with my destiny?
Since you are concerned with my future and do not value my splendor and wealth
Seeing that each year I go through fire and water to attain these honors.
Yet you are at ease in your home and in good health; should you not fear for your own end even as I.

I trust the Lord who caused my enemies to fall into snares that lay in hiding for my own footsteps
On the day that the foe came into the fortified city and slaughtered the commander like a calf and fatted cattle.
This foe was kin to my king and the treachery of a stranger is less painful than that of a friend.
Two viceroys of Spain were there together with the troops of the Zemari.
They vanquished the city and moved like a deadly disease to the mountain fortresses to ravage them
And we moved out to expel them and God proceeded to banish them in my behalf.

The beginning of the month of 'Elul found them upon the heads of

rocks, without grass and fruit.
And we made them fall to the earth like birds who have touched the heights and are no more.
They were scattered in four or five directions like olives shaken by a hired hand.
And we slew them two upon three like the pointing of a *ẓere* upon a *segol*.
We smote them with a devastating blow even the choice troops of 'Og and Sihon the Amorite
And we defeated the two, viceroys—for this is the punishment of rebels
All were annihilated save nine who fled and he (Yadair) the tenth with them.
He was sought out and carried as a prize and a gift to my king in the month of Tishri.

My friend, in times of trouble the Rock stood up in my behalf and for this I praise him,
And sing to the Lord who discerned the fear of the foe in my heart and lessened my terror.
My melodies are offered to the Healer who put balm on the hurting place and removed my pain.
He said to me: 'Are you capable of giving praise?' I replied: 'I am the David of my age! '
And he answered: 'Is Saul (also) among the prophets?' I replied: 'Mine is the heritage from Merari
And from 'Assir and 'Elkanah and 'Asaf and Misha'el and Elzafan and Sitri;
How can I not compose songs to God who cured my wounds?
From my forbear Yedutun the musician of praises I learned to glorify (God) and I am worthy of him.
Let me take sweet counsel with God in my song and He will embitter the hearts of my foes.
He is responsible for slaying my adversaries and I am beholden to entreat him with my song,
'And to work for him like a hired hand each day for He will pay my wages on time.'

[הרהורים על מעמדו במדינה – מלחמת יַדַּיְר]

שְׁעֵה מִנִּי, עֲמִיתִי וַחֲבֵרִי, / וְהַט אֹזֶן וְלֵב אֶל מַאֲמָרִי.
הֲלִי תַפְחִיד בְּמִלִּים לֹא נְכוֹנִים? / וְאֵיךְ אֶפְחַד? וְצוּר–יִשְׁעִי וְאוֹרִי!
עֲמִיתִי אַתְּ, וְאִם תַּרְבֶּה עֲלִילוֹת – / תְּהִי אֶצְלִי כְּאַכְזָרִי וְנָכְרִי.

וְאֵין טוֹבָה לְמִסְתּוֹלֵל בְּבֵיתִי, / וְאֵין שָׁלוֹם לְמִתְעוֹלֵל בְּעִירִי.
וְאִם לֹא תַעֲזֹב רָעָה בְּפִיךָ / וְתִתְאַמֵּץ כְּבֵית מֶרִי בְּמֶרִי —
פְּנוּ אֵלַי, מְיֻדָּעַי, וְשִׁמְעוּ / וּבֹרוּ אֶת דְּבָרוֹ מִדְּבָרִי:
יְרִיבֵנִי עֲלֵי חֶבְרַת מְלָכִים — / עֲנִיתִיו: זֹאת מְנָת חֶלְקִי וְתוֹרִי.
וְהִפְחִיד מֵחֲרוֹן אַפָּם וְקִצְפָּם — / הֲשִׁיבוֹתִיו: בְּאֵל מַחְסִי וְשִׂבְרִי.
וְשָׁח: מַה לְּךָ וְלִקְרָבוֹת? עֲנִיתִיו: / כְּבָר נִגְזַר מְקוֹם מוֹתִי וְקִבְרִי,
וְהָאֵל הַמְבַשֵּׂר לִי עֲלֵי יַד / שְׂרָפָיו בַּחֲלוֹם יִהְיֶה בְעֶזְרִי.
וְאִם אֶמַּק בְּחַטָּאתִי — הֲלִי יָד? / יְבוֹאֵנִי אֲשֶׁר נִכְתַּב בְּסִפְרִי!
וְיֵשׁ אָדָם אֲשֶׁר לֹא שָׁר בְּחַיָּיו / כְּתִבְנִי מֵת בְּלֹא עִתּוֹ וְזִמְרִי,
וְיֵשׁ אַחֵר אֲשֶׁר לֹא בָא בְקֶרֶב / מְרִיבָה אוֹ קְרָב, נִטְמַן כְּמִצְרִי,
וְיֵשׁ נִסְפֶּה בְּלֹא מִשְׁפָּט, וְהָיָה / בְּעוֹדוֹ חַי — וְרָעֵב וַעֲרִירִי,
חֲדַל מִנִּי מְעַט, אוּלַי אֲבַלֶּה / בְּטוּב יָמַי וְעַל רֹאשִׁי פְּאֵרִי
וְאֶשְׁתֶּה מֵי מְנוּחוֹת מִבְּאֵרִי / בְּכוֹס יֵשַׁע וְנוֹזְלִים מִן יְאוֹרִי!
הֲטוֹב לִי כִּי אֱהִי מוֹאֵס בְּכוֹסִי / וְלֹא אֶשְׂמַח בְּגוֹרָלִי וּפוּרִי?
וְאִם תָּשִׁית לְאַחֲרִיתִי לְבָבְךָ / וְלֹא יִשְׁוֶה לְךָ הוֹדִי וְעָשְׁרִי,
לְמַעַן כִּי בְכָל שָׁנָה בְּמַיִם / וְאֵשׁ אָבוֹא וּמֵהֶם רַב יְקָרִי —
הֲלֹא תִירָא כְּמוֹתִי אַחֲרִיתָךְ, / וְאַתְּ שָׁלֵו בְּתוֹךְ בֵּיתָךְ וּבָרִיא!
אֲנִי אֶבְטַח בְּאֵל הִפִּיל אֲשׁוּרַי / בְּתוֹךְ פַּחִים טְמָנוּם לַאֲשׁוּרִי
בְּיוֹם בָּא צַר לְעִיר מִבְצָר וְטָבַח / בְּתוֹכוֹ שַׂר כְּמוֹ עֵגֶל וְכִמְרִיא,
וְצַר זֶה מִשְּׁאֵר מַלְכֵּי — וְרֶעַת / רְחוֹקַי תֶּחְסַר מֵרַע שְׁאֵרִי.
וְהָיוּ שָׁם שְׁנַיִם מְנַסְּכֵי / סְפָרַד עִם גְּדוּדֵי הַצְּמָרִי
וְלָכְדוּ עִיר וְהָלְכוּ אֶל מְצוּדוֹת / לְשַׁדּוֹתָם כְּמוֹ קֶטֶב מְרִירִי,
וַיִּצָאנוּ לְהַדִּיחוֹ — וְיָצָא / אֱלֹהִים וֶהֱדִיחוֹ בַּעֲבוּרִי,
וְרֹאשׁ אֵלוּל עֲלֵי רָאשֵׁי סְלָעִים / מְצָאנוּם, לֹא מְקוֹם עֵשֶׂב וּפְרִי,
וְהוֹרַדְנוּם אֱלֵי אֶרֶץ כְּמוֹ תוֹא / אֲשֶׁר נָגַע אֱלֵי מָרוֹם וְהִמְרִיא,
וְנָכוֹצוּ לְאַרְבָּעָה חֲמִשָּׁה / כְּמוֹ זַיִת אֲשֶׁר נָקַף שְׂכִירִי,
וְחִלַּלְנוּם שְׁנַיִם מוּל שְׁלֹשָׁה / כְּמוֹ נוֹקֵד כְּתָב בִּסְגוֹל וְצֵרִי.
וְהִכִּינוּם בְּמַכָּה כִּלְּתָה אֶת / סְגֻלַּת עוֹג וְסִיחוֹן הָאֱמוֹרִי,
וְהֻכּוּ הַנְּסִיכִים הַשְּׁנַיִם — / וְזֶה תַגְמוּל אֲשֶׁר הוֹלֵךְ בְּקֶרִי.
וְתַמּוּ כֹל — לְבַד תִּשְׁעָה אֲנָשִׁים / אֲשֶׁר נָסוּ וְהוּא עִמָּם עֲשִׂירִי,
וּבִקֵּשׁ עַד אֲשֶׁר הוּבַל כְּמוֹ שַׁי / וְכִתְשׁוּרָה אֱלֵי מַלְכִּי בְּתִשְׁרִי.

יְדִידִי, בַּעֲדִי קָם צוּר בְּצָרוֹת / וְעַל כָּכָה תְּהִלּוֹתַי לְצוּרִי,
וְשִׁירוֹתַי לְאֵל חָזָה מְגוֹר צָר / בְּתוֹךְ לִבִּי וְהֵפִיג אֶת מְגוֹרִי,
וְזִמְרוֹתַי לְרוֹפֵא שָׂם צֳרִי עַל / מְקוֹם הַצִּיר וְהִדִּיחַ לְצִירִי.
וְאוֹמֵר לִי: הֲתוּכַל אַתְּ לְהַלֵּל? — / הֲשִׁיבוֹתִיו: אֲנִי דָוִד בְּדוֹרִי!
וְעָנַנִי: הֲשָׁאוּל בַּנְּבִיאִים? — / עֲנִיתִיהוּ: יְרֻשָּׁה מִמְּרָרִי
וּמֵאַסִּיר וְאֶלְקָנָה וְאָסָף / וּמִישָׁאֵל וְאֶלְצָפָן וְסִתְרִי!
וְאֵיכָה לֹא תְהִי שִׁירָה סְדוּרָה / בְּפִי לָאֵל אֲשֶׁר גָּהָה מְזוֹרִי?
וּמֵהוֹרֵי יְדוּתוּן הַמְהֻלָּל / לְנַצֵּחַ, וְיָצָאתִי לְהוֹרִי.
לְאֵל עָלַי לְהַמְתִּיק סוֹד בְּשִׁירִי — / וְלִי עָלָיו לְמָרֵר לֵב מְצֵרִי,
וְהוּא עָרֵב לְחַלֵּל צוֹרְרַי — וַ־ / אֲנִי עָרֵב לְחַלּוֹתוֹ בְּשִׁירִי,
וְלִפְעֹל לוֹ כְּמוֹ שָׂכִיר בְּכָל יוֹם — / וְהוּא יִתֵּן בְּיוֹמִי אֶת שְׂכָרִי.

## 9. Lament for Zion; the War with Yadair II

My heart is hot within me and my eyes are tearing for I long for Ḥammat and Meph'at
And to see the assembly from Siryon moving and resting as they bring with songs to Moriah bundles of spikenard.
Even the caravan of Lebanon on 'Ariel with a voice of melody scattering crumbs of myrrh and cassia like a sower.
In the days when the young lads of Zion will be at home, like the bright and shining sun on garden beds of spices
They shall gaze upon the singing maidens with looks of love on eyes painted with the color of God's work.
And the daughters did not disgrace their fathers with sin and the sons did not commit obscenities or faults.
I yearn for the prince's daughter who, in the nut-garden placed her fawn by a lily to be gathered and planted.

Behold the roaring lions who occupy it and prevent her from entering therein.
She was ruined by the hands of strangers who stripped the open flowers, the wreaths and the knobs from the city in the beautiful region
On seeing with my hearts eye my Holy of Holies a devastated heap and the foundation stone swallowed up among the rocks.
With terror in my eyes I cried bitterly and roared with an angry heart as if it had been pierced by the spear of the foe.
O God! Will You forever raise up the daughter of 'Edom who

dwells above the stars while Zion's daughter lies sunken in the depths of the sea?
Are you not angry that the daughter of Judah is naked while the sister of 'Uz has bracelets and rings?
Arise like a lion from his thicket or a tiger from his hills and lift your outstretched and well-known hand,
And heap your arrows upon Bozrah and make Teman who is full of your wide fury drink the bitter cup.

I thank You (now) with song as when the rebel and king's kin entered the fortress in his folly
And thought to save himself in his stronghold
As he entered therein,—even a curse stuck to him like leprosy.
We encamped at its base and his men on the towers were small in our eyes like locusts and worms,
But with God's sword my troops were successful while his followers were by the sword cut down.
During the day the heavens were noisy from the tumult of horses while from their movements the earth shook and trembled,
The princes dressed in fine linen touched with red were made crimson by arrows and the assembly of the proud was colored with blood.
Here I saw a crowd breaking through and hurling stones and there I heard jubilant shouts and trumpets.
And we rose up and climbed to its tip on a ladder made of bows and flying arrows which wearied the tender hearted.
We made a road to their gates for all who would plunder and we came into their courts as one enters a city that is broken in.
And we made mounds of earth colored with their blood and a highway from the dried up corpses of their lords.
As you walked you trampled with your feet upon a body or a skull and you heard the cry of the mortally wounded.
Here were those who remembered and did avenge and were laden with booty while there the groans of the wounded flowing with blood.
There they took Yadair's two companions,—one was instantly slain, the other chained in the stocks.
But (Yadair) fled with a trembling and weak heart as one bereft of his senses and was not brought to justice or to the bidding of the king.
The fugitive thinks that every tree wishes to kill him and each rock is a sword that will cut off his arm.
He escaped to a mighty potentate while his mind went mad after what he saw happening to his companions.

But sated by our victory we took him from there by a stratagem with a high hand and clear planning
I drink the cup of salvation even that of my triumph while he imbibes filthy spittle and shame in his beaker
O God with your help I hastened to the pit and my hand played upon the hole of the asp.
I put my trust and hope in You and my soul knew well your glory and grace.
I will respond to You with exultation in the great crowd while the assembly rejoices with songs over your goodness.
Thus may I continue to live and ever be preserved and saved from distress and anxiety.

[קינה על חורבן ציון; מלחמת יַדִּיר]

לְבָבִי בְּקִרְבִּי חַם וְעֵינִי מְדַמַּעַת,
לְמַעַן אֲנִי נִכְסָף לְחַמַּת וּמֵיפַעַת,
וְלִרְאוֹת עֲדַת שִׁרְיוֹן מְבִיאָה לְמוֹרִיָּה
בְּשִׁירִים צְרוֹרוֹת נֵרְדְּ, חוֹנָה וְנוֹסַעַת,
וְאֹרְחַת לְבָנוֹן עַל אֲרִיאֵל בְּקוֹל זִמְרָה
תְּפַזֵּר כְּתִיתֵי מֹר וְקִדָּה כְּזוֹרַעַת.
יְמֵי נַעֲרֵי צִיּוֹן בְּצִיּוֹן כְּשֶׁמֶשׁ עַל
עֲרוּגוֹת בְּשָׂמֶיהָ מְהִלָּה וּמוֹפַעַת,
יְשׁוּרוּן אֱלֵי שָׂרוֹת יְשׁוּרוּן בְּאִישׁוֹן חֵן
לְעַיִן בְּפוּךְ מִמַּעֲשֵׂה אֵל מְקֹרַעַת,
וְלֹא נִבְלוּ בָנוֹת בְּדֹפִי אֲבוֹתֵיהֶם,
וְלֹא פָעֲלוּ בָנִים נְבָלָה וּמִגְרַעַת.
וְאֶתְאַו לְבַת־נָדִיב בְּגִנַּת אֱגוֹז שָׁמָּה
עֲפָרִים עֲלֵי שׁוֹשָׁן לְלַקֵּט וְלָטַעַת
וְהִנֵּה אֲרָיוֹת יִשְׁאֲגוּ שָׁם, מְנָעוּהָ
אֲזַי מֵעֲבֹר אוֹתָהּ וּמִבּוֹא וּמִגַּעַת
הֲרוּסַת יְדֵי זָרִים אֲשֶׁר חִלְּצוּ מִקִּיר
יְפֵה נוֹף פְּטוּרֵי צִיץ וְלוֹיוֹת וּמִקְלַעַת.
בְּשׁוּרִי בְּעֵין לִבִּי דְּבִירִי מְעִי מַפָּל
וְאֶבֶן שְׁתִיָּה בֵּין אֲבָנִים מְבֻלַּעַת —
אֲמָרֵר בְּעֵין חָרֵד וְאָהִים בְּלֵב זָעֵף

כְּאִלּוּ חֲנִית אוֹיֵב לְבָבִי מְבַקַּעַת.
אֱלֹהִים, הֲלָעַד תַּעֲלֶה בַּת אֱדוֹם, תָּדוּר
עֲלֵי עָשׁ – וּבַת צִיּוֹן בְּלֶב יָם מְשֻׁקַּעַת?
הֲלֹא תֶאֱנַף כִּי בַת יְהוּדָה עֲרֻמָּה מִן
כְּסוּת – וַאֲחוֹת עוּץ בַּעֲלַת חָח וְטַבַּעַת?
עֲלֵה כַאֲרִי מִסֻּבְּכוֹ אוֹ כְנָמֵר מִן
הֲרָרָיו וְהָרִים יָד נְטוּיָה וְנוֹדַעַת
וְהַסְפֵּה חֲצָצֶיךָ בְּבָצְרָה וְהַשְׁקֵה כּוֹס
לְתֵימָן מְלֵאָה מֵחֲמָתְךָ וְשׁוֹרַעַת –
וְאוֹדֶה לְךָ מִשִּׁיר כְּשִׁירֵי בְּבוֹא בַעַל
מְרִי וַאֲחִי מֶלֶךְ בְּמִבְצָר בְּלִי דַעַת,
וְחָשַׁב לְהִנָּצֵל בְּנַפְשׁוֹ בְּמָעֻזּוֹ
וּבָא בוֹ – וְדָבְקָה בּוֹ קְלָלָה כְּצָרַעַת.
וְנַחְנוּ בְתַחְתִּיתוֹ וְהָיוּ בְעֵינֵינוּ
אֲנָשָׁיו בְּמִגְדָּלִים חֲגָבִים וְתוֹלַעַת,
וְהָיְתָה בְּחֶרֶב אֵל עֲדָתִי מְבַצַּעַת –
וְהָיְתָה לְפִי חֶרֶב עֲדָתוֹ מְבֻצַּעַת.
בְּיוֹם הַשְּׁחָקִים רוֹעֲשִׁים מֵהֲמוֹן סוּסִים
וְאֶרֶץ בְּשַׁעֲטָתָם נְדוּדָה וּמוּנַעַת
וְשָׂרִים לְבוּשֵׁי שֵׁשׁ מְאָדָּם מְאָדָּמִים
בְּחֵץ, וַעֲדַת רָמִים בְּדָמִים מְתֻלַּעַת,
בְּזֶה אֶחֱזֶה רִגְשַׁת מְפִיצָה וְקוֹלַעַת,
וּפֹה אֶשְׁמְעָה רִנַּת מְרִיעָה וְתוֹקַעַת.
וְקַמְנוּ וְעָלִינוּ לְרֹאשׁוֹ בְּסֻלָּם מִן
קְשָׁתוֹת וּמַעְלַת חֵץ לְלֵב רַךְ מְיַגַּעַת,
וְשַׂמְנוּ לְפִתְחֵיהֶם מְסִלָּה לְכָל שׁוֹלֵל
וּבָאנוּ בְחַצְרֵיהֶם מְבוֹא עִיר מְבֻקַּעַת.
וְשַׂמְנוּ אֲדָמָה מִדְּמֵיהֶם מְצֻבַּעַת
וְאֶרֶץ בְּפִגְרֵי רוֹזְנֵיהֶם מְבֻקַּעַת:
תְּהַלֵּךְ – וְתִרְמֹס רַגְלְךָ גֵּו וְגֻלְגֹּלֶת
וְעַל אָזְנְךָ נֶפֶשׁ חֲלָלִים מְשַׁוַּעַת.

וְנוֹטֵר וּמִתְנַקֵּם וְעָמוּס בְּמַלְקוֹחַ –
וְאוֹנֵק בְּחַבּוּרָה מְרִיקָה וְנוֹבַעַת.
וְשָׁם נִלְקְחוּ רֵעָיו שְׁנֵיהֶם – וְזֶה חָלָל
מְהֵרָה, וְזֶה רַגְלוֹ בְּמַסְגֵּר מְשֻׁקַּעַת.
וּבָרַח בְּלֵב רַגָּז וְנָמֵס, כְּמוֹ יִבְרַח
חֲסַר לֵב, וְלֹא סָר אֶל נְכוֹחָה וּמִשְׁמַעַת,
וְנָס יַחְשֹׁב כָּל עֵץ יְבַקֵּשׁ לְהָרְגֵהוּ
וְעַל כָּל צְרוֹר – חֶרֶב זְרוֹעוֹ מְגַדַּעַת.
וְנִמְלַט לְאַדִּיר רָם וְאַדִּיר, וְנַפְשׁוֹ מֵ־
אֲשֶׁר רָאֲתָה עֵינוֹ בְּרֵעָיו מְשֻׁגַּעַת,
וּמִשָּׁם לְקָחֻנוּהוּ בְּעָרְמָה וְיָד רָמָה
וְעֵצָה טְהוֹרָה מִיְשׁוּעָה מְשֻׂבַּעַת.
אֲנִי אֶשְׁתְּ כּוֹס יֶשַׁע וְכוֹס עַל יְשׁוּעָתִי
וְהוּא יֵשְׁתְּ קִיקָלוֹן וּבֹשֶׁת בְּקֻבַּעַת.
אֱלֹהַי, בְּךָ רַצְתִּי בְּרֶגֶל מְהִירָה אֶל
פְּחָתִים וְיָד עַל חוּר פְּתָנִים מְשַׁעְשַׁעַת,
וְשַׂמְתִּי בְךָ כִסְלִי וְשִׂבְרִי, וְנַפְשִׁי אֶת
הֲדָרְךָ וְחַסְדְּךָ מְבִינָה וְיוֹדַעַת.
לְךָ אֶעֱנֶה בִּשְׂפַת רְנָנוֹת בְּקָהָל רַב
וְעֵדָה עָלַי טוּבְךָ בְּשִׁירִים מְרוֹעַעַת.
וְכָכָה תְחִי נַפְשִׁי וְתִהְיֶה לְעוֹלָם מִן
מְצוּקָה וְצָרָה נֶעֱזֶרֶת וְנוֹשַׁעַת!

## 10. On Lifting the Siege at Lorca

Though she cannot speak, send a carrier pigeon,
With a small letter tied to her wings,
Adorned with red waters of saffron and with frankincense
perfumed.
When she rises and takes flight send with her another
Lest an eagle meet her or she fall into a snare,
Or she tarry and not make haste, the other will then speed away.
When she reaches the house of Joseph, on his roof-top she will coo
And when descending on his hands, he'll play with her as with a
bird

And loosening her wings he'll read this in the letter:
'Know my son that the cursed crew of rebels has since fled.
They were scattered upon the hills like chaff on a wind-swept field.
Strewn among the highways like sheep without a pastor,
They did not realize their hopes against their enemies.
When we went to destroy them they fled in the night
And were killed, even slaying one another at the river crossing.
They were frustrated in their designs against the fortified city
And were disgraced like thieves caught in the act.
Shame covered their faces like a garment;
Humiliation stuck to them like the lobe to the liver.
They drank contempt in a beaker and sucked an intoxicating cup!

There was anguish in my heart like a woman who first gives birth.
But the Lord placed a balm thereon like rain in a time of drought.
Then did my eyes become bright and mine enemies' gloomy;
I sing with a happy heart and he delivers a dirge.
A voice of rejoicing is in my house while he bitterly bewails.

To You my rock and high tower, to You my soul is singing
In times of distress my prayers were set before You.
My son, place your heart in God's glorious hand
Rise up and recite my song of praise among the people called to assembly.
Set it as an emblem tied upon your hand
Upon your heart inscribe it with iron pen and lead.

[הנצחון על יד לורקה]

שְׁלַח יוֹנָה מְבַשֶּׂרֶת – / וְאִם אֵינָהּ מְסַפֶּרֶת –
בְּאִגֶּרֶת קְטַנָּה אֱל / כְּנָפֶיהָ מְחֻבֶּרֶת,
מְאֻדֶּרֶת בְּמֵי כַרְכֹּם / וּבִלְבוֹנָה מְקֻטֶּרֶת.
וְעֵת תָּעוּף וְתִתְנַשֵּׂא / שְׁנֵה אוֹתָהּ בְּאַחֶרֶת,
לְמַעַן אִם פְּגָשָׁהּ נֵץ / וְאִם תִּפֹּל בְּמִכְמֹרֶת
וְתִתְאַחֵר וְלֹא תָחִישׁ – / תְּהִי שֵׁנִית מְמַהֶרֶת.
וְעֵת תִּגַּע לְבֵית יוֹסֵף / תְּצַפְצֵף עַל מְרוֹם קֶרֶת
וְעֵת תֵּרֵד עֲלֵי יָדָיו / יְשַׂחֵק בָּהּ כְּצִפֹּרֶת
וְיַתִּיר אֶת כְּנָפֶיהָ / וְכֹה יִקְרָא בְאִגֶּרֶת:
בְּנִי, דַּע כִּי כְבָר בָּרְחָה / עֲדַת קָמִים מְאֹרֶרֶת,

וְנָפוֹצָה עֲלֵי הָרִים / כְּמֹץ חֶלְקָה מְסֹעֶרֶת,
וּבִדְרָכִים כְּמוֹ צֹאן מְ־ / בְּלִי רוֹעֶה מְפֻזֶּרֶת,
וְלֹא חָזְתָה בְאוֹיַבְתָּהּ / אֲשֶׁר הָיְתָה מְשָׁעֶרֶת.
בְּלֶכְתֵּנוּ לְהַשְׁמִידָם / אֲזַי בָּרְחוּ בְּאַשְׁמֹרֶת,
וְנֶהֶרְגוּ וְהָרְגוּ אִישׁ / לְרֵעֵהוּ בְּמַעְבֶּרֶת;
וּבוֹשׁוּ מֵאֲשֶׁר קִוּוּ / בְּעִיר חוֹמָה מְסֻגֶּרֶת,
וְהוֹבִישׁוּ כְּמוֹ גַּנָּב / אֲשֶׁר נִמְצָא בְּמַחְתֶּרֶת,
וְעָטוּ עַל פְּנֵיהֶם אֶת / כְּלִמָּתָם כְּאַדֶּרֶת,
וְהַבֹּשֶׁת דְּבֵקָה בָּם / כְּמוֹ כָבֵד לְיֹתֶרֶת,
וְשָׁתוּ בּוּז בְּקֻבַּעַת / וּמָצוּ כוֹס מְשַׁכֶּרֶת!
וְהָיָה חִיל בְּתוֹךְ לִבִּי, / כְּחִיל אִשָּׁה מְבַכֶּרֶת,
וְשָׂם הָאֵל צְרִי עָלָיו, / כְּמוֹ מָטָר בְּבַצֹּרֶת –
וְאָז אוֹרוּ שְׁתֵּי עֵינַי / וְאוֹיַבְתִּי שְׁחַרְחֹרֶת,
אֲנִי אָשִׁיר בְּטוּב לֵבָב – / וְהִיא קִינִים מְדַבֶּרֶת,
וְקוֹל שָׂשׂוֹן בְּתוֹךְ בֵּיתִי – / וְהִיא בִּבְכִי מְמָרֶרֶת!
לְךָ, סַלְעִי וּמִשְׂגַּבִּי, / לְךָ נַפְשִׁי מְזַמֶּרֶת,
לְךָ הָיְתָה בְּצָרָה תַּ־ / חֲנוּנֶיהָ מְסַדֶּרֶת!
בְּנִי, שִׂים לִבְּךָ אֶל יַד / אֱלֹהֵי הַמְּהֻדֶּרֶת,
וְקוּם וּקְרָא תְהִלָּתִי / בְּמִקְרָא עָם וּבַעֲצֶרֶת,
וְשִׁית אוֹתָהּ כְּטוֹטֶפֶת / עֲלֵי יָדְךָ מְקֻשֶּׁרֶת,
וְתִכָּתֵב בְּלִבָּתְךָ / בְּעֵט בַּרְזֶל וְעוֹפֶרֶת!

## 11. The Death of Naja

**How often, O Mighty One of Jacob, has my soul tearfully cried out to You and in a little while it laughed with a cup of salvation!**
**'Agag plotted to give renown to ‘Amalek,—but the hand (of God) upon the throne erased his name even as was his colleague's.**
**The adder who lifted up his heart at the sea has perished; he trusted in his navy but the fire of God was kindled in wrath against him.**
**My brother and friend, sip the cups of victory and sing to God with them and give me drink and kiss me also.**

[על מות אויבו נג׳א]

כַּמָּה, אֲבִיר יַעֲקֹב, נַפְשִׁי לְךָ צָעֲקָה
בִּבְכִי – וְכִמְעַט עֲלֵי כוֹס יֶשְׁעֲךָ צָחֲקָה!
זָמַם אֲגַג לַעֲשׂוֹת שֵׁם לַעֲמָלֵק – וְיָד
עַל כֵּס, כְּמוֹ שֵׁם חֲבֵרוֹ, אֶת שְׁמוֹ מָחֲקָה.
אָבַד שְׁפִיפוֹן אֲשֶׁר גָּבַהּ לְבָבוֹ בְיָם,
בָּטַח בְּמֵימָיו – וּבוֹ אֵשׁ אֵל בְּאַף נִשְּׂקָה.
אָחִי וְרֵעִי, שְׁתֵה כוֹסוֹת יְשׁוּעָה, וְשִׁיר
לָאֵל עֲלֵיהֶן, וְהַשְׁקֵנִי וְגַם לִי שְׁקָה!

# C. In the Service of the King

## 12. At Court

Does your king anger you with bitter words and evil deeds
And you hope that he has turned from his wrath?
But can the wisest of men break an earthen jar
And guarantee that he will once again put together the shreds?

הֲתַכְעִיס מַלְכְּךָ בִּמְרִי וְחַטָּאת / וְתוֹחִיל כִּי יְהִי שָׁב מִכְּעָסָיו?
וְאֵיךְ יִשְׁבֹּר כְּלִי חֶרֶשׂ חֲכַם לֵב / וְיִבְטַח עוֹד לְחַבֵּר אֶת חֲרָשָׂיו?

## 13. The Monarch's Favors

A monarch will not favor you unless he hopes to be
At ease while you labor and exert yourself in his service.
You are caught in his tongs: With one hand he brings you into
The flames,—while protecting you from the fire which with both hands he sets against you.

לֹא יַעֲבִידְךָ מוֹשְׁלְךָ עַד יְקַוֶּה כִּי / יִשְׁקֹט וְאַתְּ תִּיגַע וְתִיעַף בְּמַעְבָּדָיו,
אַתָּה כְּמֶלְקָחָיו: בְּיָדוֹ יְבִיאֲךָ תּוֹךְ / הָאוּר – וְיִשְׁמֹר מִשְּׂרֵפָה בְּךָ יָדָיו!

## 14. Dread Your Great King

Dread your great king whether he be resting or scolding
And fear his wrath both in your own home or in the gates.
He is pacified like a child; he rages like a boor.
He will strike you and laugh; he will slay and not care.
His anger is like a blazing fire consuming the trees of the forest.

גּוּר מַלְכְּךָ הָרַב, אִם נָח וְאִם גָּעַר,
וִירָא חֲמָתוֹ תּוֹךְ חֲדָרְךָ וּבַשַּׁעַר.
יִרְצֶה כְּמוֹ נַעַר, יִכְעַס כְּמוֹ בַעַר,
יַכֶּה – וְהוּא יִשְׂחַק, יָמִית – וְלֹא שָׂעַר,
קִצְפּוֹ כְּלַבַּת אֵשׁ תִּבְעַר עֲצֵי יַעַר.

## 15. He Promotes the Clowns

Fickleness in a king is like that of a drunkard
He is appeased when he should be angry; he is wroth when he ought to be forgiving.
Occasionally he exalts the wise, though more often
He humbles them and promotes the clowns.

הֵפֶךְ בְּמֶלֶךְ כְּמוֹ הֵפֶךְ בְּשִׁכּוֹרִים:
יִרְצֶה מְקוֹם אַף, וְיִתְאַנַּף מְקוֹם רָצוֹן,
פַּעַם יְנַשֵּׂא מְתֵי חָכְמָה, וְיַשְׁפִּיל אֶת
חָכָם פְּעָמִים – וְיִשָּׂא אֶת מְתֵי לָצוֹן.

# D.
# To His Son Joseph

## 16. A Letter on the Eve of the Battle of Lorca

Joseph, all that I endured and the anguish I suffered,—was for your sake.
Were it not for you,—I would have already roamed the world and lived like many others of your generation.
This is my letter,—its words are written with honesty and who can teach equity as well as your father?
I wrote it,—while death facing us laughed with a mouth wide and long
And me not knowing whether it was in waiting for us or our adversaries, on the morrow when they would attack.
If it is decreed, my son, that you not see me again, nor I you
Give heed to my letter while sitting, or standing, and when you sleep,—may it awaken you.
May it be your master and guide when sages and teachers will not wish to help you,
With your life and possessions and in all ways fear your Creator and Rock.
Acquire understanding and good sense for they are your praise and glory.
Fear your mother and speak kindly to your uncle and cousin and honor your friend
Be beloved by all creatures, and before you gain wealth,—acquire a good name in your community.

Joseph, give alms to each who asks according to his request, and if you have not,—speak gently to him.
And to all who are in want, give a portion of your goods yet remember your (own) needs when making your bequest.
Be brave, for valor will bring you honor but do not rest upon my laurels,
Nor exalt yourself with the excellence of your forbears and do not despise your subordinates.
That which I have omitted from this testament, seek out and study and you will be blessed.
If God will allow me to return I will enlighten you and may He remove you from evil.

יְהוֹסֵף, כֹּל אֲשֶׁר אֶשָּׂא וְאֶסְבֹּל / וְכֹל אָבוֹא בְּצָרָה – בַּעֲבוּרָךְ!
וְלוּלֵא אַתְּ, כְּבָר שַׁטְתִּי בְתֵבֵל / וְחָיִיתִי כְּמוֹ רַבִּים בְּדוֹרָךְ.
כְּתָבִי זֶה – כְּתָב יֹשֶׁר אֲמָרָיו, / וּמִי יוֹרֶה לְךָ יֹשֶׁר כְּהוֹרָךְ?
כְּתַבְתִּיהוּ – וְהַמָּוֶת מְצַחֵק / לְנֶגְדֵּנוּ בְּפֶה רָחַב וְאָרַךְ,
וְלֹא אֵדַע, בְּקוּם הַצַּר לְמָחָר, / הֲלָנוּ אִם לְצָרֵינוּ יְעֹרַךְ,
וְאִם נִגְזַר, בְּנִי, כִּי לֹא לְעוֹלָם / תְּשׁוּרֵנִי וְכִי עוֹד לֹא אֲשׁוּרָךְ.
תְּנָה לִבָּךְ בְּשִׁבְתָּךְ אֶל כְּתָבִי / וְקִימָתָךְ, וְאִם תִּישַׁן – יְעִירָךְ,
וְיוֹם לֹא יִדְרְשׁוּ רַבִּים וּמוֹרִים / לְהוֹעִילָךְ – יְהִי רַבָּךְ וּמוֹרָךְ!
בְּכָל הוֹנָךְ וְכָל נַפְשָׁךְ וְעַל כָּל / דְּרָכֶיךָ יְרָא יוֹצְרָךְ וְצוּרָךְ,
קְנֵה בִינָה וְשֵׂכֶל, כִּי תְבוּנָה – / תְּהִלָּתָךְ וְהַשֵּׂכֶל – הֲדָרָךְ.
יְרָא אִמָּךְ, וְדַבֵּר טוֹב לְדוֹדָךְ / וְלִשְׁאֵרָךְ, וְכַבֵּד אֶת חֲבֵרָךְ.
וְהִתְאַהֵב לְכָל נִבְרָא, וְטֶרֶם / קְנוֹתָךְ הוֹן – קְנֵה שֵׁם טוֹב בְּעִירָךְ.
יְהוֹסֵף, תֵּן לְכָל אוֹהֵב כְּלִבּוֹ, / וְאִם אַיִן – עֲנֵהוּ מַעֲנֶה רַךְ,
וְתֵן חֵלֶק לְכָל חָסֵר בְּהוֹנָךְ / וְעֵת מַתָּן – זְכֹר אֶת מַחֲסוֹרָךְ!
עֲשֵׂה חַיִל וְאַל תִּבְטַח עֲלֵי מָה / עֲשִׂיתִיו, כִּי עֲשֵׂה חַיִל – יְקָרָךְ,
וְתִתְגַּדֵּל וְרוֹמָה עַל גְּדֻלַּת / אֲבוֹתֶיךָ, וְאַל תָּבוּז צְעִירָךְ.
וְלַמּוּסָר טְעָמִים לֹא זְכַרְתִּים, / דְּרֹשׁ אוֹתָם וְדַבֵּר בָּם – תְּבֹרַךְ,
וְאִם יָשִׁיב יְשִׁיבֵנִי אֱלֹהִים, / אֲנִי אוֹרָךְ וְאֵל מֵרַע יְסִירָךְ!

## 17. A Writing Exercise

**Your splendid writing was arranged like the carbuncle (on the breastplate of the High Priest.)**
**And its even rows were like embroidery upon a cloak**
**It was a delight to the eyes like the first ripening green figs**
**And its scent was like that of myrrh upon a perfumed bride.**
**Write and read and give heed to the Law in curtained ark.**
**For if you will persevere,—I will add much to your pay and wages.**
**Joseph if with an iron pen you write your letter**
**(Know that) you are inscribed and engraved upon my liver and not upon the caul.**
**And my love for you is bound to the walls of my heart and to its heirs;**
**My reproof is revealed to you even as my love is concealed.**

כְּתִיבָתְךָ מְהֻדֶּרֶת / כְּבָרֶקֶת מְסֻדֶּרֶת,
וְטוּרֶיהָ מְיֻשָּׁרִים / כְּמוֹ רִקְמָה בְּאַדֶּרֶת,
וְנֶחְמָדִים לְעֵינַיִם / כְּמוֹ פַּגֵּי מְבַכֶּרֶת,
וְרֵיחָמוֹ כְּרֵיחַ מוֹר / עֲלֵי כַלָּה מְקֻטֶּרֶת.
כְּתֹב וּקְרָא וְשִׂים לִבְּךָ / לְדָת אָרוֹן וְכַפֹּרֶת,
וְאִם תּוֹסִיף – לְךָ אוֹסִיף / מְחִיר הַרְבֵּה וּמַשְׂכֹּרֶת.
יְהוֹסֵף, אִם כְּתַבְתָּמוֹ / בְּעֵט בַּרְזֶל בְּאִגֶּרֶת –
מְכֻתָּב אַתְּ וְחָרוּת עַל / כְּבֵדִי, לֹא בְּיֹתֶרֶת,
וְלָךְ אַהֲבָה לְקִיר לִבִּי / וּמוֹרָשָׁיו מְחֻבֶּרֶת
וְתוֹכַחְתִּי מְגֻלָּה לָךְ / וְאַהֲבָתִי מְסֻתֶּרֶת.

## 18. Take This Book

Joseph, take this book that I have selected for you from the choice works in the language of the Arabs.
I have copied it,—while the killing spear was sharpened by our hands and the sword drawn.
And death decrees one army to be exchanged for another, even (life's) time (for its demise).
But I cease not from teaching you though death's mouth is opened all about me,
In order that wisdom may come upon you,—for it is dearer to me than discovering my foes defeated.
Take it and reflect upon it and quit the crowds who deride language and speech.
Know that the man of understanding is like a tree of sweet fruit whose leaves are healing remedies,
While the fool is like the tree of the forest whose limbs and branches will be consumed by fire in the end.

יְהוֹסֵף, קַח לְךָ סֵפֶר בְּחַרְתִּיו / לְךָ מִטּוּב לְשׁוֹן קֵדָר וְעֵיפָה!
כְּתַבְתִּיו – וַחֲנִית הֶרֶג מְלֻטָּשׁ / בְּיָדֵינוּ וְהַחֶרֶב שְׁלוּפָה,
וְהַמָּוֶת יְצַו צָבָא לְהַחֲלִיף / בְּצָבָא אֶת צְבָאִים בַּחֲלִיפָה.
וְלֹא אֶחְדַּל לְהַשְׂכִּילְךָ, וְאִם עַל / סְבִיבִי פָּעֲרָה פִּיהָ אֲסִיפָה!
לְמַעַן מְצָאֲךָ חָכְמָה – מְיֻפֶּה / לְנַפְשִׁי מִמְּצֹא צָרַי נְגִיפָה.

קְחָה אוֹתוֹ וְשִׂיחַ בּוֹ וְצֵא מִן / קְהִלַּת לַעֲגֵי לָשׁוֹן וְשָׂפָה,
וְדַע כִּי כָל נְבוֹן דָּבָר כְּמוֹ עֵץ / פְּרִי מָתוֹק וְעָלֵהוּ תְּרוּפָה,
וְהַפֶּתִי כְּעֵץ יַעַר אֲשֶׁר סוֹף / נְצָרָיו וַעֲנָפָיו אֶל שְׂרֵפָה.

## 19. Advice to a Husband

If your wife would dominate and rule you like a husband
Beat her regularly.
Do not, my son, be a wife to your wife
She shall be your woman and you a man to her!

הַךְ אִשְׁתְּךָ מַכַּת בְּלִי סָרָה, אִם / תִּמְשֹׁל בְּךָ כָּאִישׁ וְתָרִים רֹאשָׁהּ.
אַל נָא, בְּנִי, אַל נָא תְהִי אַתְּ אֵשֶׁת / אִשְׁתְּךָ וְתִהְיֶה אִשְׁתְּךָ – אִישׁ אִישָׁהּ!

## 20. In an Alcove

Joseph moved his father's heart by responding
To his requests whether easy or difficult.
Once he said; "Let us go to the garden
For it is full of flowers and blossoms.
For I planted there an alcove for my repose
And set it apart for my relief.
It is circled about with a canal
Like the heavens overarching the earth."
And we went out to the garden beds
Arranged like rows in a scroll
(Each patron has a highway to his heart
Even the way to the opening thereof by all petitioners.)
And we sat in the shade of the pomegranate and chestnut trees
As if in a castle and avoided the terebinth and oak,
While underneath us the grasses made our beds
And the leaves were the covering above our heads.
Then the cup-bearer filled our goblets with red wine
And placed them on multi-colored vessels made of bulrushes
Which he sent to the drinker who, like a bridegroom
Awaited the arrival of his bride's litter upon the waters.
And they drank and returned the empty goblets
To the cup-bearer who refilled them as before.
The latter did not touch with his hand the one who drank
Nor say to him, "Here, drink! " There was no tumult.

It was wonderful and a sight to behold.
One failing to witness this has not seen excellence,
For there is nothing that surpasses
Friends drinking in an alcove overlaid with garden growth.

יְהוֹסֵף יַט לְבַב אָבִיו בְּמִלָּה / לְמִשְׁאֶלֶת כְּבֵדָה אוֹ נְקַלָּה
וְאָז אָמַר "הֲלֹא נֵלֵךְ לְגַן כִּי / בְּנִצָּנָיו וּבִפְרָחָיו מְמֻלָּא
וְשָׂם כִּכָּר לְמַרְגּוֹעֵי נְטַעְתִּיו / וְשַׂמְתִּיו לַהֲנָחָתִי סְגֻלָּה
סְבִיבוֹתָיו תְּעָלָה הָעֲגֻלָּה / כְּשָׁמַיִם עֲלֵי אֶרֶץ עֲגֻלָּה".
וְיָצָאנוּ אֱלֵי גִנַּת עֲרוּגוֹת / עֲרוּכוֹת בָּהּ כְּמוֹ טוּרֵי מְגִלָּה
בְּכָל נָדִיב מְסִלּוֹת יֵשׁ בִּלְבָבָם / וְאֶל פִּתְחָם לְכָל שׁוֹאֵל מְסִלָּה.
וְיָשַׁבְנוּ בְּצֵל רִמּוֹן וְעַרְמוֹן / בְּאַרְמוֹן לֹא בְצֵל אֵלוֹן וְאֵלָה,
וְתַחְתֵּינוּ לְמַצָּעוֹת עֲשָׂבִים / וְהֶעָלִים לְמַעְלָה רֹאשׁ חֻתְּלָה.
וְהַמַּשְׁקֶה יְמַלֵּא כוֹס בְּאֹדֶם / וְיָשִׂים עַל כְּלִי גֹמֶא מְטֻלָּא
וְאֶל שׁוֹתֶה כְּמוֹ חָתָן יְשַׁלַּח / עֲלֵי מַיִם בְּאַפִּרְיוֹן כְּכַלָּה,
וְיִשְׁתֵּהוּ וְאֶל כּוֹסָיו יְשִׁיבוֹ / וְאֶל מַשְׁקֶה אֲזַי שָׁב כַּתְּחִלָּה,
וְלֹא יִגַּע בְּהוֹשִׁיט יָד לְשׁוֹתֶה / וְלֵאמֹר לוֹ "שְׁתֵהוּ!" אֵין הֲמֻלָּה.
פְּלִיאָה הִיא וּמַרְאִיתָהּ גְּדוֹלָה / וּמִי לֹא שָׁר כְּזֹאת לֹא שָׁר גְּדֻלָּה
וְכִפְעֻלַּת שְׁתֹה אַחִים בְּכִכָּר / עֲלֵי יוּבַל בְּגִנָּה אֵין פְּעֻלָּה!

# E.
# In Mourning for his Brother Isaac

### 21. "Does Isaac Live?

On the way to see my brother, when they said that in his illness
he is crushed and low
A messenger of evil tidings stood in my path and was silent.
Whereupon I spoke to him: "Tell me, why are you still.
Does Isaac live?" He answered: "He is already dead."
I replied: "Silence, may dust fill your mouth!

May you be notified of every distress and affliction and may your father and mother be bereaved over you!
Did I not bring a physician who healed many others like him and sustained them from sickness?
How can he die, the great one of his age, accepted of the multitude of his brethren and seeking the welfare of your people,
Perhaps he sleeps?" He replied: "Will he awake be he prince or pauper who has fallen ill and died?"

בְּלֶכְתִּי לַחֲזוֹת אָחִי, בְּדַבֵּר / אֲנָשִׁים כִּי בְחָלְיוֹ דַךְ וְהֻמַּךְ –
מְבַשֵּׂר רַע בְּדַרְכִּי קָם וְדָמַם, / וְשַׂחְתִּי לוֹ "אֱמֹר לִי, מָה הֲדַמָּךְ?
הֲיִצְחָק חַי?" הֱשִׁיבַנִי "כְּבָר מֵת". / עֲנִיתִיו "הַחֲרֵשׁ–עַפְרָא בְּכַמָּךְ!–
וְתִתְבַּשֵּׂר בְּכָל צָרָה וְצוּקָה / וְאוֹתְךָ יְשַׁכְּלוּ הוֹרְךָ וְאִמָּךְ.
הֲלֹא רוֹפֵא הֲבִיאוֹתִי, וְרַבִּים / כְּמוֹתוֹ מֵחֳלִי רִפֵּא וְסָמַךְ,
וְאֵיךְ יָמוּת גְּדוֹל דּוֹרוֹ וְרָצוּי / לְרֹב אֶחָיו וְדוֹרֵשׁ טוֹב לְעַמָּךְ,
וְיָשֵׁן הוּא?" הֱשִׁיבַנִי "הֲיֵעוֹר / אֲשֶׁר חָלָה וּמֵת, אִם שַׂר וְאִם מָךְ?"

## 22. A Curtain of Stones

O first born of my mother, the prince of death has dealt violently with you and from this world, at sunset, drove you away.
In the evening there will be between us a curtain of stones and dusty earth.
Your wealth will not aid you, nor your glory on the day of your misfortune, nor your purse or cup.
I kissed you and you did not respond, though you lay upon your bed like a man of health.
And I cried out and you did not answer, for your tongue has ceased from speaking.
You will sleep the sleep of ages which the Rock has destined for all his creatures.
And in a ripe old age He has made you sip the deadly cup and in a little while I (too) will drink from it!

בְּכוֹר אִמִּי, בְּכוֹר מָוֶת חֲמָסְךָ / וּמִזֶּה עֵת נְטוֹת שֶׁמֶשׁ יְנִיסְךָ,
וְלָעֶרֶב יְהִי בֵּינִי וּבֵינְךָ / אֲבָנִים וַעֲפַר אֶרֶץ לְמָסָךְ,
וְלֹא הוֹעִיל לְךָ הוֹנְךָ וְהוֹדְךָ / בְּיוֹם אֵידְךָ, וְלֹא כִיסְךָ וְכוֹסָךְ.
נְשַׁקְתִּיךָ – וְלֹא שַׁתָּ לְבָבְךָ, / וְאַתְּ שׁוֹכֵב כְּאִישׁ בָּרִיא בְּעַרְשָׂךְ,
וְצָעַקְתִּי – וְלֹא תָשִׁיב, לְמַעַן / לְשׁוֹנְךָ מִלְּדַבֵּר סָר וְחָשַׂךְ.
וְיָשַׁנְתָּ שְׁנַת עוֹלָם אֲשֶׁר צוּר / עֲלֵי כָל מַעֲשָׂיו הִפִּיל וְנָסַךְ,
וְהִשְׁקוּךָ בְּכֶלַח כּוֹס תְּמוּתָה / וְכִמְעַט קָט אֲנִי שׁוֹתֶה בְּכוֹסָךְ!

## 23. I Carried Him to his Grave

O my tongue, I make a request of you: By my life, please raise up a cry of lament
For my brother and father even father to all who were crushed in judgment and to the plundered widow,
For the patron who opened his doors to every passer-by though all others were closed,
Who shepherded both bear and cow alike and none were violent or vile.
I washed him and dressed him and placed him on the bed, while from my mouth was the voice of a woman in labor.
And I carried him to his grave, and my garments were rent on the left side of my cloak
My loved ones were seated about me while I arose, went down and lowered him into the grave.
And they said: "Time will yet be good to you and you will be at rest." With anguish I replied to them:
"Cursed be the goodness of this life even all contentment, after my brother!
O God take my life since sorrow such as this I cannot bear!"

לְשׁוֹנִי, אֶשְׁאֲלָה מִמֵּךְ שְׁאֵלָה: / בְּחַיַּי הַעֲלִי נָא קוֹל יְלָלָה
עֲלֵי אָחִי וְאָבִי וַאֲבִי כָל / רְצוּץ מִשְׁפָּט וְאַלְמָנָה גְזוּלָה,
וְעַל נָדִיב אֲשֶׁר פָּתַח דְּלָתָיו / לְכָל עוֹבֵר, וְכָל דֶּלֶת נְעוּלָה;
אֲשֶׁר הִרְעָה כְּאֶחָד דֹּב וּפָרָה / וְאֵין טוֹרֵף וְאֵין עוֹשֶׂה נְבָלָה.
רְחַצְתִּיהוּ וְהִלְבַּשְׁתִּיו וְשַׂמְתִּיו / בְּמִטָּה וַעֲלֵי פִי – קוֹל כְּחוֹלָה,
וְהוֹלַכְתִּיו אֱלֵי קִבְרוֹ, וּמַדַּי / קְרוּעִים וַעֲטִיפָתִי שְׂמֹאלָה,
וְיָשְׁבוּ אוֹהֲבַי סָבִיב וְקַמְתִּי / וְיָרַדְתִּי וְהוֹרַדְתִּיו שְׁאוֹלָה.
וְאָמְרוּ "עוֹד יְיֵטִיב הַזְּמָן לָךְ / וְתָנוּחַ". הֲשִׁיבוֹתִים בְּחִילָה

"עֲלֵי טוֹב הַזְּמָן הַזֶּה וְעַל כֹּל / מְנוּחָה אַחֲרֵי אָחִי קְלָלָה!
אֱיָלוּתִי, קְחָה נַפְשִׁי, לְמַעַן / נְשֹׂא יָגוֹן כְּמוֹ זֶה לֹא יְכוֹלָה!"

## 24. A Day Ago I Buried You

Lo, I return with my spirit in torment
May God have mercy upon you, my brother!
A day ago I buried you
But even now my complaint is bitter.
Greetings I bring you! Do you not hear
When I call to you with all my might?
Answer me: Do you not recognize
The response of my crying lament?
Are your bones starting to wither
And your teeth loosening in the jaw?
Has your moistness fled in the night
Even as mine is running in my tears?
O first born of my father, I have left you
As security in the hand of my Creator
Whose assurance I trust
That you will go in peace.

אֲהָהּ, שַׁבְתִּי בְּצַר רוּחִי, / אֱלֹהִים יְחָנְךָ, אָחִי!
קְבַרְתִּיךָ בְּיוֹם אֶמֶשׁ / וְגַם הַיּוֹם מְרִי שִׂיחִי.
לְךָ שָׁלוֹם! הֲלֹא תִשְׁמַע / בְּקָרְאִי לָךְ בְּכָל כֹּחִי?
הֲשִׁיבֵנִי: הֲתַכִּיר מַ־ / עֲנֵה קִינִי בְּהַצְרִיחִי?
הֲרָפְתָה מִמְּךָ עֶצֶם / וּמַכְתֵּשׁ מִמְּקוֹם לֶחִי,
וְנָס לֵחָךְ בְּלַיְלָה, כִּי / כְבָר נָס מִבְּכִי לֵחִי?
עֲזַבְתִּיךָ, בְּכוֹר אָבִי, / לְפִקָּדוֹן בְּיַד גֹּחִי,
וְאֶבְטַח כִּי אֱלֵי שָׁלוֹם / תְּהִי הוֹלֵךְ לְמַבְטִיחִי!

## 25. Within the Earth They Have Locked You Up

Is there a sea between us that I may not come to visit you
Nor hasten with a trembling heart and sit beside your grave?
If I do not, then truly I will be a traitor to your love!

**O my brother, I sit beside your grave facing you.**
**There is an ache within my heart for you like the agony I felt upon your death!**
**If I greet you I do not hear your reply**
**And you do not go out to meet me on the day that I come to your plot of land.**
**You do not laugh with joy at my approach, nor I at yours.**
**And I do not see your features, nor you mine,**
**Since the pit is your home and the grave your dwelling place!**
**First born of my father and son of my mother, peace be to you in your future**
**And may the spirit of God rest upon you and upon your soul!**
**I go back to my place for within the earth they have imprisoned you.**
**I slumber for a time and then awake, but yours is the sleep of eternity.**
**And until the day of my release is come my heart is in flames by your departure!**

הֲיָם בֵּינִי וּבֵינֶךָ / וְלֹא אֶטֶּה לְחַלּוֹתְךָ
וְלֹא אָרוּץ בְּלֵב חָרֵד / וְאֵשֵׁב עַל קְבוּרָתְךָ?
אֱמֶת, אִם אֶעֱשֶׂה כָּזֹאת / אֱהִי בוֹגֵד בְּאַחֲוָתְךָ!
אֲהָהּ, אָחִי, אֲנִי יוֹשֵׁב / עֲלֵי קִבְרְךָ לְעֻמָּתְךָ,
לְךָ מַכְאוֹב בְּתוֹךְ לִבִּי / כְּמַכְאוֹבִי בְּמִיתָתְךָ.
וְאִם אֶתֵּן לְךָ שָׁלוֹם – / וְלֹא אֶשְׁמַע תְּשׁוּבָתְךָ,
וְלֹא תֵצֵא לְפָגְשֵׁנִי / בְּיוֹם בּוֹאִי לְאַדְמָתְךָ,
וְלֹא תִשְׂחַק בְּקִרְבָתִי / וְלֹא אֶשְׂחַק בְּקִרְבָתְךָ,
וְלֹא תִרְאֶה תְּמוּנָתִי / וְלֹא אֶרְאֶה תְמוּנָתְךָ,
לְמַעַן כִּי שְׁאוֹל בֵּיתְךָ / וּבַקֶּבֶר מְעוֹנָתְךָ –
בְּכוֹר אָבִי וּבֶן אִמִּי, / שְׁלוֹמִים לְךָ בְּאַחֲרִיתְךָ,
וְרוּחַ אֵל תְּהִי נָחָה / עֲלֵי רוּחֲךָ וְנִשְׁמָתְךָ!
אֲנִי הוֹלֵךְ לְאַרְצִי, כִּי / בְּאֶרֶץ סָגְרוּ אוֹתְךָ.
וְאָנוּם עֵת וְאִיקַץ עֵת – / וְאַתְּ לָעַד בְּנוּמָתְךָ,
וְעַד בּוֹא יוֹם חֲלִיפָתִי / בְּלִבִּי אֵשׁ פְּרִידָתְךָ!

# F.
# On His Life

## 26. The Promise

I remember your good tidings on the day of distress and anguish;
You are good and righteous both in word and deed!
I remember the good tidings which comfort me when misfortune
Comes and I hope for your help and support:
When You sent Seraphs to your servant, while yet a boy lying upon
His bed, to inform him of your manifold goodness.
They sat before me whereupon Michael said:
"This is the word of God who pleads your cause:
Whenever you pass over dangerous waters, I will be with you
Rivers will not drown you on the day that your foe approaches."
Even Gabriel his colleague spoke of what he had heard
Concerning me within your chariot and environs:
"When you walk through fire, you shall not be burned
I shall speak to the flame that it never kindle upon you."
These are the tidings upon which I rely like a sword in hand.
Swords I see but it is in yours that I trust.

יוֹם צַר וּמָצוֹק אֲנִי זוֹכֵר בְּשׂוֹרָתְךָ –
טוֹב אַתְּ, וְצֶדֶק בְּמוֹ פִּיךָ וּבִלְבָבְךָ!
אֶזְכֹּר בְּשׂוֹרָה אֲשֶׁר הִיא לִי לְנַחֵם בְּבוֹא
צָרָה וְאוֹחִיל לְיֶשְׁעֲךָ וְשִׂגּוּבְךָ:
תִּשְׁלַח לְעַבְדְּךָ – וְהוּא שׁוֹכֵב בְּעַרְשׂוֹ וְהוּא
נַעַר – שְׂרָפִים לְבַשְּׂרֵנִי בְּרֹב טוּבְךָ.
יָשְׁבוּ לְנֶגְדִּי וּמִיכָאֵל אֲזַי שָׂח בְּכֹה
״אָמַר יְיָ אֲשֶׁר יָרִיב לְךָ רִיבְךָ:
כִּי תַעֲבֹר יוֹם בְּמֵי צָרָה – אֲנִי אִתְּךָ,
לֹא יִשְׁטְפוּךָ נְהָרוֹת יוֹם קְרֹב אוֹיִבְךָ״.
גַּם גַּבְרִיאֵל חֲבֵרוֹ בִּשְּׂרַנִי אֲשֶׁר
שָׁמַע בְּמֶרְכַּבְתְּךָ עָלַי וּבִסְבִיבְךָ:

״כִּי תֵלְכָה לָךְ בְּמוֹ אֵשׁ, לֹא תְכַוֶּה לְךָ –
אֹמַר לְלַהַב וְלֹא יִבְעַר לְעוֹלָם בְּךָ״.
זֹאת הַבְּשׂוֹרָה אֲשֶׁר אֶתְמֹךְ כְּחֶרֶב בְּיָד,
אֶרְאֶה חֲרָבוֹת – וְאֶשָּׁעֵן עֲלֵי חַרְבְּךָ!

## 27. Will You Remember This Only?

Samuel, approach the One seated upon the cherubs with free-will offerings of your lips like rain upon the grass
And may the acclaim of the Rock your redeemer within your mouth and heart be beloved.
When you go upon the way, remember what He has done for you upon the thoroughfares
And praise God who favored you and say: "Blessed are You who rewards the righteous!'
Remember the signs which He showed you here, like the miracles for his pure ones close to him.
On the day that kings gave chase to kill you upon horses thick as clouds
And went about in devious ways designed to ambush you from all sides,
You fled and fell into the river whose banks overflowed like a philanthropist's generosity,
But they were disappointed in their hopes as they returned frustrated with bitter sadness.

Will you remember this only? Will you not recall when He gave you light for nine months in the dark recesses,
And curdled you like cheese in the womb and poured you out, fat like milk.
He nursed you to your fill,—though not by mouth, and He brought forth your waste,—though not through excretory channels.
He prepared your creation within it and brought you forth at the end of the appointed days.

Will you remember this only? Will you not recall his actions at your birth, during the days when you were nursed on milk.
For you without understanding the days were as nights and morning like evening.
You did not discern between far and near and knew not truth from falsehood.

You could not do for yourself so He put you in charge of generous parents.
And placed love for you in their hearts to feed you though they be hungry,
And to protect you, with the approaching frost at night even to guard you by day from the heat.
Afterward He gave you intelligence to speak and you tender in age, your branches moist.
And He guided you and taught you to walk and you jumped like a grasshopper.

Will you remember this only? Will you not recall when He gave you knowledge and good sense like the hoary ones with age.
And He made you wise with his Scripture and Law, they being designated the first among the sciences,
And gave you to know the lore of the Greeks and helped you understand the wisdom of the Arabs
To open eloquently among the famous the doors of intelligence that heretofore were not penetrated.
He made your name great and mighty across the sea and in the lands of the west.

Will you remember this only? Will you not recall that He placed your throne above the distinguished stars,
And bestowed much riches according to the good hand of God even silver like the trees of the forest and gold like common stones,
And garments of fine linen and purple and embroidered work and ornamental wares were dragged into your house.
He gave you a heart wide as the sea and your hands were fresh like a rain shower.
He taught you how to reply nobly when standing before the king so as to save a life from the pit
And in peacetime, the proper conduct of peace even wise strategy in seasons of war.
He instructed you how to ignite the flames of conflict or put out the heated passions in the councils
Even to tread upon an enemy with an angry spirit as one presses grapes in a wine cellar.

Will you remember this only? Will you not recall when He stood up for you in time of trouble and redeemed you speedily,
And sated your sword with blood like water drawn from wells of rejoicing

On the day when distress and fear were hot like an oven giving off flames from all sides.
And all were gloomy and each heart like wax and every face was pale.
And arrows and spears sent down like rain mingled in the air,
Even upon the chiefs and horsemen and nobles swords opened their mouths wide.
He saved you from the approaching disaster though none among your dear ones could help.
His deeds multiplied defying count or telling nor could they be contained in a book.

O God give your servant words to tell the glory of your excellence upon your grace and goodness.
In your grace,—You bestowed your kindness upon him in times of distress, though he was heavy with sin,
And in your goodness,—which he found like water in the desert and grapes in the wilderness.
I will speak of your deeds to all that are standing or sitting and to each passerby,
And tongues will be filled with their telling and books replete with their records.
They will go on the highways with travelers to Zoan and to the lands of Lehavim.

O God the servant did perversely yet You supported him with precious wealth and embroidered tapestries
And with a great name like that of the pious who tremble and are anxious at your words.
Yet he went astray like the wicked after his heart and eyes and turned to the proud ones.
Erase his guilt and hear his prayer and may the utterances of his lips be agreeable before You.
Does it profit You that you remember the transgressions of your familiars and the debts of your loved ones?
And if his guilt testifies against him,—may the angels be his righteous defenders.

O God there are themes in my lines which my detractors treat with abuse.
Yet they have not drawn as from deep waters but have contrived as with stolen waters.
They are to be compared to broken cisterns,—though they be hewed out and filled with all goodness.

Even their interpretation is revealed to You as is my heart known to You, for You try the heart.

O God destroy not your creation, and do not transfer healing for pain,
And may my loved ones not be ashamed of me nor the dogs laugh at me in the day of calamity.
Cover me with your pinions and your shade, according to my desire and not that of my foes
And sweeten my years until death and dulcify the clods of earth in my grave.

שְׁמוּאֵל, קַדְּמָה יוֹשֵׁב כְּרוּבִים / בְּנִדְבַת פֶּה כְּמָטָר עַל עֲשָׂבִים,
וְיִהְיוּ מַהְלְלֵי הַצּוּר גְּאָלָךְ / בְּתוֹךְ פִּיךָ וְלִבְּךָ נֶאֱהָבִים,
וְעֵת תֵּלֵךְ עֲלֵי נָתִיב זְכֹר אֵת / אֲשֶׁר עָשָׂה לְךָ עַל הַנְּתִיבִים,
וּבָרֵךְ אֵל גְּמָלָךְ טוֹב וְשִׂיחַ / "מְבֹרָךְ אַתְּ, מְשַׁלֵּם טוֹב לְטוֹבִים!"
זְכֹר אוֹתוֹת אֲשֶׁר עָשָׂה לְךָ פֹה / כְּאוֹתוֹתָיו לְבָרְיו הַקְּרוֹבִים —
בְּיוֹם רָדְפוּ מְלָכִים אַחֲרֶיךָ / לְהָרְגֶךָ עֲלֵי סוּסִים כְּעָבִים,
וְיָצְאוּ מֵעֲקַלְקַלּוֹת נְתָנוּם / לְךָ מִפֹּה וּמִפֹּה מַאֲרָבִים.
וּבָרַחְתָּ וְנָפַלְתָּ בְנָהָר, / גְּדוֹתָיו יִגְרוּ כִּידֵי נְדִיבִים,
וּבוֹשׁוּ מֵאֲשֶׁר קִוּוּ, וְשָׁבוּ / בְּפַח נֶפֶשׁ וּבִמְרִירוּת עֲצָבִים.
הֲזֶה תִזְכֹּר? הֲלֹא תִזְכֹּר בְּהִלּוֹ / לְךָ תִּשְׁעָה בְּמַחְשַׁכֵּי קְרָבִים,
וְהִקְפִּיאֲךָ בְּבֶטֶן כַּגְּבִינָה / וְהִתִּיךְ בָּךְ כְּמוֹ חָלָב חֲלָבִים,
וְהֵינִיקְךָ לְשָׂבְעָה לֹא עֲלֵי פֶה / וְהוֹצִיא רַעֲךָ לֹא עַל נְקָבִים,
וְהֵכִין אֶת יְצִירָתְךָ בְּתוֹכָהּ / וְהוֹצִיאֲךָ לְקֵץ יָמִים חֲשׁוּבִים.
הֲזֶה תִזְכֹּר? הֲלֹא תִזְכֹּר פְּעָלָיו / בְּיַלְדוּתְךָ יְמֵי יֶנֶק חֲלָבִים,
וְהַיָּמִים בְּעֵינֶיךָ כְּלֵילוֹת, / בְּלִי דַעַת, וּבֹקֶר כַּעֲרָבִים,
וְלֹא תַכִּיר קְרוֹבִים מֵרְחוֹקִים / וְלֹא תֵדַע אֱמֶת מִן הַכְּזָבִים,
וְלֹא תוּכַל עֲשׂוֹת טוֹבָה לְנַפְשְׁךָ / וְהִפְקִידְךָ בְּיַד אָבוֹת מְטִיבִים.
וְנָתַן לְךָ בְּלִבּוֹתָם חֲנִינָה / לְהַשְׂבִּיעֲךָ, וְלוּ הָיוּ רְעֵבִים,
וְלִשְׁמָרְךָ בְּבוֹא קֶרַח בְּלַיִל / וְלִשְׁמָרְךָ בְּיוֹמָם מִן שְׁרָבִים,
וְהִשְׂכִּילְךָ אֱלֵי יָמִים לְדַבֵּר — / וְאַתְּ רַךְ וַעֲנָפֶיךָ רְטוּבִים —
וְהִנְהִיגְךָ וְהוֹלִיכְךָ בְּרֶגֶל / וְהָיִיתָ מְנַתֵּר כַּחֲגָבִים.
הֲזֶה תִזְכֹּר? הֲלֹא תִזְכֹּר בְּשׁוּמוֹ / לְךָ מַדָּע וְשֵׂכֶל טוֹב כְּשָׂבִים,

וְהֶחְכִּימְךָ בְּמִקְרָאוֹ וְדָתוֹ / אֲשֶׁר הֵמָּה בְּרֹאשׁ חָכְמוֹת נְקוּבִים,
וְהוֹדִיעֲךָ תְּבוּנַת הַיְּוָנִים / וְהִשְׂכִּילְךָ בְּחָכְמַת הָעֲרָבִים,
לְפַתֵּחַ בְּצַחוּת בֵּין נְקוּבִים / בְּשֵׁם פִּתְחֵי תְבוּנָה לֹא נְקוּבִים,
וְעָשָׂה אֶת שְׁמָךְ גָּדוֹל וְעָצוּם / בְּעֵבֶר יָם וְאַרְצוֹת מַעֲרָבִים.
הֲזֶה תִזְכֹּר? הֲלֹא תִזְכֹּר בְּנָתְנוֹ / לְךָ כֵּס עַל בְּנֵי עָשׁ הַחֲשׁוּבִים,
וְעֹשֶׁר רַב כְּיַד הָאֵל, וְכֶסֶף — / כְּעֵץ יַעַר, וְכָאֶבֶן — זְהָבִים,
וּבֶגֶד בּוּץ וְאַרְגָּמָן וְרִקְמָה / וּמַכְלוּלִים בְּתוֹךְ בֵּיתְךָ סְחוּבִים.
וְנָתַן לִבְּךָ רָחָב כְּמוֹ יָם / וְכַפְּךָ רַעֲנָנָה כָּרְבִיבִים,
וְהוֹרְךָ לַעֲנוֹת, עֵת קוּם מְלָכִים, / נְגִידִים מִשְּׁאוֹל נֶפֶשׁ מְשִׁיבִים,
וְעִתּוֹתֵי שְׁלוֹמִים — דָּת שְׁלוֹמִים, / וְתַחְבּוּלוֹת — בְּעִתּוֹתֵי קְרָבִים
לְהַבְעִיר אוּר קְרָבוֹת, אוֹ לְכַבּוֹת / בְּמוֹעֵצוֹת קְרָבוֹת כַּלְּהָבִים,
וְלִדְרֹךְ בַּחֲמַת רוּחַ מְשַׂנְאִים / כְּמוֹ דוֹרֵךְ עֲנָבִים בַּיְקָבִים.
הֲזֶה תִזְכֹּר? הֲלֹא תִזְכֹּר בְּקוּמוֹ / לְךָ בַּצַּר בְּפִדְיוֹנִים קְרוֹבִים
וְרִוָּה חַרְבְּךָ מִדָּם כְּמַיִם / אֲשֶׁר מִמַּעְיְנֵי שָׂשׂוֹן שְׁאוּבִים.
וְיוֹם צָרָה וּפַחַד חַם כְּתַנּוּר / אֲשֶׁר מִזֶּה וּמִזֶּה לוֹ שְׁבִיבִים,
וְכָל נֶפֶשׁ שְׁחַרְחֹרֶת, וְכָל לֵב / כְּמוֹ דוֹנַג, וְכָל פָּנִים צְהֻבִּים,
וְחִצִּים וַחֲנִיתוֹת הַשְּׁלוּחִים / כְּמוֹ מָטָר בְּאַוִּיר נֶעֱרָבִים,
וְעַל רָאשִׁים וְרִכְבֵי סוּס וְשָׂרִים / חֲרָבוֹת פָּעֲרוּ פִּיּוֹת רְחָבִים —
גְּאָלְךָ מִיְּדֵי צָרָה קְרוֹבָה / וְאֵין גּוֹאֵל לְךָ מִן הַקְּרוֹבִים,
וְגָדְלוּ מַעֲשָׂיו מִסְּפֹר וְסַפֵּר / וּמִשּׁוּמָם בְּתוֹךְ סֵפֶר כְּתוּבִים.
אֱלֹהִים, תֵּן לְעַבְדָּךְ פֶּה לְהַגִּיד / כְּבוֹד הוֹדָךְ עֲלֵי חֶסֶד וְטוֹבִים:
עֲלֵי חֶסֶד — בְּטוֹבָתָךְ גְּמַלְתּוֹ / בְּעִתּוֹת צַר וְהוּא כָבֵד בְּחוֹבִים,
וְעַל טוֹבִים — בְּצִמָּאוֹן כְּמַיִם / וּבַמִּדְבָּר מְצָאָם כַּעֲנָבִים.
אֲחַוֶּה אֶת פְּעָלֶיךָ לְכָל קָם / וְכָל יוֹשֵׁב וְכָל עוֹבֵר וְשָׁבִים,
וְיִמָּלְאוּ בְּסִפְרָתָם לְשׁוֹנוֹת / וְיִמָּלְאוּ בְחֻקּוֹתָם כְּתָבִים,
וְיֵלְכוּ עַל דְּרָכִים עִם אֲנָשִׁים / אֱלֵי צֹעַן וְאֶל אֶרֶץ לְהָבִים.
אֱלֹהִים, הֶעֱוָה עֶבֶד סְעַדְתּוֹ / בְּהוֹן יָקָר וּמַרְבַדִּים חֲטוּבִים
וְשֵׁם גָּדוֹל כְּשֵׁם זַכִּים אֲשֶׁר אֶל / דְּבָרֶיךָ חֲרֵדִים וַעֲצֵבִים,
וְזָנָה אַחֲרֵי לִבּוֹ וְעֵינָיו / כְּמַרְגִּיזִים וּפָנָה אֶל רְהָבִים.
מְחֵה פִשְׁעוֹ, שְׁמַע שִׂיחוֹ, וְיִהְיוּ / הֲגִיגֵי פִיו לְפָנֶיךָ עֲרֵבִים!
הֲטוֹב לָךְ כִּי תְהִי פוֹקֵד מְרָדִים / עֲלֵי דוֹדִים, וְחוֹבִים עַל אֲהוּבִים?

וְאִם עָנוּ פְשָׁעִים בּוֹ – יְלִיצוּן / צְדָקָה בַעֲבוּרוֹ הַכְּרוּבִים.
אֱלֹהִים, יֵשׁ בְּשִׁירוֹתַי דְּבָרִים / עֲלֵיהֶם דִּבְּרוּ עָתָק מְרִיבִים
וְלֹא דָלוּם כְּמוֹ מַיִם עֲמֻקִּים, / אֲבָל דִּמּוּם אֱלֵי מַיִם גְּווּבִים
וְאֶל בּוֹרוֹת מְשֻׁבָּרִים – וְהֵמָּה / מְמֻלָּאִים בְּכָל טוּבָה, חֲצוּבִים,
וּפִתְרוֹנָם לְךָ גָלוּי וְלִבִּי / כְּמוֹ תֵדַע – וְאַתְּ בּוֹחֵן לְבָבִים.
אֱלֹהִים, מַעֲשֶׂיךָ אַל תְּחַבֵּל / וְאַל תָּמִיר רְפוּאָה בַכְּאֵבִים,
וְאַל תּוֹבִישׁ יְדִידַי בִּי וְאַל נָא / בְּיוֹם אֵיד יִשְׂחֲקוּ עָלַי כְּלָבִים,
וְסֹךְ עָלַי בְּאֶבְרָתְךָ וְצִלְּךָ / כְּחֶפְצִי, לֹא כְמוֹ חֵפֶץ יְרִיבִים,
וְהַמְתִּיק לִי עֲדֵי מָוֶת שְׁנוֹתַי / וְהַמְתִּיק לִי בְּתוֹךְ קִבְרִי רְגָבִים!

## 28. The Mountain of Sand

Do you remember the mountain pass of sand which I crossed alone while fleeing from you and afraid?
Even today I am in transit over you,—but behind me are tens of thousands who obey me like their father
And wait for my utterances as for the rain and attend to my wisdom as to prophecy.
Because of this bless them for me my God,—may they follow after me willingly today.

הֲתֵדַע, מַעֲבַר הַחוֹל, בְּעָבְרִי / בְּךָ חָרֵד וּבוֹרֵחַ בְּמַקְלִי?
וְהַיּוֹם אֶעֱבֹר בָּךְ – וַאֲחוֹרַי / רְבָבוֹת כַּאֲבִיהֶם יִשְׁמְעוּ לִי,
וְיוֹחִילוּ לְאִמְרֵי פִי כְּמָטָר, / וְיַקְשִׁיבוּ כְּאֶל חָזוֹן לְשִׂכְלִי,
וְיַעַן בָּרְכֵם אֵלִי לְרַגְלִי – / לְרָצוֹן נִמְשְׁכוּ הַיּוֹם בְּחַבְלִי.

## 29. The Hour

She said: "Be happy that God has helped you reach
The age of fifty in this world," not knowing
That to me there is no difference between my life's
Past and that of Noah about whom I heard.
For me there is only the hour in which I am present in this world:
It stays for a moment and then like a cloud moves on.

אָמְרָה: ״שְׂמַח בַּעֲבוּר הַגִּיעֲךָ אֵל אֱלֵי
שָׁנִים חֲמִשִּׁים בְּעוֹלָמָךְ״ וְלֹא יָדְעָה
כִּי אֵין חֲלֻקָּה בְּעֵינַי בֵּין יְמוֹתַי אֲשֶׁר
עָבְרוּ וּבֵינוֹת יְמֵי נֹחַ אֲשֶׁר אֶשְׁמְעָה.
אֵין לִי בְּעוֹלָם לְבַד שָׁעָה אֲנִי בָהּ, וְהִיא
תַעְמֹד כְּרֶגַע וְאַחַר כֵּן כְּעָב נֶסְעָה.

### 30. At Age Sixty

When in the night he heard me cry that I had not yet slept he said to me:
"Why is your weeping so bitter?" I replied, "Because I am sixty years old.
The age of sixty differs from previous years; it removes my perversity with its own.
And after sixty, laughter will no longer be upon my mouth nor singing on my lips."

וְאוֹמֵר לִי בְּשָׁמְעוֹ אֶת בְּכוֹתִי / בְּלֵיל לֹא טָעֲמוּ עֵינַי שְׁנָתִי:
״עֲלֵי מַה זֶּה בְּמַר תִּבְכֶּה?״ עֲנִיתִיו / ״לְמַעַן כִּי שְׁנַת שִׁשִּׁים שְׁנָתִי,
שְׁנַת שִׁשִּׁים מְשֻׁנָּה מִשְּׁנוֹתַי / בְּעִקְשׁוּתָהּ מְסִירָה עִקְּשׁוּתִי,
וּמִשִּׁשִּׁים וּמַעְלָה לֹא יְהִי עוֹד / שְׂחוֹק עַל פִּי וְרִנָּה עַל שְׂפָתִי״.

### 31. In My Latter Days

Is there to be found one among my friends who shares my grief and is there among my neighbors one skilled in large lament?
And (failing this) will the gazelle trade its legs for mine that I may run upon them to the crocodile who will teach me how to mourn o'er my youth?

After the passing of sixty one years will I have a hairbreath's desire for my singing women?
And after the heavens have shut up the bright clouds of my young years,—will the dew of youth come down to rest upon my vital powers?

After the lights of my young manhood have been dimmed,—will they as once before pour the oil of tender age upon my tapers?
The graves of my companions have spoken that I be in them on the

morrow for with them I pitched my tent in my dwellings abroad.

And if I do not return to my young life,—take a spade and begin to prepare my grave!
The sorrows of my old age have raised upon my heart a burning fire; their tongues have whitened my hair.

And the weakening pains have stirred illness in my knees,—and see I stumble on straight paths even in my own courts.
I cry over my soul for it is exceedingly precious and it is fitting for me to bewail and bemoan that which I value.

And I look upon my beard grown white as my hair in place of my youth;—old age is like the soot upon my kettles.
Had I power over it,—I would have hastily bound it with rope so that it would no longer threaten to whiten my black hair.

If the fire of grief rages within my skull, then would its healing be,—the wine of grapes in my presses.
Yet in old age the springs of my youth have been shaken out of my beard and senility has made me contemptuous to my young girls!

Would that I were like God and know,—whether the day of my fears is near or far off,
And when I shall be without life, dust in my grave and at what time shall my spirit revive and be breathed into my clods of earth (again).

For my heart says that I shall live again, and if my flesh is pained,—then will the Lord God heal my bruises.
And He will transfer strength in place of my weakness and give me the power of eagles' wings in my limbs.

Thus will God allow me in his goodness and mercy, for while yet I live, I have put my trust in the Lord even my hopes.
Men may say that there is peace in the grave, but I am anxious lest I be attacked there for my sins.

Those that call death, "a walk to the ancestors" are right, for the fathers and mothers are there.
Will you hurry with my corpse from the shade of my roof and my dwelling place to the darkness of the grave on the day of my death?

And why will you burden my flesh with burial shrouds,—will I mourn there together with that which is tied about me?
Why will you immerse me in purifying water,—when tomorrow my stench will make filthy my girdle.

O God, ages had already passed even generations upon earth and I had not yet been born.
And later, You remembered me in mercy and I came forth into my family without requesting You to give me leave.

After my exit, You delivered me to misfortune, the cause of all that befell me, even like a rock for my anguish.
You have created me in the world, beautiful in appearance,—but in my latter days You change my form.

However, righteous are your deeds and your words are faithful,—while the breath of my mouth is perverse even my utterance.
Take for me a scroll and give pen and ink in my hand that I may write this day all that has happened to me

And read it and let my eyes flow like springs of water for in the grave they will no longer bring forth tears.
Let me cry my friends over the beautiful figure which they rush to the house wherein are assembled the sons of men.

The bright and honored one is for all her glory covered with dust and my mouth is closed and my eyelids shut.
For then I shall be still in the coffin, like a rock at the bottom of the sea, even my tongue which tells of my achievements,

And my eye which has seen wondrous things will then be consumed by decay in its socket and rot in my grave.
There will be no power of speech in my mouth nor hearing in my ear, and my hand will be idle even my running feet.

And worst of all, even more distressing than all else is the ascent from my earthly grave to stand before judgment.
For all my deeds are weighed in the balance, on the one scale my merits on the other my sins.

Perhaps an angel will defend me with a good word to raise my sins and lower my merits
Who will at my trial remind the Rock of my studies in the Law and investigations in the Torah.

**So that I may hear: "God has already accepted with favor your deeds and your credits outweigh your transgressions."**
**And rejoice when God comes in his glory to take me and be happy when my lights will be gathered in.**

הֲנִמְצָא בְרֵעַי מַר לְבָבוֹ לְמָרוֹתַי
וְאִם אֶמְצְאָה בַעֲלַת נְהִי רַב בְּגֵרוֹתַי?
וְאִם יַחֲלִיף רַגְלָיו צְבִי לִי, וְאָרוּץ בָּם
לְתַנִּים וְיוֹרוּנִי סְפֹד עַל בְּחוּרוֹתַי?
הֲיֵשׁ אַחֲרֵי אַחַת וְשִׁשִּׁים עֲבַרְתִּימוֹ
בְּנַפְשִׁי מְקוֹם חֵפֶץ כְּשַׂעְרָה בְשָׂרוֹתַי,
וְאַחַר עֲצֹר שַׁחַק עֲנַן אוֹר עֲלוּמַי – טַל
עֲלוּמִים זְמָן יוֹרִיד וְיַשְׁכִּיב בְּאוֹרוֹתַי?
וְאַחַר כְּהוֹת נֵרוֹת בְּחוּרַי – הֲיֵשׁ לִיצֹק
כְּמֵאָז מְאוֹר שֶׁמֶן בְּחוּרִים בְּנֵרוֹתַי?
קְבוּרוֹת חֲבֵרַי דִּבְּרוּ כִּי אֲנִי בָהֶם
לְמָחָר, וְעִמָּם אָהֳלִי אַט בְּגֵרוּתַי.
וְאִם אֵין אֲנִי שָׁב אֶל נְעוּרַי אַחֲרַנִּית,
קְחוּ אֵת וְהָחֵלוּ לְהָכִין קְבוּרוֹתַי!
יְגוֹנֵי זְקוּנִים הֶעֱלוּ עַל לְבָבִי אֵשׁ
יְקוֹדִים – לְשׁוֹנוֹתָם מְאִירוֹת בְּשַׂעְרוֹתַי,
וְצִירֵי חֲלוּשָׁה עוֹרֲרוּ מַחֲלֵי בִרְכַּי –
וְהִנֵּה אֲנִי כוֹשֵׁל בְּמִישׁוֹר בְּחַצְרוֹתַי!
אֲנִי אֵבְךְ נַפְשִׁי, כִּי יְקָרָה מְאֹד נַפְשִׁי,
וְלִי נָאֲוֶה לִסְפֹּד וְלִבְכּוֹת יְקָרוֹתַי.
וְאֶרְאֶה בְּהִתְלַבֵּן זְקָנִי כְּמוֹרָשַׁי,
מְקוֹם שַׁחֲרוּת – זֹקֶן כְּפִיחַ בְּסִירוֹתַי.
וְלוּ אֵרְדְּ בּוֹ – כִּמְעַט אֲסַרְתִּיו בְּמֵיתָר, עַד
אֲשֶׁר לֹא יְנוֹפֵף יָד לְהַלְבִּין שְׁחוֹרוֹתַי.
וְלוּ אֵשׁ יְגוֹנִים לְהַטָּה קָדְקֳדִי, הָיוּ
צְרִי אֵשׁ יְגוֹנִים – מֵי עֲנָבִים בְּפוּרוֹתַי,

וְאוּלָם בְּזִקְנָה נִנְעֲרוּ מֵי נְעוּרַי מִן
זְקֻנִי, וְזִקְנָה נִאֲצַתְנִי לִנְעוּרוֹתַי!
וּמִי יִתְּנֵנִי כֶאֱלֹהִים וְאֶתְבּוֹנֵן -
הֲקָרוֹב וְאִם רָחוֹק יְהִי יוֹם מְגוּרוֹתַי
וְכַמָּה אֱהִי עָפָר בְּקִבְרִי בְּלִי רוּחַ,
וּמָתַי תְּחִי רוּחִי וְתוּפַח בְּעַפְרוֹתַי.
וַיֹּאמַר לְבָבִי כִּי אֶחִי עוֹד, וְאִם יִכְאַב
בְּשָׂרִי – יְרַפֵּא אֵל אֱלֹהִים חֲבוּרוֹתַי,
וִיתֵּן אֱיָל חֵלֶף לְחָלְשִׁי וְיִתֶּן לִי
כְּכֹחַ בְּאֶבְרוֹת הַנְּשָׁרִים בְּאֶבְרוֹתַי,
וְכֵן יַעֲשֶׂה לִי אֵל בְּטוּבוֹ וְחַסְדּוֹ, כִּי
בְּאֵל מַחֲסִי שַׂמְתִּי בְּעוֹדִי וְשִׂבְרוֹתַי.
וַיֹּאמְרוּ אֲנָשִׁים כִּי מְנוּחָה בְּקֶבֶר יֵשׁ
וְאֶדְאַג אֲנִי פֶּן אֶפְגְּעָה בוֹ בְּסָרוֹתַי,
וְהֵם יִקְרְאוּ מָוֶת ״הֲלִיכָה אֱלֵי אָבוֹת״
וְצָדְקוּ, לְמַעַן שָׁם אֲבוֹתַי וְהוֹרוֹתַי.
עֲלֵי מָה בְּיוֹם מוֹתִי תְּחִישׁוּן בְּגוּפָתִי
אֱלֵי צֵל שְׁאוֹל מִצֵּל מְעוֹנִי וְקוֹרוֹתַי?
וְלָמָּה תְּצוּרוּן עַל בְּשָׂרִי בְּתַכְרִיכֵי
קְבוּרָה – וְשָׁם אֶבְלֶה אֲנִי עִם צְרוֹרוֹתַי?
וְלָמָּה בְּמַיִם תִּטְבְּלוּנִי לְהִטַּהֵר –
וּמָחָר תְּטַנֵּף צַחֲנָתִי חֲגוֹרוֹתַי?
אֱלֹהִים, כְּבָר עָבְרוּ זְמַנִּים וְדוֹרוֹת עַל
אֲדָמָה וְהָיִיתִי כְּאַיִן בְּדוֹרוֹתַי
וְאַחַר פְּקַדְתַּנִי לְרָצוֹן – וְיָצָאתִי,
לְבַל אֶשְׁאֲלָה צֵאת מִמְּךָ, אֶל מְכוּרוֹתַי;
וְאַחַר יְצִיאָתִי לְהַוּוֹת נְתַתַּנִי
וּמָקוֹר לְמִקְרוֹתַי וְכִצְרוֹר לְצָרוֹתַי.
וְאַתָּה יְצַרְתַּנִי בְּעוֹלָם יְפֵה מַרְאֶה –
וְאַתָּה בְּאַחֲרִיתִי תְּשַׁנֶּה יְצִירוֹתַי,
וְאוּלָם צְדָקָה מַעֲשֶׂיךָ, וְאִמְרָתְךָ

אֱמוּנָה, וְרוּחַ פִּי מְעֻקָּל וְאִמְרוֹתַי.
קְחוּ לִי מְגִלָּה וַעֲשׂוּ לִי דְיוֹ וָעֵט
לְיָדִי, וְאַשְׁחִירָה כְּהַיּוֹם בְּקוֹרוֹתַי.
וְאֶקְרָא וְתִזַּלְנָה כְּעֵינַי מְאוֹרוֹתַי
לְמַעַן בְּקֶבֶר לֹא אֲדַמַּע מְאוּרוֹתַי,
וְאֶבְכֶּה עֲלֵי צוּרָה יְפֵיפָה יְאִיצוּן בָּהּ
לְמוֹעֵד בְּנֵי אָדָם חֲבֵרַי וְחַבְרוֹתַי,
וְיִפְעָה כְבוּדָה כָּל כְּבוּדָהּ בְּכַסּוּתָהּ
בְּעָפָר וּבִסְתֹּם פִּי וַעֲצֵם שְׁמוּרוֹתַי,
וְכִי אָז יְהִי דוּמָם בְּאָרוֹן, כְּמוֹ אֶבֶן
בְּלֶב־יָם, לְשׁוֹנִי הַמְסַפֵּר גְּבוּרוֹתַי,
וְעֵינַי אֲשֶׁר חָזְתָה פְּלָאִים אֲזַי תֵּעַשׁ
בְּחוֹרָהּ בְּרִקָּבוֹן וְתִמַּק בְּנִקְרוֹתַי,
וְכִי אֵין בְּחֵךְ טַעַם וְשִׂיחַ, וְאֵין שֵׁמַע
לְאָזְנִי, וּבָטְלָה יָד וּבָטְלוּ מְמַהֲרוֹתַי.
וְרָעָה אֲשֶׁר רָעָה וּמָרָה עֲלֵי כָּל זֹאת –
עֲלוֹתִי לְמִשְׁפָּט מִן רְגָבַי וְקִבְרוֹתַי
וְכִי כָל פְּעֻלּוֹתַי שְׁקוּלוֹת בְּמֹאזְנַיִם
בְּכַף זֹאת זְכִיּוֹתַי וּבְזֹאת מְרוֹרוֹתַי.
וְאוּלַי יְהִי מַלְאָךְ וּמֵלִיץ בְּדָבָר טוֹב
לְהָרִים עֲוֹנוֹתַי וְהַשְׁפֵּל יְשָׁרוֹתַי
וְיַזְכִּיר בְּהִשָּׁפְטִי לְצוּרִי חֲקִירוֹתַי
בְּדָתֵי תְעוּדוֹתַי וְדָרְשִׁי בְּתוֹרוֹתַי
וְאֶשְׁמַע "כְּבָר רָצָה אֱלֹהִים פְּעָלֶיךָ
וְתֵרֵד בְּכָזֹאת מֵעֲבָדַי בְּשׁוּרוֹתַי".
וְאֶשְׂמַח בְּצֵאתִי אֶל כְּבוֹד אֵל לְאָסְפֵנִי,
וְאֶשְׂמַח בְּהֵאָסֵף יְרֵחִי וְאוֹרוֹתַי.

# G.
# Rescue at Sea

## 32. Rescue at Sea

Can he who stumbles and falls stand again; can the wanderer and
he who is lost sleep in peace?
For me whose foot has slipped and whose joints have swayed is it
possible to be raised up again?
By my soul, I believe that help will come even comfort to a
tumultuous life;
By their souls, there is none to help or comfort in my distress as
they behold my confusion.
They think that the day of anguish will never change even as a
wilderness cannot be inhabited.
Yes the Lord does lift up those whom He has bent and made low
and his are the secret things and his way is hidden!

Hear my words and know that not for nothing did God sustain me
upon the earth.
Receive the evil days with a kind heart, a closed mouth and
guarded thoughts.
Let your ears be stopped up to transgressors and your eyes be
closed to whores
Like Ḥofni at Shiloh or Zimri with the Midianite woman and 'Onan
with his sister-in-law.
Hear my words and magnify God in the home and on the way
while laying down and rising up.
And hurry, make haste and fear and tremble and be filled with
dread
Of the one God who does not give birth nor is born living eternally
without likeness, male or female.
Exert yourself to discover his will and from fear of his rebuke find
no rest.

I am the man who descended into the sea depths and for most of
the year the sea is stormy.
And I chose to go down in the month of 'Av, for then the waves
do not break in anger.
We pulled along with oars and a breeze blew the corn of the field
and its standing ears.

And behold the sea was like my servant, performing my desires and the wind my maid-servant.
The heavens were like clear sapphire and the waters like oil, good and smooth,
And the sailors told tales to one another of what they witnessed at sea and of its secrets.
One recalled a huge and wonderful beast and another remembered an animal.
Whereupon the captain replied: 'You don't know the wonders of the sea and you haven't told us anything.
There is a beast named Qorḥa who is not overshadowed by any animal of the deep.
All predators who meet up with her are devoured or slain,
And she overturns all ships, like a hitched wagon even a mighty navy! '

No sooner had he finished telling about her than she advanced howling and bustling.
I heard her and it was a tumultuous voice even the sound of thunder was a whisper in my ears.
I looked upon this frightening apparition whose measurements appeared to be that of a fish;
Like Leviathan of the legends, like the tortuous serpent, like a palm-tree in stature.
Its head was the size of an oared galley, behind a face rising like a hill.
Its eyes were like reservoirs of water, its nostril like an oven and its forehead a parapet;
Its mouth was deep and wide like a cave which empties a river into itself in thirst.
Its lips were like two bottles of skin inflated and between them a mouth like a coat of mail.
Its body was white and its back green; its neck was like a tower and its belly a stack of wheat.
Its fin was like a polished sword its scales a buckler, red.
To those who saw her she looked to be like Tyre in the heart of the sea or like Dumah.
She swam around the boat while no one moved or said a word.
She reached its edge and stood on its tail like a cedar or a climbing vine.
Thereupon each man's heart melted like wax and streamed like water in a flood.
And I calmed and quieted my soul which had become like a ewe-lamb, dumb on the day of slaughter.

I remembered God and others with me recalled gods like 'Ashima.
I said: 'Truly, one way or another, sins will ensnare the guilty soul.
And if Jonah swallowed by the sea, was spit out on the dry land for his righteousness,–what can I expect?
O God, defer (your anger) for this happening has awakened me, who was in slumber.
But if this is to be my fate then may it atone for my numerous transgressions! '
She then submerged into the deep waters like the armies which the Lord cast down into the sea
And came underneath my boat to overturn it, while each man's heart died and all breathing stopped.
Whereupon the Lord rebuked her, and she returned instantly to the innermost depths of the sea,
While He saved the little worms on the plank of wood covered with pitch,
And brought back the dead from the grave and rescued with a high and uplifted hand those about to be swallowed up.
All who knew the sea were amazed saying: 'By what merit were these spared and why?'
For never before has a ship been delivered from the hands of Qorḥa the angry one!'
I replied: 'Indeed God's redemption is unfailing to those who know the glory of his majestic splendor.
For He saves his familiars and reaps vengeance upon those who anger him.
His is the sea and its life even the waters of the great deep and He suspends them in space.
And what is any living thing compared to the Rock who formed her even gave her strength and made her powerful.'

I am obliged to God with the gratitude of the redeemed; it will be set upon my lips and studied.
And I am thankful, that my Rock has no beginning like things created and there is no end to him.
I am grateful that the resurrection is a certainty and that the dead will be awakened from the earth,
And that Moses and his Torah which is in our hands is truthful and with perfection written,
And that the words of our sages are just and their lore and the study thereof is pleasant,
And that there is reward in the world to come for the pure and the dead are recompensed for their hidden sins,

**And that God is ruler on dry land and on the seas, in the heavens and over ‘Ayish and Kimah;**
**His fear is set upon me even his faultless Torah within my heart.**

הֲלַכּוֹשֵׁל וְלַנּוֹפֵל תְּקוּמָה / וְלַנּוֹדֵד וְלָאוֹבֵד תְּנוּמָה?
וְאִם יֶשׁ לִי, בְּמוֹט רַגְלִי, וְאִם יֵשׁ / לְקַרְסֻלַּי אֲשֶׁר מָעַד תְּרוּמָה?
בְּנַפְשִׁי – כֹּל אֲשֶׁר יָבוֹא בְעֶזְרָה / וְנֶחָמָה לְכָל נֶפֶשׁ הֲלוּמָה,
בְּנַפְשָׁם – אֵין אֲשֶׁר יָבוֹא בְּיוֹם בּוֹא / מְהוּמָתִי וְרָאוּ בִי מְהוּמָה.
יְדַמּוּ כִּי לְעוֹלָם אֵין תְּמוּרָה / לְיוֹם צָרָה וְלֹא תֵשֵׁב שְׁמָמָה –
וְאֵל יָרִים אֲשֶׁר הֵשַׁח וְהִשְׁפִּיל, / וְלוֹ סוֹדוֹת וְדַרְכּוֹ נַעֲלָמָה!
שְׁמַע מִלָּה, וְדַע כִּי לֹא לְקַלָּה / יְחַיֵּנִי אֱלֹהִים עַל אֲדָמָה,
וְקַבֵּל אֶת יְמֵי רָעָה בְּלֵב טוֹב / וּפֶה סָגוּר וּמַחְשָׁבָה חֲסוּמָה,
וּמִשּׁוֹנִים תְּהִי אָזְנְךָ כְּבֵדָה, / וּמִזּוֹנִים תְּהִי עֵינְךָ עֲצוּמָה
כְּמוֹ חָפְנִי בְּשִׁילֹה אוֹ כְזִמְרִי / בְּמִדְיָנִית וְאוֹנָן בְּיִבְמָה.
שְׁמַע מִלָּה וְהַגְדֵּל יָהּ בְּבַיִת / וּבַדֶּרֶךְ וּבִשְׁכִיבָה וְקִימָה,
וְהִבָּהֵל וְהִדָּחֵף וְגוּרָה / וְהֵחָרֵד וְהִמָּלֵא בְאֵימָה
לְאֵל רִאשׁוֹן בְּאֵין מוֹלִיד וְנוֹלָד / וְחַי לָעַד בְּלִי דוֹמֶה וְדוּמָה,
וְלִמְצֹא אֶת רְצוֹנוֹ לֵךְ וְשׁוּבָה / וּמִירֹא גַעֲרָתוֹ שֵׁב וְקוּמָה.
אֲנִי הָאִישׁ אֲשֶׁר יָרַד בְּתוֹךְ יָם, / וְיֵשׁ לַיָּם בְּרֹב שָׁנָה נְהָמָה,
וּבָחַרְתִּי לְרִדְתּוֹ אָב, לְמַעַן / בְּאָב לֹא יִשְׁבְּרוּ גַלָּיו בְּחֵמָה.
וְנִמְשַׁכְנוּ בְּמִשּׁוֹטוֹת, וְרוּחַ / תְּנוֹפֵף שִׁבֳּלֵי שָׂדֶה וְקָמָה,
וְהִנֵּה יָם כְּעַבְדִי יַעֲשֶׂה אֵת / אֲשֶׁר אֶחְפֹּץ וְהָרוּחַ כְּאָמָה,
וְשָׁמַיִם כְּסַפִּירִים טְהוֹרִים / וְהַמַּיִם כְּשֶׁמֶן טוֹב וְחֵמָה.
וּמַלָּחִים יְחַוּוּ זֶה לְזֶה אֵת / אֲשֶׁר רָאוּ בַיָּם מִתַּעֲלוּמָה,
וְזֶה יַזְכִּיר דְּבַר חַיָּה גְדוֹלָה / וְנִפְלָאָה, וְזֶה יַזְכִּיר בְּהֵמָה,
וְרַב חוֹבֵל יְשִׁיבֵם "לֹא יְדַעְתֶּם / פְּלִיאַת יָם וְלֹא שַׁחְתֶּם מְאוּמָה!
וְשָׁם חַיָּה, שְׁמָהּ קַרְחָה, אֲשֶׁר הִיא / בְּכָל חַיּוֹת מְצוּלָה לֹא עֲמוּמָה,
וְכָל חַיָּה אֲשֶׁר חַיּוֹת שְׁאֵרָהּ / בְּפָגְעָהּ בָּהּ אֲכוּלָה אוֹ הֲמוּמָה;
וְהוֹפֶכֶת לְפִיהָ כָל סְפִינָה / וְצִי אַדִּיר כְּמֶרְכָּבָה רְתוּמָה".
וְלֹא כִלָּה לְסַפֵּר פָּעֳלָהּ עַד / אֲשֶׁר בָּאָה, וְהִיא גוֹעָה וְהוֹמָה.
שְׁמַעְתִּיהָ – וְהָיָה קוֹל הֲמוּלָּה / וְקוֹל רַעַם בְּאָזְנַי קוֹל דְּמָמָה,

וְהִבַּטְתִּי אֱלֵי צוּרָה אֲיֻמָּה, / אֲבָל הָיְתָה בְּתֹכֶן דָּג רְקוּמָה:
כְּלִוְיָתָן אֲשֶׁר סֻפַּר, כְּנָחָשׁ / עֲקַלָּתוֹן, כְּמוֹ תָמָר בְּקוֹמָה.
וְרֹאשׁ לָהּ כָּאֳנִי שַׁיִט בְּמִדָּה / עֲלֵי פָנִים מְנֻשָּׂאִים בְּרָמָה,
וְעֵינַיִם כְּמַעְיָנִים, וְנָחִיר / כְּמוֹ כִבְשָׁן, וְלָהּ רַקָּה כְּחוֹמָה,
וּפֶה עָמֹק וְרָחָב כַּמְּעָרָה – / תְּעַר נָהָר אֱלֵי תוֹכוֹ בְּצָמָא.
וּבִשְׂפָתוֹת כְּנֹאד עַל נֹאד נְפוּחִים / וּבֵינֵיהֶם כְּפִי תַחְרָא פְרוּמָה,
וְגוּף לָבָן, וְגַב יָרֹק, וְצַוָּאר / כְּמוֹ מִגְדָּל וּבֶטֶן כַּעֲרֵמָה,
וּבִסְנַפִּיר כְּמוֹ חֶרֶב לְטוּשָׁה / וְקַשְׂקֶשֶׂת כְּסֹחֵרָה אֲדֻמָּה,
וְגִזְרָתָהּ לְמַשְׁגִּיחִים כְּמוֹ צַר / אֲשֶׁר הָיְתָה בְּלֵב יָם אוֹ כְדֻמָּה.
וְשָׁטָה מִסְּבִיבוֹת לַסְּפִינָה, / וְאֵין מַגִּיד וְאֵין נוֹאֵם נְאִימָה,
וְהִגִּיעָה לְצִדֶּיהָ וְעָמְדָה / עֲלֵי זָנָב כְּאֶרֶז אוֹ שְׁדֵמָה.
אֲזַי נָמֵס לְבַב כָּל אִישׁ כְּדוֹנַג / וְכַמַּיִם וְשִׁבֹּלֶת זְרוּמָה,
וְשִׁוִּיתִי וְדוֹמַמְתִּי לְנַפְשִׁי / כְּרָחֵל יוֹם טְבֹחַ נֶאֱלָמָה
וְזָכַרְתִּי אֱלֹהִים – וַאֲחֵרִים / לְנֶגְדִּי יִזְכְּרוּ אֵל כַּאֲשִׁימָא.
וְאָמַרְתִּי: אֱמֶת, כָּזֹה וְכָזֶה / עֲוֹנוֹת יִלְכְּדוּ נֶפֶשׁ אֲשֵׁמָה,
וְאִם נִבְלַע בְּיָם יוֹנָה וְהוּקָא / בְּצִדְקָתוֹ בְּיַבָּשָׁה – אֲנִי מָה?
אֱלֹהִים, הַאֲרֵךְ לִי, כִּי אֲשֶׁר בָּא / הֱקִיצַנִי וְהָיִיתִי בְנוּמָה,
וְאִם הוּא זֶה גְמוּל יָדִי, תְּהִי בוֹ / סְלִיחַת מַעֲוָתִי הָעֲצוּמָה!
אֲזַי שָׁקְעָה בְּלֵב יַמִּים כְּחִיל / אֲשֶׁר הָאֵל בְּיָם יָרָה וְרָמָה
וְתַחַת לָאֳנִי בָּאָה לְהָפְכוֹ / וּמֵת כָּל לֵב וְאָבְדָה כָּל נְשָׁמָה.
אֲבָל גָּעַר אֱלֹהִים בָּהּ, וְשָׁבָה / כְּרֶגַע אֶל מְצוּלַת יָם פְּנִימָה,
וְהוֹשִׁיעַ לְתוֹלָעִים קְטַנִּים / עֲלֵי שׂוֹכָה בְּמוֹ זֶפֶת קְרוּמָה,
וְהֵשִׁיב מִשְּׁאוֹל מֵתִים, וְהִצִּיל / מְבֻלָּעִים בְּיַד נִשֵּׂאת וְרָמָה.
וְתָמְהוּ כָּל נְבוֹנֵי יָם וְאָמְרוּ: / בְּמַה זֶּה נִמְלְטוּ אֵלֶּה וְלָמָּה?
וְלֹא הָיְתָה פְלֵיטָה לָאֳנִיָּה / לְפָנִים מִיְּדֵי קַרְחָה זְעוּמָה!
עֲנִיתִים: כֵּן, גְּאֻלַּת אֵל לְיוֹדְעַי / כְּבוֹד הוֹדוֹ מְהֻדֶּרֶת שְׁלֵמָה,
וְהוּא עוֹשֶׂה לְמַכִּירָיו תְּשׁוּעָה / וְהוּא עוֹשֶׂה בְמַרְגִּיזָיו נְקָמָה,
אֲשֶׁר לוֹ יָם וְחַיָּתוֹ וּמֵימֵי / תְּהוֹם רַבָּה וְתוֹלָם עַל בְּלִימָה.
וּמַה חַיָּה לְנֶגֶד צוּר נְסָכָהּ / וְשָׂם לָהּ עֹז וְשָׂם לָהּ תַּעֲצוּמָה?
אֲנִי אוֹדֶה לְאֵל תּוֹדַת גְּאוּלִים / תְּהִי עַל פִּי מְשֻׁנֶּנֶת וְשׂוּמָה
וְאוֹדֶה כִּי לְצוּרִי אֵין תְּחִלָּה / כְּנִבְרָאִים וְכִי אֵין לוֹ חֲתִימָה,

וְאוֹדֶה כִּי אֱמֶת הִיא הַתְּחִיָּה / וְכִי מֵתִים יָקִיצוּן מֵאֲדָמָה,
וְכִי מֹשֶׁה וְתוֹרָתוֹ אֲשֶׁר הִיא / בְּיָדֵנוּ אֱמֶת וּבְתֹם רְשׁוּמָה,
וְכִי דִבְרֵי חֲכָמֵינוּ יְשָׁרִים / וְתַלְמוּדָם וּמִשְׁנָתָם נְעִימָה,
וְיֵשׁ שָׂכָר לְעוֹלָם בָּא לְזַכִּים / וְתַגְמוּלִים לְמֵתִים עַל עֲלוּמָה,
וְאֵל שַׁלִּיט בְּיַבֶּשֶׁת וְיַמִּים / וּבִשְׁחָקִים וְעַל עַיִשׁ וְכִימָה,
וְיִרְאָתוֹ עֲלֵי פָּנַי נְתוּנָה / וְתוֹרָתוֹ בְּתוֹךְ לִבִּי תְּמִימָה.

# H. Prayer

### 33. Establish the Promise

**Lord bare today your right arm**
**And rescue the children of Abraham from 'Edom.**
**And to those who flaunt their pride and haughtiness before You**
**Gird yourself with strength to rebuke them in anger.**
**Annul the covenant made by those who fail to do your will**
**And establish the promise given to David the monarch of your kingdom.**
**Upon those who stretch forth their hands against your flock**
**Send your wrath, like a raging and consuming fire!**

אֱלֹהַי, חֲשֹׂף הַיּוֹם זְרוֹעַ יְמִינֶךָ
וּמִכַּת אֱדוֹם חַלֵּץ בְּנֵי אַב הֲמוֹנֶךָ!
וְלַלּוֹבְשִׁים גֵּאָה וְגָאוֹן לְפָנֶיךָ –
בְּעֶבְרָה וּבִגְעָרָה לְבַשׁ אֶת גְּאוֹנֶךָ.
וְהָפֵר בְּרִית שׂוּמָה לְעוֹבְרֵי רְצוֹנֶךָ,
וְהָקֵם שְׁבוּעָתְךָ לְדָוִד קְצִינֶךָ,
וְעַל עָם, אֲשֶׁר שׁוֹלְחִים יְדֵיהֶם בְּצֹאנֶךָ,
תְּשַׁלַּח – כְּאֵשׁ תִּיקַד וְתִבְעַר – חֲרוֹנֶךָ!

## 34. Answer Me

Build me up like a tower on the heights of your sanctuary,
And set me like a seal upon your heart.
Make me drunk with the blood of the foe on the day of war
And satisfy me with his flesh on the night of redemption.
Place the cup of salvation upon my right hand
That my tongue may give voice in joy to a song of love.
For nearly a thousand years I have declared my sorrow
With many tears and with fasting,—will You not answer me?

עַל מְרוֹם קָדְשְׁךָ כְּמִגְדָּל בְּנֵנִי / וַעֲלֵי לִבְּךָ כְּחוֹתָם תְּנֵנִי,
מִדְּמֵי צַר בְּיוֹם קְרָב שַׁכְּרֵנִי, / וּבְשָׂרוֹ בְּלֵיל פְּדוּת שַׂבְּעֵנִי.
כּוֹס יְשׁוּעוֹת תְּנָה עֲלֵי יַד יְמִינִי, / שִׁיר יְדִידוּת שְׁמַע בְּרַנֵּן לְשׁוֹנִי.
זֶה כְּאֶלֶף לְךָ אֲחַוֶּה יְגוֹנִי / וּבְבִכְיָה וְצוֹם הֲלֹא תַעֲנֵנִי?

## 35. Arise, Awake

O evil queen, give up your reign;
Rule over your foes, O condemned Sarah.
O fawn of S'nir, too long have you slept
Ailing in bed, arise, awake.
Be healed, for there is balm for your affliction.
Be lifted up, for there is a reward for your righteousness.

מַלְכָּה רְשָׁעָה, מִמְּלֹךְ הִתְאַחֲרִי, / שָׂרָה שְׂנוּאָה – עַל מְשַׂנְאַיִךְ שְׂרִי!
עָפְרַת שְׂנִיר, אָרְכָה תְנוּמָתֵךְ עֲלֵי / עֶרֶשׂ חֳלִי, הִתְנַעֲרִי הִתְעוֹרְרִי,
הִתְרַפְּאִי, כִּי יֵשׁ לְמַכָּתֵךְ צֳרִי, / הִתְנַשְּׂאִי, כִּי יֵשׁ לְצִדְקָתֵךְ פְּרִי.

## 36. Day of Redemption

Shake yourself free, shake yourself free
And be apprised that the day of redemption is nigh!
Your mourning time is ended and your anguish
Has been removed, healing now exists for you.
Rise up, you who are tossed about and reeling
And repay those who have made you stagger.
Now he is visible who in a vision was foretold

That like a lion he shall stand.
Zion, like a withered tree
Will henceforth give fruit.
They will be abashed who once put you to shame
And no longer will call you: 'The rebellious people.'

הִתְנַעֲרִי, הִתְנַעֲרִי, / וּבְיוֹם פְּדוּת הִתְבַּשְּׂרִי!
שָׁלְמוּ יְמֵי אֶבְלֵךְ, וְסָר / צִלֵּךְ, וְנִמְצָא לָךְ צֳרִי.
קוּמִי, שְׁכוּרָה סֹעֲרָה, / וּמְשַׁכְּרַיִךְ שַׁכְּרִי.
עַתָּה אֲשֶׁר נִרְאָה "וְלֹא / עַתָּה" יְהִי קָם כַּאֲרִי.
צִיּוֹן, אֲשֶׁר הָיְתָה לְעֵץ / יָבֵשׁ, תְּהִי עוֹשָׂה פְּרִי,
בּוֹשׁוּ מְבִישַׁיִךְ, וְעוֹד / לֹא יִקְרְאוּ לָךְ: עַם מְרִי.

## 37. He Who Stretched Out the Heavens

He who stretched out the heavens
Upon his earth like a tent
And set his dwelling in the glitter of amber,
Surrounded by fire and flame
Who covers himself with dread
And no one exits or enters,
Forgive my sins and keep distant
Those who accuse me of evil and slander.
God is greatly to be feared in the assembly of the saints!

O Lord, a cloud is your garment,
Even the gloomy mist.
And light abides with You
And You are knowledgeable in the darkness.
Moreover You have created the sweet things
As well as that which is bitter and tasteless,
And every root and branch
Even things of primary and secondary importance.
To You the heavens bow down,
Even the mighty and lowly ones.
And if I continually rehearse your praise
It is for You redundant and superfluous.
But why do You visit sins
Upon a premature worm?
Scatter my transgressions like chaff,

And as smoke from a window!
God is greatly to be feared in the assembly of the saints!

He who measured the dust of the earth
And the mire of the streets with a ḥomer;
Who gauged the heavens with a span
And the waters with an ‘omer;
Who made a skin for the heavens
With his stars like that of a leopard.
He gives us birth and causes death
And there is no one to oppose or change him.
All who fall into his net
Are like the wild oxen and chamois caught in a snare.
And all creatures are like sheep
Who need his protection and keeping.
We speak vanities and lies
But whatever He says is accomplished.
And a brightness surrounds him
Even a fierce wind which makes your hair stand
And lights that are green and black,
And white as wool.
And one fire rages in the midst of another
And each consumes his neighbor.
God is greatly to be feared in the assembly of the saints!

The seraphs prostrate themselves before You
As well as angels and seers,
And in fear they come out of hiding
From their caves and hollow rocks.
And the shining stars
Are turned to darkness.
But You allow sovereignty to monarchs
And give grace to those who have beauty.
Also by your wrath are they destroyed
In an instant they are removed.
Moreover You enfeeble the strong and fortify the weak,
Even bestow loving kindness upon hundreds and thousands.
Give of your goodness to the treasured people
Though they be stained with sin.
God is greatly to be feared in the assembly of the saints!

The heavens strong as a molten mirror
Tremble before You.
Even the giants prostrate themselves

And the haughtiness of the great ones is made low.
Whereas men will speak and go back on their word
Your decrees are carried out.
When You gaze upon the earth
She trembles in her pillars.
And her foundations are revealed
And the channels of the waters appear.
A voice of thunder emanates from You,
Even the path of the lightning.
And You have set up statutes and ordinances
Which are engraved upon our hearts.
Yet we have performed them foolishly
Like those who scorn and lack refinement.
Pull off the sins and transgressions
Which have stuck to our bodies.
And if our offenses are many
Your forgiveness we know is great.
God is greatly to be feared in the assembly of the saints!

He who sends out his ice
In morsels even as bread in abundance
And who tears apart his rain clouds
Like a used-up garment.
Send honor to them that fear You
And a torch of destruction to the wicked;
Make white the sins that were red
As scarlet or strawberry,
And do not sell your congregation
To strangers forever.
Grant a healing I pray
Unto a people contrite and broken,
Bereaved and driven out
Without a bill of divorcement.
Betroth her to yourself anew with faithfulness
And write for her the marriage document.
God is greatly to be feared in the assembly of the saints!

אֲשֶׁר נָטָה שְׁחָקִים / עֲלֵי אַרְצוֹ כְקֻבָּה
וְשָׁת שְׁכְנוֹ בְחַשְׁמַל / וּבֵינוֹת אֵשׁ וְלַבָּה
וְאֵימָה לוֹ חֲתֻלָּה / וְאֵין יוֹצֵא וְאֵין בָּא —
סְלַח פֶּשַׁע וְהַרְחֵק / מְלִיצֵי חֵטְא וְדִבָּה,

אֵל נַעֲרָץ בְּסוֹד / קְדוֹשִׁים רַבָּה!

אֱלֹהַי, עָב לְבוּשְׁךָ / וְעָנָן וַעֲרָפֶל,
וְהַנֹּגַהּ יְגוֹרְךָ / וְתֵדַע מַה בְּאֹפֶל.
וְאַתְּ בּוֹרֵא מְתוּקִים / וְכָל מָרוֹר וְתָפֵל,
וְכָל שֹׁרֶשׁ וְעָנָף / וְכָל עִקָּר וְטָפֵל,
וְלָךְ שַׁחוּ גְבֹהִים / וְכָל נִשָּׂא וְשָׁפֵל.
וְאִם אֹמַר וְאַגְדִּיל – / לְךָ יֶתֶר וְכֶפֶל!
וְאֵיךְ תִּפְקֹד חֲטָאִים / עֲלֵי תוֹלָע וְנֶפֶל?
זְרֵה חֶטְאִי כְּמוֹ מֹץ / כְּעָשָׁן מֵאֲרֻבָּה!

אֲשֶׁר כָּל הָעֲפָרִים / וְטִיט חוּצוֹת וְחֹמֶר
וְשָׁת שַׁחַק כְּעֹבֶר / וְהָעוֹלָם כְּעֹמֶר,
וְשָׁת גֶּלֶד שְׁחָקִים / וְכוֹכָבָיו כְּנָמֵר,
וְהוּא מוֹלִיד וּמֵמִית / וְאֵין מַמְרֶה וּמֶמֶר.
וְכֹל יִפֹּל בְּרִשְׁתּוֹ / כְּתוֹא מִכְמָר וְזֶמֶר,
וְכָל נִבְרָא כְּמוֹ צֹאן / וְהוּא נוֹצֵר וְשׁוֹמֵר.
וְלָנוּ שָׁוְא וְכָזָב / וְהוּא אוֹמֵר וְגוֹמֵר,
וְנֹגַהּ לוֹ תְסוֹבֵב / וְרוּחַ כֹּל תְּסַמֵּר
וְאוֹר יָרֹק וְשָׁחוֹר / וְאוֹר לָבָן כְּצֶמֶר
וְאֵשׁ תִּבְעַר בְּתוֹךְ אֵשׁ / וְאֶת כָּל אֵשׁ מְכַבָּה.

לְךָ שַׁחוּ שְׂרָפִים / וּמַלְאָכִים וְצוֹפִים,
וּמֵאֵימָה יְבוֹאוּן / בְּתוֹךְ חוֹרִים וְכֵפִים,
וְכוֹכָבִים מְאוֹרִים / בְּחֹשֶׁךְ מַחֲלִיפִים.
וְאַתְּ מַמְלִיךְ מְלָכִים / וְנוֹתֵן חֵן לְיָפִים,
וּמִזַּעְמָךְ אֲבוּדִים / כְּרֶגַע נֶאֱסָפִים,
וְאַתְּ תַּעְטִיף קְשׁוּרִים / וְאַתְּ תִּקְשֹׁר עֲטוּפִים.
וְאַתְּ גּוֹמֵל חֲסָדִים / לְמֵאוֹת וַאֲלָפִים –
גְּמֹל טוֹב עַם סְגֻלָּה, / וְאִם מֵחֵטְא עֲקֻבָּה.

לְךָ רָפוּ שְׁחָקִים / אֲשֶׁר כִּרְאִי חֲזָקִים,
וְלָךְ שַׁחוּ נְפִילִים / וְשָׁפֵל רוּם עֲנָקִים.

וְכֹל יָמִיר וְיַחֲלִיף – / וְאַתְּ גּוֹזֵר וּמֵקִים.
וְאַתְּ מַבִּיט לָאָרֶץ / וְתִרְעַד מִן יְצוּקִים,
וְיִגָּלוּ יְסוֹדוֹת / וְיֵרָאוּ אֲפִיקִים,
וּמִמְּךָ קוֹל רְעָמִים / וּמִשְׁלַחַת בְּרָקִים.
וְשַׂמְתָּ חֹק וּמִשְׁפָּט / בְּלִבֵּנוּ חֲקוּקִים,
וְהִסְכַּלְנוּ עֲשׂה בָם / כְּמוֹ לֵצִים וְרֵיקִים.
נְתֹץ פֶּשַׁע וְעָוֹן / לְגוּפֵנוּ דְבֵקִים,
וְאִם רַב הֶעֱוִינוּ, / סְלִיחָתְךָ מְרֻבָּה.

אֲשֶׁר יַשְׁלִיךְ קְרָחָיו / כְּלֶחֶם רַב וּפָתּוֹת
וְקוֹרֵעַ חֲזִיזָיו / כְּמוֹ בִגְדֵי שְׁחִיתוּת –
שְׁלַח כָבוֹד לְחָרֵד / וְלַפִּיד בּוּז לְעַשְׁתּוּת
וְהַלְבֵּן חֵטְא מְאָדָם / כְּשָׁנִי אוֹ כְמוֹ תוּת,
וְאַל תִּמְכֹּר עֲדָתְךָ / לְזָרִים לַצְּמִיתוּת
וְהַעֲלֵה נָא אֲרוּכָה / לְעַם נִדְכֶּה וְכָתוּת
וְלִשְׁכוּלָה גְרוּשָׁה / בְּלִי סֵפֶר כְּרִיתוּת –
תְּאָרְשֶׂהָ בֶּאֱמוּנָה / וְתִכְתֹּב לָהּ כְּתֻבָּה.

# I.
# Life in Granada

## 38. Street Scene

I passed by the street of the butchers where they kept sheep and oxen
And cattle numerous as the fish of the sea and many fowl whose day of misfortune had come
Where blood congealed upon blood and slaughterers were in abundance shedding blood.
And next to it were the fishermen, with their catches from the sea as plentiful as the sand and lying in the vessels of the men who snared them.
Close by them was the street of bakers,—who work by day and do not sleep at night.
Here men baked and there they ate, from this side they dragged their catches,

From that one they carried to their homes;—whereupon my heart understood their mystery.
And I spoke to those who stood about: "Why do you continue to prevail over these living things all during the course of their existence?
What difference is there between them and yourselves, in their death and birth,
Their sleeping and waking, sitting and standing?
Were it not that God gave them as food for you, He would not have annihilated them.
Had he given them the temperament they would have put an end to those who eliminate them!
Even as you they breathe and have a heart which makes them function upon the earth.
There is never a time when one among them does not die or is in the process of giving birth.
Think about this, you who are pure and you princes who take pride in your honor:
If you would understand the mystery of the world know that this is all there is to man!

עָבַרְתִּי עַל שׁוּק טַבָּחִים – / בּוֹ צֹאן וּשְׁוָרִים עַל יָדָם
וּמְרִיאִים רַב כִּדְגַת הַיָּם / וָעוֹף לָרֹב, בָּא יוֹם אֵידָם,
בּוֹ דָם קָפָא עַל גַּב דָּם, בּוֹ / שׁוֹחֲטִים רַבִּים יָרִיקוּ דָם.
וּלְצִדּוֹ – צָדִים וּדְגַת יָם / כַּחוֹל, בִּכְלִי כָּל אִישׁ צָדָם,
וּלְצִדָּם שׁוּק מַאֲפֶה – בַּיּוֹם / אוֹפֶה וּבַלַּיְלָה לֹא רָדַם.
מִזֶּה אוֹפִים, מִזֶּה אוֹכְלִים, / מִזֶּה מוֹלִיכִים אֶת צֵידָם,
מִזֶּה נוֹשְׂאִים אֶל בָּתֵּיהֶם – / וַיָּבֶן לִבִּי אֶת סוֹדָם,
וָאֹמַר לָעוֹמְדִים: עַל מָה / כֹּה יִכְלוּ אֵלֶּה מֵעוֹדָם?
מָה הֶבְדֵּל בֵּין אֵלֶּה לָכֶם / בִּגְוִיעָתָם וּבְמוֹלָדָם
וּבְנוּמָתָם וּבַהֲעִירָם / וּבְמוֹשָׁבָם וּבְמַעֲמָדָם?
לוּלֵי כִּי צוּר הוּא הִטְעִימָם / לָכֶם, אָכֵן לֹא הִשְׁמִידָם,
אִלּוּ נָתַן בָּהֶם רוּחַ – / הֵם הֶאֱבִידוּ אֶת מַאֲבִידָם!
לָהֶם נֶפֶשׁ כָּכֶם גַּם לֵב / כָּכֶם עַל אֶרֶץ לַהֲנִידָם,
לֹא נִמְצָא עֵת לֹא מֵת בּוֹ מֵת / אוֹ עֵת לֹא יוֹלִיד מוֹלִידָם.
לָזֹאת יָשִׂימוּ לֵב זַכִּים / וּנְסִיכִים גָּאוּ בִכְבוֹדָם:
אִם יָבִינוּ סוֹד הָעוֹלָם, / יֵדְעוּ כִּי זֶה כָּל הָאָדָם!

## 39. A Study Group in the Synagogue

Will destiny be cruel to Rabbi and Rava,
And is there contention between him and the Talmud?
Is this why he put in the mouth of the fool
Well-fed, well-dressed and distinguished looking,
Even every boor, the notion that he is
Mephiboshet and Rav Hai Gaon is Ziva his servant?
They think that by the grace of fringes and beard
And turban they are men qualified to head the academy!

Do you remember my brother when we both went
To the synagogue on Hoshana Rabba.
And we heard an ass braying and the shrieks
Of oxen and they were all howling close by.
And I said: "Who is it that has turned the house of God
Into a stable;—it is indeed a sin and a crime!"
And they replied: "There are no asses or cattle in the house of the Lord
These are men engaged in study of a tractate in the Talmud!"
Whereupon I exclaimed: "Will you thus barter away the law
And the testimony,—and I whither shall I go?"
Angrily we then entered the house of God,—
(Would that we had lost our way!)
And there was the teacher and his students, their heads
Swaying like lonely trees in the desert.
With their mouths they insulted Hillel and Shammai
And slapped the face of Rabbi 'Aqiva
The teacher elaborated upon the text for the benefit of the students
And with difficulty seized a response from them.
As I sat there I was enraged by
What I saw and my spirit was depressed.
I then reverently greeted the teacher
But he replied as one who would quarrel and bear enmity.
Then I began to recite the morning prayers
With a loud voice like that of a multitude and armed host.
Were he to give thanks to God that he was created a man
And not a woman,—I would respond to him:
"Do you really think that you belong among men?
Even God testifies against you that you are a woman!"

הֲיִרְהַב הַזְּמָן בִּרְבִּי וְרָבָא / וְאִם בֵּינָיו וּבֵין תַּלְמוּד מְרִיבָה?
וְלָכֵן סִדְּרוֹ עַל פִּי פְתָאִים, / מְתֵי בֶטֶן וַאֲדֶרֶת וְשֵׂיבָה,
וְכָל בַּעַר אֲשֶׁר יֹאמַר ״אֲנִי הוּא / מְפִיבֹשֶׁת, וְרַב הַאי כְּצִיבָא״ —
יְדַמּוּ כִּי בְצִיצִיּוֹת וְזָקָן / וּמִגְבַּעַת יְהִי אִישׁ רֹאשׁ יְשִׁיבָה!
זְכֹר, אָחִי, בְּלֶכְתֵּנוּ שְׁנֵינוּ / אֱלֵי בֵית הַתְּפִלָּה יוֹם עֲרָבָה
וְשָׁמַעְנוּ חֲמוֹר נוֹעֵר וְצוֹוַחַת / בְּנֵי בָקָר, וְהֵם גּוֹעִים, קְרוֹבָה.
וְשַׁחְתִּי ״מִי אֲשֶׁר שָׁת בֵּית אֱלֹהִים / כְּבֵית רֶפֶת—וְהִיא חַטָּאת וְחוֹבָה?״
וְאָמְרוּ ״אֵין חֲמוֹר וּמְרִיא בְּבֵית אֵל, / אֲבָל קוֹרִין בְּמַסֶּכֶת וּבָבָא!״
וְאָמַרְתִּי ״הֲמִירוֹתֶם תְּעוּדָה / וְתוֹרָה, וַאֲנִי אָנָה אֲנִי בָא?״
וּבָאנוּ זוֹעֲמִים אֶל בֵּית אֱלֹהִים — / וּמִי יִתֵּן וְנִטְעֶה בַנְּתִיבָה! —
וְהִנֵּה רַב וְתַלְמִידִים מְנִידִים / לְרָאשֵׁיהֶם כְּעַרְעָר בָּעֲרָבָה,
בְּפִיהֶם גִּדְּפוּ הִלֵּל וְשַׁמַּאי / וְהִכּוּ עַל לְחִי רַבִּי עֲקִיבָא,
וְהָרַב יַאֲרִיךְ לָהֶם טְעָמִים / וִיטָרֵף מִלְּשׁוֹנָם אוֹת וְתֵבָה.
וְיָשַׁבְתִּי וּפָנַי זוֹעֲפִים מִן / אֲשֶׁר אֶרְאֶה וְנַפְשִׁי בִי עֲצֵבָה,
וְשָׁאַלְתִּי שְׁלוֹם הָרַב בְּכָבוֹד — / וְעָנַנִי כְּאִישׁ מָדוֹן וְאֵיבָה.
וְהֵחֵל לַעֲנוֹת מֵאָה בְרָכוֹת / בְּקוֹל עָבֶה כְּקוֹל הָמוֹן וְצָבָא,
יְבָרֵךְ אֵל לְמַעַן אִישׁ בְּרָאוֹ / וְלֹא אִשָּׁה — הֲשִׁיבוֹתִיו תְּשׁוּבָה:
״הֲתָשִׁית נַפְשְׁךָ מִן הַזְּכָרִים? / וְאֵל יָעִיד בְּךָ כִּי אַתְּ נְקֵבָה!״

# J.
# Of Wine and its Pleasures

## 40. On Parting from Friends

Hear me physician, who put to flight my body's hurt,
Have you a remedy for the pain of separation from my friends?
And you who gaze at the stars, can you see
In them that which is hidden deep inside me?
It is my fault,—and because of it the mighty God
Has taken and exiled you from my neighborhood.
He has afflicted with your separation,—for I am weak
Like the young saplings smitten by the locusts.
A pair of evils beset me when you parted
And one or the other awakens my grief.
At times I am silent and controlled

But often my tears like a stream surround me.
When I am silent,—my friends have quarrel with me
And when I weep,—my family is vexed.
How much longer can I bear the bruising pain
That overcomes me from each side!
And so I will not send anyone to inquire as to your well-being,
And will not forward to you my letters of love.
Since you do not look upon me,—I am envious
Of all who are favored by your gaze, though they be my adversaries.
Though if they saw you their quarrel
With me would end and they would follow in my path,
Therefore I am jealous of all
That you behold, even the letters that I write.

שְׁמַע, רוֹפֵא, אֲשֶׁר הֵנִיס כְּאֵבַי: / הֲיֵשׁ אֶצְלָךְ צֳרִי לִנְדוֹד אֲהוּבַי?
וְאַתְּ, חוֹזֶה בְכוֹכָבִים, הֲתָבִין / בְּכוֹכָבִים אֲשֶׁר צָפְנוּ קְרָבַי?
אֲנִי חַבְתִּי – וְאֵל אַמִּיץ לְקָחָךְ / וְהִגְלָךְ מִשְּׁכוּנָתִי בְּחוֹבַי
וְהִכַּנִי בְנוּדָךְ – וַאֲנִי רַךְ – / כְּמַכַּת רֹאשׁ עֲלוֹת לֶקֶשׁ בְּגוֹבַי.
שְׁתַּיִם נִקְבְּצוּ עָלַי בְּלֶכְתָּךְ / וְזֹאת אוֹ זֹאת תְּעוֹרֵר אֶת עֲצָבַי:
אֲנִי שׁוֹתֵק וּמִתְאַפֵּק פְּעָמִים, / וְעִתִּים מִבְּכִי נַחַל סְבִיבַי,
וְעֵת אֶדֹּם – יְרִיבוּנִי חֲבֵרַי, / וְאִם אֶבְכֶּה – יְרִיבוּנִי קְרוֹבַי.
וְאֵיךְ אוּכַל נְשֹׂא אַחַת בְּרֹאשִׁי / תְּשׁוּפֵנִי וְאַחַת עַל עֲקֵבַי!
וְלֹא אֶשְׁלַח אֲשֶׁר יִרְאֶה שְׁלוֹמָךְ / וְלֹא אֶשְׁלַח לְךָ כִּתְבֵי אֲהָבַי,
לְמַעַן לֹא תְשׁוּרֵנִי – וְאֶחְמֹד / לְכֹל תָּשׁוּר, וְלוּ הָיוּ יְרִיבַי,
אֲשֶׁר לוּ יֶחֱזוּךְ – יַחְדְּלוּ מִן / מְרִיבָתִי וְיֵלְכוּ עַל נְתִיבַי.
וְעַל כָּכָה אֲנִי חוֹמֵד לְכֹל מַה / תְּשׁוּרֵהוּ – עֲדֵי אֶחְמֹד כְּתָבַי!

### 41. Leave the Hidden Things

My friend, all your years are sleep
Both good and bad are dreams.
Therefore shut your eyes and ears,
(May the Lord give you strength!)
And leave the hidden things
In your world to those who understand them.
Rather give me a cup of old wine to drink

From the hand of a young maid skilled on the 'alamot.
Let it be as old as the age of Adam, and if not
Then as young as the days of Noah.
May its perfume be like that of myrrh and calamus
And its appearance like fine gold and coral;
Like the wine of David for whom queens were prepared
In innocence and pleasant concubines.
He sang happily on the day it was placed in a pitcher
And raised up splendid tones upon the lyre
As he said: "Wine like this shall be stored and preserved
And placed for safe-keeping in jugs tightly sealed
For those who would drink with a merry heart
While holding the cup with sober hands,
Even keeping in mind the rule in Qohelet written:
'And fear the troubles that come after death'."

יְדִידִי, כָּל שְׁנוֹתֶיךָ תְּנוּמוֹת / וְטוֹבָתָם וְרָעָתָם חֲלוֹמוֹת,
וְעַל כָּכָה אֱטֹם אֹזֶן וְעַיִן / עֲצֹם – יִתֵּן לְךָ אֵל תַּעֲצוּמוֹת! –
וְהַנִּיחַ דְּבָרִים נַעֲלָמִים / בְּעוֹלָמָךְ לְמֵבִין תַּעֲלוּמוֹת,
וְהַשְׁקֵנִי יְשִׁישָׁה בַּאֲשִׁישָׁה / בְּכַף עַלְמָה מְטִיבָה בַּעֲלָמוֹת
יְשָׁנָה מִן יְמוֹת אָדָם, וְאִם לֹא – / חֲדָשָׁה מִן יְמֵי אִישׁ הָאֲדָמוֹת!
יְהִי רֵיחָהּ כְּרֵיחַ מוֹר וְקָנֶה / וּמַרְאֶהָ – כְּמַרְאֵה פָּז וְרָאמוֹת,
כְּיֵין דָּוִד הֱכִינוּהוּ מְלָכוֹת / בְּנִקָּיוֹן וּפִילַגְשִׁים נְעִימוֹת,
וְיוֹם הֻנַּח בְּנֵבֶל – שָׁר בְּצַחוּת / וְצַחְצָחוֹת עֲלֵי נִבְלוֹ יְרִימוֹת
וְשָׂח "כָּזֶה יְהִי אָצוּר וְשָׁמוּר / וְאָסוּר בַּחֲבִיּוֹת הַחֲתוּמוֹת
לְכָל שׁוֹתֶה בְּלֵב טוֹב מֵי עֲנָבִים / וְאוֹחֵז כּוֹס בְּיָדַיִם חֲכָמוֹת,
וְשׁוֹמֵר דָּת בְּקֹהֶלֶת כְּתוּבָה / וְחָרֵד מִתְּלָאוֹת אַחֲרֵי מוֹת".

## 42. A Place for Festivities

Do you know what I have done for the wise
And for the sages who walk in perfect ways,
And for young men who fear the Lord and are beautiful
To look at, even for the boys among them?
I prepared a place for festivities as I declared:
"Come and spend your days in pleasantness,

Let us be happy before the time of separation,—
For destruction is poised at the side of all beings,—
Since companionship and life are sisters
While parting and death are their twins."
Thus they approached their couches of purple
Weave and magnificent embroidery
And the vessels of wine and various delicacies were
In the hands of nobles, wise as we.
Upon the plants of aloe-trees, even its branches
Young turtle-doves played noisily together,
And during the day the garden beds were sated
With rain and they brought out their hidden plants.
There we were in a good disposition with no
Anxiety as we carried out our plans.

I sent for the musician and he came
In a hurry with his violin and his gaily decorated lyre.
And I held on to the open wine flask
Almond shaped and overlaid with precious stones.
And called to my household that they come to drink
Of the produce of choice vines and the posterity of the vineyards,
Even of the world's light squeezed into a pitcher
Like Tamar pressed between her brothers-in-law.
And they emptied the flask filled like a woman with child,
Though no embryo was present therein.
They brought out that which was preserved since the vintage
  season
And what was kept closed for years in deep jugs.
It was like an old man when his bones stick out
But whose color is blushing red like that of a boy.
It was perfumed but not from the powders of frankincense;
Its odor was sweet but not of the chief spices.
It had the appearance of fire, but poured itself out like water.
It looked like a simpleton but it led wise men astray
And like lightning,—though the latter at times brings with it rain
And sometimes fails to do so.
They poured wine into their bodies in the black night
And emerged enlightened out of their dark garments
But when the wine glow advanced upon the light of day
They were unable to look upon the heavens.
They thought they had a hold upon the wine, but it deceived them
With the flattery of its lips and not by the power and dread of its
  hand.
It made them speak though remaining silent itself

And caused the notables to dance like gazelles and young wild oxen.
By their consent it instantly removed their intelligence
While their knowledge was completely driven into exile.
They consider a poor man as if he ruled over princes
And a fool by virtue of his appearance, his discernment and his scent
As though he had dominion over the wise.
Then they go into hiding with their cups as bright as onyx stones
And glow even more than pearls from the wine
Preserved in flasks like faces red;
They were clothed by its light as a garment
Whose brightness settled and fixed itself upon their foreheads.
They sent the wine coursing downward into their mouths
And it got the upper hand over princes and nobles.
Then they lay down toward evening as if
Beaten down by the sledge hammer of Ya'el.

I awakened them in the morning and there was no one
Who could stand up or lift his head;
Their legs were as if without toes,
Their necks lacking bones.
Then they asked me: "Who are you and what do you want?"
As they began to stir like one shaken from a dream.
I replied: "Give heed to my words
Which testify for you, my friends and foes, alike
And let them be heard in all the streets and upon
The highest places of the city for none will refute or deny them:
I am a descendant of Q'hot and the progeny of M'rari,
Men of renown and best in discernment.
My father and the prophet Samuel
Of old were interconnected by blood lines
Even Moses, God's prophet and my father
Were related by family and flesh.
The former I will call, "Father" and he will say,
"Son" to me, when the nations are assembled.
Whoever finds a flaw in my pedigree for purposes of derision,
Investigate him and discover a man full of blemishes!
Indeed I have wealth and great honor but with God
Alone is mighty strength and power.
And I have eloquence that surpasses the Levites
And status higher than that of the priests.
I rule over treasures of gold
And have dominion over hoards of rich apparel.

The wise are silent in my presence
And men of understanding as if laden with guilt.
They stand closed-mouth
When I pass by, even their eyes are shut.
They remain dumbfounded before me
Even wise men of mighty capabilities.
And I expounded upon noble themes
Though their subject matter was obscure,
And I delivered precious rhymes
To which none are comparable in the world.
Moreover, and best of all,
In all my efforts I have not done aught in anger.
And if I have sinned under compulsion or in secret
May God forgive me for these.

הֲתֵדַע אֶת פְּעָלַי לַחֲכָמִים / וְלִזְקֵנִים בְּאָרְחוֹתָם תְּמִימִים
וּבַחוּרִים מְתֵי יִרְאָה וְטוֹבִים / בְּמַרְאֵיהֶם וְלִצְעִירִים לְיָמִים?
הֲכִינוֹתִי מְקוֹם מִשְׁתֶּה וְשַׁחְתִּי / "עֲלוּ, בַּלּוּ יְמֵיכֶם בַּנְּעִימִים,
עֲלוּ, נָשִׂישׂ בְּטֶרֶם בּוֹא פְרִידָה – / וְאֵיד נָכוֹן לְצַלְעֵי כָל יְקוּמִים,
וְהַחֶבְרָה וְהַמִּחְיָה – אֲחָיוֹת, / וְהַפֵּרוּד וְהַמָּוֶת – תְּאוֹמִים".
אֲזַי בָּאוּ אֱלֵי מַצָּע מְשֻׁבָּץ / בְּאַרְגָּמָן וּמַכְלוּלִים רְקוּמִים
וְאֶל כֵּלִים וְאֶל מִינֵי מְגָדִים / בְּיַד שׁוֹעִים כְּמוֹתֵנוּ עֲרֵמִים
עֲלֵי מַטַּע אֲהָלִים – עַל עֲנָפָיו / בְּנֵי תוֹר שׂוֹחֲקִים יַחַד וְהוֹמִים,
וְיוֹם רָווּ בְּיֵין עָבִים וְשָׁכְרוּ / וְהוֹצִיאוּ צְפוּנֵיהֶם תְּלָמִים.
וְיָשַׁבְנוּ בְּמוֹשָׁב טוֹב, וְאֵין בּוֹ / כְּבַד לֵב, וַהֲפִיקוֹנוּ זְמָמִים:
וְשָׁלַחְתִּי לְבֶן־יוּבַל וּמִהַר / בְּכִנּוֹרוֹ וּמִנָּיו הַשְּׁלֵמִים,
וְתָמַכְתִּי בְּאֵם אֶקְדָּח פְּתוּחָה / מְשֻׁקֶּדֶת מְעֻלֶּפֶת לְשָׂמִים,
וְקָרָאתִי בְּנֵי בֵיתִי וְקָמוּ / לְבֶן־שׂוֹרֵק וְנֶכֶד הַכְּרָמִים,
אֱלֵי עָשׁוּק, מְאוֹר עוֹלָם בְּכַדּוֹ – / כְּתָמָר הָעֲשׁוּקָה בֵּין יְבָמִים.
וְהֵרִיקוּ מְעֻבֶּרֶת מְלֵאָה – / וְלֹא הָיְתָה מְלֵאָה בַעֲצָמִים,
וְהִתִּירוּ אֲסִיר בָּצִיר וְעָצוּר / שְׁנָתַיִם בְּלֵב כַּדִּים אֲטוּמִים,
וְהִנֵּה שָׁב זְמַן שִׂפָּה בְשָׂרוֹ – / אֲבָל עֵינוֹ מְאָדָּם כַּעֲלָמִים!
מְקֻטָּר – לֹא בְּאַבְקַת הַלְּבוֹנָה, / מְרֻקָּח – לֹא בְּרָאשֵׁי הַבְּשָׂמִים,
כְּמַרְאֵה אֵשׁ וּמִשְׁתַּפֵּךְ כְּמַיִם / דְּמוּת פֶּתִי וּמֵסִית הָעֲרוּמִים,
וְכַבָּרָק וְתוֹכוֹ יֵשׁ גְּשָׁמִים – / וְיֵשׁ בָּרָק וְאֵין עִמּוֹ גְּשָׁמִים.

שְׁפָכוּהוּ עֲלֵי גוּפָם בְּלַיִל / וְיָצְאוּ מִלְּבוּשׁ חָשְׁכָם עֲרוּמִּים,
וְלֹא יָכְלוּ, בְּעֵת נוֹסַף מְאוֹרוֹ / עֲלֵי אוֹר יוֹם, לְהַבִּיט אֶל מְרוֹמִים.
וְתָפְשׂוּ בוֹ, אֲבָל הִטָּם בְּחֵלֶק / שְׂפָתָיו, לֹא בְחֹזֶק יָד וְאֵימִים,
וְדִבֶּר בָּם – וְהוּא דוֹמֵם – וְהִרְקִיד / יְקָרִים כַּצְּבִי וּכְבֶן רְאֵמִים.
וְלִרְצוֹנָם בְּפֶתַע סָר תְּבוּנָם / וְדַעְתָּם הָגְלְתָה הָגְלַת שְׁלוֹמִים,
וְרָאוּ דַל – וְלוֹ שִׁלְטוֹן עֲלֵי שַׂר, / וּפֶתִי – לוֹ מְלוּכָה עַל חֲכָמִים
בְּמַרְאֵהוּ וְטוּב טַעְמוֹ וְרֵיחוֹ / וְהָחְבְּאוּ בְכוֹסוֹת הַשְּׁהָמִים
וְאָדְמוּ מִפְּנִינִים עַל יְדֵי מָךְ / אֲסִיר הַכַּד כְּמוֹ פָּנִים אֲדֻמִּים
כְּאִלּוּ אוֹר אֲשֶׁר לוֹבֵשׁ וְנֹגַהּ / בְּרַקּוֹתָם מְדֻבָּקִים וְשׁוּמִים.
שְׁלָחוּהוּ עֲלֵי פִיהֶם בְּמוֹרָד – / וְעָלָה הוּא לְרֹאשׁ שָׂרִים וְרָמִים,
וְהִשְׁכִּיבָם לְעֵת עֶרֶב, כְּאִלּוּ / בְּמַקֶּבֶת בְּיַד יָעֵל הֲלוּמִים.
הֲקִימוֹתִים לְעֵת בֹּקֶר, וְאֵין בָּם / אֲשֶׁר יָקוּם וְרֹאשָׁם לֹא מְרִימִים,
כְּאִלּוּ אֵין לְרַגְלֵיהֶם בְּהוֹנוֹת / וְאֵין לָהֶם בְּצַוָּארָם גְּרָמִים.
וְאָמְרוּ לִי "אֱמֹר, מִי אַתְּ וּמַה לָּךְ?" / וְנִעְּרוּ כְּנֵעוֹר מִן חֲלוֹמִים.
עֲנִיתִים אָז "תְּנוּ אֹזֶן לְמֵלִין / יְעִידוּן בָּם מְיֻדָּעִים וְקָמִים,
וְיִשָּׁמְעוּ בְּכָל חוּצוֹת וְעַל גַּב / מְרוֹם קֶרֶת וְאֵין מַכְלִים וּמַדְמִים:
אֲנִי נֶכֶד קְהָת וּשְׁאֵר מְרָרִי, / מְתֵי הַשֵּׁם מְטִיבֵי הַטְּעָמִים,
וּמֵאָבִי וּמִבֶּן־צוּף שְׁמוּאֵל / לְפָנִים הֶעֱרוּ דָמִים בְּדָמִים,
וּבֵין אָבִי וּבֵין מֹשֶׁה נְבִיא אֵל / שְׁאֵר בָּשָׂר וְקִרְבַת הַלְּחוּמִים,
אֲנִי אֶקְרָא שְׁמוֹ "אָבִי", וְהוּא לִי / "בְּנִי" יִקְרָא בְּהִקָּבֵץ עֲמָמִים.
וּמִי יִמְצָא בְיַחְסִי מוּם לְשִׁמְצָה – / חֲקֹר: תִּמְצָא אֱנוֹשׁ מָלֵא בְּמוּמִים!
וְלִי עֹשֶׁר וְכָבוֹד רַב – וְלָאֵל / לְבַדּוֹ עֹז וְתַעְצוּמוֹת עֲצוּמִים –
וּפִתְחוֹן פֶּה עֲלֵי פִיּוֹת עֲרֵבוֹת / וּמַשָּׂא רֹאשׁ עֲלֵי רָאשִׁים כְּסוּמִים,
וּמַמְלָכָה עֲלֵי גִנְזֵי זְהָבִים / וּמֶמְשֶׁלֶת עֲלֵי גִנְזֵי בְרוֹמִים.
בְּמוֹשְׁבֵי חֲכָמִים מַחֲרִישִׁים / וּמַשְׂכִּילִים כְּאִלּוּ הֵם אֲשֵׁמִים,
וְיָקוּמוּ בְּפִיפִיּוֹת חֲסוּמוֹת / בְּעֵת עָבְרִי וְאִישׁוֹנִים עֲצוּמִים,
וְיִוָּתְרוּ לְנֶגְדִּי נֶאֱלָמִים / חֲכָמִים לַעֲשׂוֹת חַיִל אֲלוּמִים.
וְאֶחְשֹׂף הַדְּבָרִים הַנְּגִידִים – / וְהָיוּ עִנְיְנֵיהֶם נַעֲלָמִים,
וְאַטִּיף הַחֲרָזִים הַיְּקָרִים – / וְאֵין לָהֶם בְּתֵבֵל אָח וְדוֹמִים.
וְעַל כָּל זֹאת וְטוֹב מִזֹּאת וּמִזֹּאת / בְּכָל יָכְלִי פְּעָלַי לֹא זְעוּמִים,
וְאִם אֶפְשַׁע בְּאֹנֶס אוֹ בְנֶעְלָם, / יְכַפֵּר אֵל אֲנָסִים וַעֲלוּמִים!"

## 43. A Ransom

I will be a ransom for the young lad who arose at night
To the sound of the ʿud and the excellent flute players,
Who saw a cup in my hand and said:
"Drink the wine from between my lips!"
While the moon like the letter yod was written
Upon the garment of dawn with colors of gold.

אֱהִי כֹפֶר לְעֹפֶר קָם בְּלַיִל / לְקוֹל כִּנּוֹר וְעוּגָבִים מְטִיבִים
אֲשֶׁר רָאָה בְּיָדִי כוֹס וְאָמַר / "שְׁתֵה מִבֵּין שְׂפָתַי דַּם עֲנָבִים!"
וְיָרֵחַ כְּמוֹ יוֹד נִכְתְּבָה עַל / כְּסוּת שַׁחַר בְּמֵימֵי הַזְּהָבִים.

## 44. The Face of Darkness Flees

Come at dawn and see the curtain
Of sky dotted with silver and fine gold,
While the face of darkness flees like a black man
Before a light-skinned maiden.

And to the voices of high-flying birds drink
From the hand of a young maid in splendid attire
The wine which reflects in the cup the light of sun
And whose fragrance is like myrrh and cassia.

קוּמָה בְּשַׁחַר וְשׁוּר יְרִיעַת / שַׁחַק בְּכֶסֶף וּפָז נְקֻדָּה
וּפְנֵי אֲפֵלָה כְּמוֹ שְׁחַרְחֹר / נָס מִפְּנֵי נַעֲרָה בְּרֻדָּה,
וּשְׁתֵה לְקוֹל צִפֲּרֵי שְׁחָקִים / מִיַּד פְּנִימָה וְכַף כְּבוּדָּה
יַיִן מְאוֹרוֹ בְּכוֹס כְּמוֹ אוֹר / שֶׁמֶשׁ וְרֵיחוֹ כְּמֹר וְקִדָּה.

## 45. Look at the Morning Light

Tell me, my friend,
When can I give you my wine to drink?
The call of the cock awoke me,
And I am unable to sleep.
Come out and look at the morning light
Like a thread of scarlet in the east.

Hurry and give me drink,
Before the rise of dawn,
Of spiced wine and juice of pomegranate,
In a cup held by the perfumed hand of a young maid,
Who will sing to me of many things,
Both life giving and death dealing.

מְיֻדָּעִי, הֲבִינֵנִי / לְמָתַי אַשְׁקְךָ יֵינִי?
קְרָא שֶׁכְוִי הֱקִיצַנִי / וְאֵין שֵׁנָה בְּאִישׁוֹנִי.
צְאוּ וּרְאוּ בְּמִזְרָח אֶת / מְאוֹר בֹּקֶר כְּחוּט שָׁנִי
וְהָאִיצוּ בְּטֶרֶם יַ־ / עֲלֶה שַׁחַר וְהַשְׁקוּנִי
בְּכוֹס מִיַּד מְרֻקָּחָה / עֲסִיס רִקְחִי וְרִמּוֹנִי
וְתָשִׁיר לִי דְבָרִים – אִם / יְחַיּוּנִי יְמִיתוּנִי.

## 46. Gamblers

It is red in appearance and sweet to drink,
Vintage of Spain but famous as far as India.
Weak in the cup, but when it reaches the brain
It subdues mighty men and rules over them.

The mourner, whose blood is mingled with his tears,
The blood of grapes will chase away his grief.
Friends when passing the cup from hand to hand,
Are like gamblers for a precious stone.

מְאָדָּם בְּמַרְאֵהוּ וְעָרֵב לְשׁוֹתֵהוּ
וּמָזוּג בְּאִסְפַּמְיָא – וְזִכְרוֹ אֱלֵי הֹדּוּ,
וְחַלָּשׁ בְּאַגָּנָיו, אֲבָל בַּעֲלוֹתוֹ אֶל
רָאשִׁים – אֲזַי יִרְדֶּה בְּרָאשִׁים אֲשֶׁר יֵרְדוּ.
וְשָׁכוּל אֲשֶׁר דָּמָיו מְסוּכִים בְּדִמְעוֹתָיו –
יְגוֹנָיו בְּדַם אֶשְׁכּוֹל יְנוּסוּן וְיִדְּדוּ.
כְּאִלּוּ יְדִידִים עֵת יְסֻבּוּם אֲשִׁישׁוֹתָיו
מִיָּד לְיָד גּוֹרָל עֲלֵי יַהֲלֹם יַדּוּ.

## 47. Captured Without a Net

The eyes of the young lad who serves me have ravished my heart;
His master has been captured without a net.
Though waters can quench the fires of love
My desire for you is yet like a flame within me.
Come my friend, come take the bright cup
Of sweet juice of pomegranate at the time of dawn
From the hands of the cup-bearer like wheels of gold
Beset with chrysolite and black marble,
And listen to the voice of the turtle-dove and to winged birds
Intone their songs upon the high places of the city
While the image of stars in the morning dawn
Appears like sapphires upon a pale garment.

לִבְּבוּנִי עֵינֵי צְבִי לִי שֵׁרֵת / לֵב אֲדוֹנָיו יָצוּד בְּלֹא מִכְמֹרֶת.
אִם יְכַבּוּ מַיִם אֲהָבֵי דוֹדִים – / לָךְ בְּקֶרֶב לִבִּי כְּאֵשׁ בּוֹעֶרֶת!
קוּם, יְדִידִי, קוּמָה קְחָה כוֹס אֶקְדָּח / מֵעֲסִיס רִמּוֹנִי בְּעֵת אַשְׁמֹרֶת
מִיְּדֵי עֹפֶר הֵם גְּלִילֵי זָהָב / מֻלְּאוּ בַּתַּרְשִׁישׁ וּבַסּוֹחֶרֶת
וּשְׁמַע קוֹל הַתּוֹר וְכָל עוֹף כָּנָף / נָתְנוּ קוֹלָם עַל מְרוֹמֵי קֶרֶת –
וְדְמוּת כּוֹכָבִים בְּכַנְפֵי שַׁחַר / כִּדְמוּת סַפִּירִים עֲלֵי אַדֶּרֶת.

## 48. Her Translucent Glass

Receive from the young maid the wine in her translucent
Glass like fire flaming up amidst the hail.
She has lips like threads of scarlet, and her palate tastes like good
Wine while her mouth like her body has a fragrant scent.
The tips of her fingers are red from the blood of her victims, therefore
Her hand is half crimson and half bdellium.

קַח מִצְּבִיָּה דְמֵי עֵנָב בְּאֶקְדָּחָה
בָּרָה, כְּמוֹ אֵשׁ בְּתוֹךְ בָּרָד מְלֻקָּחָה.
בַּעֲלַת שְׂפָתוֹת כְּחוּט שָׁנִי, וְחֵךְ לָהּ כְּיֵין
הַטּוֹב, וּפִיהָ כְגוּפָתָהּ מְרֻקָּחָה.
מִדַּם חֲלָלִים קְצֵה יָדָהּ מְאָדָּם – לְכֵן
חֶצְיָהּ כְּאֹדֶם וּמַחְצִיתָהּ בְּדֹלָחָה!

## 49. Cold Days Have Come

The month of 'Av has ended even 'Elul and their heat is gone;
Also Tishri is gathered in and like them has passed.
Cold days have come and the new wine
Is red and its voice is still in the vat.
Therefore my friend, go among our companions
So that each may do as he intends.

Some said: Look at the clouds giving rain
And hear the thunder of the heavens on high,
And see the frost and the bonfire's flame;
One descends while the other lifts and rises.
Come, drink from the cup and drink again
From the pitcher, night and day.

מֵת אָב וּמֵת אֱלוּל וּמֵת חֻמָּם, / גַּם נֶאֱסַף תִּשְׁרִי וּמֵת עִמָּם,
בָּאוּ יְמֵי הַקֹּר, וְהַתִּירוֹשׁ / אָדַם וְקוֹלוֹ בַּכְּלִי דָמַם.
לָכֵן, יְדִידִי, סֹב אֱלֵי רֵעִים, / כָּל אִישׁ וְאִישׁ יַעַשׂ אֲשֶׁר זָמַם!
אָמְרוּ: חֲזֵה עָבִים בְּהַגְשִׁימָם / וּשְׁמַע שְׁמֵי מָרוֹם בְּהַרְעִימָם
וּרְאֵה כְּפוֹר וּלְשׁוֹן מְדוּרָה – זֶה / יֵרֵד וְזֶה יַעַל וְיִתְרוֹמָם.
קוּמָה, שְׁתֵה בַכּוֹס וְשׁוּב וּשְׁתֵה / בַכַּד, וּבַלַּיִל וְגַם יוֹמָם!

## 50. Pluck the Roses

Behold the cold days have already passed
And the season of winter's rains is buried.
The young turtle-doves are seen in our land;
They call to one another from the tips of branches.
Therefore, my companions, keep the covenant
Of friendship make haste and do not defy me.

Come to my garden and pluck
The roses whose perfume is like pure myrrh.
And by the blossoms and gathering of swallows
Who sing of the good times, drink ye
Wine in measures like the tears I shed over parting
With friends and as red as the faces of blushing lovers.

הִנֵּה יְמֵי הַקֹּר כְּבָר עָבְרוּ / וִימֵי רְבִיעָה הַסְּתָו קָבְרוּ,
נִרְאוּ בְּנֵי הַתּוֹר בְּאַרְצֵנוּ / מֵרֹאשׁ עֲנָפִים זֶה לְזֶה יִקְרוּ.
לָכֵן, מְיֻדָּעִים, בְּרִית רֵעִים / שִׁמְרוּ וְהָאִיצוּ וְאַל תַּמְרוּ!
בּוֹאוּ לְגַנָּתִי וְשׁוֹשַׁנִּים — / רֵיחָם כְּרֵיחַ מָר־דְּרוֹר בִּצְרוּ,
וּשְׁתוּ, עֲלֵי צִצִּים וְקוֹל סִיסִים / לָשִׁיר עֲלֵי טוּב הַזְּמָן חָבְרוּ,
יַיִן כְּדִמְעָתִי עֲלֵי פֵרוּד / רֵעִים וְכִפְנֵי אוֹהֲבִים חָפְרוּ.

## 51. Garments of the King's Daughters

**Let us get together now that the time is evenly**
**Divided between night and day**
**And look upon the face of the earth as it puts on**
**The multi-colored garments of the king's daughters,**
**And drink wine by the roses**
**Whose bloom is like scarlet or blood-red,**
**And see its leaves, growing**
**Joined together and suited to each other,**
**Like the faces of perfumed pretty maidens**
**Opening into faces blushing red.**

הִתְקַבְּצוּ, כִּי הַזְּמָן תָּמִים / עַתָּה כְּקַו לֵילוֹת כְּקַו יָמִים,
וּרְאוּ פְּנֵי אֶרֶץ אֲשֶׁר לָבְשָׁה / סוּתֵי בְּנוֹת מֶלֶךְ מְרֻקָּמִים,
וּשְׁתוּ דְּמֵי עֵנָב עֲלֵי וֶרֶד / צִצָּיו כְּשָׁנִי אוֹ כְמוֹ דָמִים,
וּרְאוּ פְּנֵי עָלָיו אֲשֶׁר צָמְחוּ / יַחְדָּו מְחֻבָּרִים וּמַתְאִימִים —
כִּפְנֵי יְפַת תֹּאַר מְבֻשָּׂמִים / דָּבְקוּ אֱלֵי פָנִים מְאָדָּמִים.

## 52. Among the Spikenard

**Go and eat your bread with joy, my friend**
**And with a merry heart drink your wine.**
**Stand up and dance like a gazelle or antelope**
**Among the spikenard and aloes by the waters of the pond,**
**And sing a song with gusto in the company of friends**
**Like a turtle-dove and swallow at the rise of dawn.**
**Come and let your mouth and speech be filled with laughter**
**For your works have already found favor with God.**

לֵךְ יְדִידִי, אֱכֹל בְּגִיל לַחְמֶךָ / וּבְלֵב טוֹב שְׁתֵה דְמֵי עִנְּבֶיךָ!
קוּם וְדַלֵּג כְּמוֹ צְבִי אוֹ יְעֵלִים / בֵּין אֲהָלִים וְנֵרְדְּ עַל מֵי בְרֵכָה

עִם חֲבֵרִים יְצַפְצְפוּ שִׁיר בְּרֹהַב / פֶּה, כְּמוֹ תוֹר וְסִיס בְּעֵת סוּר חֲשֵׁכָה.
קוּם וּמַלֵּא שְׂחוֹק לְשׁוֹנְךָ וּפִיךָ, / כִּי כְבָר נִרְצוּ לְאֵל מַעֲשֶׂיךָ!

## 53. Left Alone

Come my friend, the wine has already imprisoned
In the dungeon of sleep all who would pry and interrupt.
And none are with me save one who drinks with a merry heart
Upon a blossom bed of vines fresh and almond shaped.

And a young boy is present to bear the wine
While another hastens diligently to empty the pitchers.
And the hand of a lad plays upon the 'ud with a
Pen minus the ink as if he were writing and pointing.

And the earth seems to us like a maiden
At play and the world like a dancer,
Even the heavens like an armed host resting at night
While each man makes a bonfire in front of his tent.

יְדִידִי, קוּם! כְּבָר אָסְרוּ אֲשִׁישׁוֹת / בְּבוֹר נוּמָה לְכָל עוֹיֵן וּפוֹקֵד
וְאֵין עִמִּי לְבַד שׁוֹתֶה בְּלֵב טוֹב / עֲלֵי נִצַּת סְמָדַר לַח וְשָׁקֵד,
וְעֶלֶם סַב וּמַשְׁקֶה כּוֹס, וְעֶלֶם / לְהָרִיק הַחֲבִיּוֹת רָץ וְשׁוֹקֵד,
וְכַף עֹפֶר בְּעֵט מֵאֵין דְּיוֹ עַל / פְּנֵי כִנּוֹר כְּכַף כּוֹתֵב וְנוֹקֵד.
וְהָאָרֶץ בְּעֵינֵינוּ כְּעַלְמָה / מְשַׂחֶקֶת וְהָעוֹלָם כְּרוֹקֵד –
וְשָׁמַיִם כְּחַיִל נָם בְּלַיִל / וְכָל אִישׁ שָׁם לְעֻמַּת אָהֳלוֹ קֵד.

## 54. Take a Cup

Take a cup from the young gazelle and say to him: "Get
A bottle and run to the pitcher, fill it and bring it here!"
For there is a pain close to my heart, and
The pitcher contains the healing balm to remove it.

Whoever is generous and continues thus
Or tender-hearted,–(for he will prevail like a lion)
Does well for the sick at heart and men will attend
Him as they do to king and prophet.

In the cup is my inheritance and portion, for it is

My friend whom I desire and am reciprocated.
I will dwell wherever I find goblets of wine
There will I spend the night and be glad.

קַח מִצְּבִי כּוֹס וֶאֱמֹר לוֹ ״קְחָה
בַקְבּוּק וְרוּץ לַכַּד וּמַלֵּא וְהָבִיא!״
כִּי יֵשׁ כְּאֵב סָמוּךְ לְלִבִּי, וְיֵשׁ
בַּכַּד צֳרִי שָׁמוּר לְהָסִיר כְּאֵבִי,
הַבָּא בְלֵב נָדִיב – וְיוֹסִיף נְדִי־
בוּת, אוֹ בְלֵב רַךְ־לֵב – וְיִגְבַּר כְּלָבִיא,
מֵיטִיב לְבַב רַע־לֵב, וְלוֹ יִשְׁמְעוּן
לְבּוּת כְּמוֹ שָׁמְעָם לְמֶלֶךְ וְנָבִיא.
בַּכּוֹס מְנָת חֶלְקִי וְכוֹסִי, וְהוּא
דוֹדִי אֲשֶׁר חָפֵץ אֲנִי בוֹ וְהוּא בִי.
בִּמְקוֹם אֲשֶׁר אֶמְצָא גְבִיעִים אֲנִי
שׁוֹכֵן וְשָׁם אָלִין וְיִיטַב לְבָבִי!

## 55. Drive Away Grief

If you desire to be happy, even as
I am, then hear what I have to say.
I will teach you the way of happiness.
But if you do not believe me you are doomed to sighs and
affliction:

'There are five things that fill the heart
With delight and drive away grief:
A graceful form, a garden, wine, the ripple
Of a stream and a poet, these awaken joy within me.'

אִם תְּאַוֶּה, כְּמוֹ נְאַוֶּה לְנַסֵּךְ / יֵין שְׂמָחוֹת, שְׁמַע הֲגִיגֵי לְשׁוֹנִי:
אוֹרְךָ אֶת נְתִיב שְׂשׂוֹנִים, וְאִם לֹא / תַאֲמִין לִי, אֲחִי אֲנָחוֹת וְעֹנִי,
כִּי חֲמִשָּׁה יְמַלְאוּ הַלְּבָבוֹת / בַּשְּׂמָחוֹת וְהֵם יְנִיסוּן יְגוֹנִי:
יַעֲלַת־חֵן וְגַן וְיַיִן וְרִגְשַׁת / מֵי נְחָלִים וְשִׁיר יְעִירוּן שְׂשׂוֹנִי.

## 56. Among the Ruins

Upon the tents of Arab princes now in ruins
The clouds poured out showers of water,
And the winds, fathers to thunder swayed them,
And the rains, sisters of lightning raised grasses around them

After the storm, friends drank toasts there,—
Light wine in golden goblets,
Until they knew not how to distinguish
Between the light of day and the dark ruins.

אָהֳלֵי בַת נְשִׂיא עֲרָב הַחֲרֵבִים – / יָצְקוּ בָם בְּנֵי נְשִׂיאִים רְבִיבִים,
וְהֱנִיעוּם אֲבוֹת רְעָמִים וְאַחְיוֹת / הַבְּרָקִים וְהֶעֱלוּ בָם עֲשָׂבִים.
אַחֲרֵי יָצְקוּ לְךָ שָׁם אֲהוּבִים / מֵי זְהוּבִים בְּתוֹךְ גְּבִיעֵי זְהָבִים,
עַד אֲשֶׁר אֵין בְּךָ תְּבוּנָה לְהַבְדִּיל / בֵּין מְאוֹרֵיהֶם וּמַחֲשַׁכֵּי עֲרָבִים.

## 57. A Fire I See

The rains gave birth to the
Vines who then brought forth the
Grapes; therefore from the children of
'Eshkol purchase two jugs of wine.

Then go to the storehouse filled
With barrels and be enterprising
Saying to all who are oppressed
And taunted: "Open your mouths!"

Then pour from tho jug into the cup
And from there into his mouth and say:
"A fire I see in my cup but
It is not consumed, like the burning bush!"

חִבְּלוּ בְנֵי עָבִים בְּנוֹת / גֶּפֶן, וְהוֹלִידוּ בְנֵי
אֶשְׁכּוֹל – וְלָכֵן מִבְּנֵי / בָנָיו שְׁנֵי כַדִּים קְנֵה
וּלְכָה אֱלֵי אוֹצָר מְמֻ־ /לָּא בַחֲבִיּוֹת וַחֲנֵה

וֶאֱמֹר "פְּתַח פִּיךָ!" לְכָל / נִגַּשׁ וְכָל אִישׁ נַעֲנֶה
וַיִּצֹק בְּכוֹס מִכַּד, וְצַק / מִכּוֹס אֱלֵי פֶּה וַעֲנֵה
"אֶרְאֶה בְכוֹסִי אֵשׁ וְלֹא / יִבְעַר – כְּמוֹ אֵשׁ בַּסְּנֶה!"

### 58. Let This be the Reward

Yours is the duty to make right your deeds
And to give you reward will upon him lie.
Do not spend (all) your days in his service
But do a time for God and times for yourselves;
Give no rest to wine in your nights!
Put out the candle-light and be lit up with your cups;
Despise the voice of singers but make music with your jugs.
And if in the grave there is no song, wine, or friend,—woe
Fools, let this be the reward for your labors.

עֲלֵיכֶם לְפוֹעַלְכֶם לְיַשֵּׁר פְּעֻלֵּיכֶם –
וְלָכֶם יְהִי עָלָיו לְשַׁלֵּם גְּמוּלֵיכֶם.
וְאַל בַּעֲבוֹדָתוֹ תְּבַלּוּ יְמוֹתֵיכֶם,
אֲבָל עֵת עֲשׂוּ לָאֵל וְעִתִּים עֲשׂוּ לָכֶם.
תְּנוּ לוֹ חֲצִי הַיּוֹם וְחֶצְיוֹ לְמַעְשֵׂיכֶם
וְאַל תִּתְּנוּ פוּגַת לְיַיִן בְּלֵילֵיכֶם!
וְכַבּוּ מְאוֹר הַנֵּר – וְאוֹרוּ בְכוֹסֵיכֶם,
וְקוּצוּ בְקוֹל שָׁרִים – וְשִׁירוּ בְנִבְלֵיכֶם.
וְאִם אֵין בְּקֶבֶר שִׁיר וְחֶמֶר וְחָבֵר – הוֹי
פְּתָאִים, יְהִי זֶה חֶלְקְכֶם מֵעֲמָלֵיכֶם!

# K.
# Aphorism From Ben Mishle

### 59. Today

I crave for your mercies today,—never mind that they are preserved for me in your treasure house.
To be sure I am promised for tomorrow eighty pieces of silver,—give me but eight of the eighty, now!

Of what value is it to the man who dies today of thirst to know that tomorrow rain will descend from the clouds?
And who can say that when your goodness arrives I will not be lying in the grave among the dead?

חֲסָדֶיךָ לְיוֹם כָּזֶה אֲקַו – לֹא / הֶיוֹתָם לִי בְּאוֹצָרְךָ צְפוּנִים.
יְעַדְתַּנִי לְמָחָר בַּשְּׁמֹנִים – / תְּנָה לִי כֹה שְׁמֹנָה מִשְּׁמֹנִים!
וּמַה בֶּצַע לְמֵת הַיּוֹם בְּצָמָא / בְּגֶשֶׁם יִרְעֲפוּ מָחָר עֲנָנִים?
וּמִי יֹאמַר, בְּבוֹא טוּבְךָ, אֲשֶׁר לֹא / אֱהִי שׁוֹכֵב בְּקֶבֶר בֵּין יְשֵׁנִים?

## 60. When You are Poor

When you are poor,—ride a lion's back to get
Your food, and do not beg from others.
Be not envious, for desire will
Sadden your heart before it does others.

בְּעֵת תִּדַּל – רְכַב עַל גַּב אֲרִי אֶל / מְזוֹנֶיךָ, וְאַל תִּשְׁאַל לְאִישִׁים,
וְאַל תַּחְמֹד, לְמַעַן כִּי בְחָמְדְךָ / לְבָבְךָ תַּעֲצִיב – טֶרֶם אֲנָשִׁים.

## 61. Because of His Wealth

Because of his wealth, the rich man's friends increase and of him
The mighty ask for favors and through his possession he prospers.
The poor man tries to succeed, but his poverty gets set
And leaps heavily upon his back and puts him down.

בְּהוֹן יִרְבְּיוּן אוֹהֲבֵי עָשִׁיר, וְאֶת פָּנָיו
יְחַלּוּ גְדוֹלִים, וּבוֹ יֵצֵא וּבוֹ יָבוֹא,
וְרָשׁ יַעֲמֹד לַעֲשׂוֹת חַיִל – וְיָקוּם רֵשׁ
וְיִדְלַג בְּכֹבֶד עֲלֵי כִתְפוֹ וְיוֹשִׁיבוֹ!

## 62. My Son

My son, do not devise evil in your heart against your friend
And do not bring him to disgrace.
Take not even the wisest women into your confidence
And do not experiment by drinking deadly drugs.

בְּנִי, אַל תְּהִי חוֹרֵשׁ עֲלֵי רֵעֲךָ רָעָה
בְּלִבְּךָ, וְאַל תָּבִיא חֲבֵרְךָ לְבִזָּיוֹן,
וְאַל תַּעֲמֵד נָשִׁים חֲכָמוֹת עֲלֵי סוֹדְךָ
וְאַל תֵּשְׁתְּ סַמִּים הַמְמִיתִים לְנִסָּיוֹן.

## 63. Beware of the Poet

**He will incite you to evil with dream-like talk**
**And with words of poetry he will urge you to deception.**
**My son, not every dream comes true**
**Neither are all the words of the poet veritable!**

יְסִיתְךָ רַע בְּשִׂיחִים כַּחֲלוֹמִים / וְדִבְרֵי שִׁיר לְרַמּוּתְךָ יְעוֹרֵר.
בְּנִי, לֹא כָל חֲלוֹם יָקוּם וְגַם לֹא / אֱמֶת הוּא כֹּל אֲשֶׁר אָמַר מְשׁוֹרֵר!

## 64. Woman

**Walls and enclosures are made for the woman**
**She is in her glory in a prepared bed and with spinning yarn;**
**Her face reflects the harlotry of the highways,**
**Therefore do we weave for her a veil and a covering.**

לְאִשָּׁה נַעֲשׂוּ קִירוֹת וְטִירוֹת, / וְתִפְאַרְתָּהּ – פְּרֹשׂ מִטָּה וּמַטְוֶה,
וּפָנֶיהָ כְּעֶרְוָה עַל דְּרָכִים – / וְלָהֶם נֶאֱרַג צָעִיף וּמַסְוֶה.

## 65. The Baby Birds

**Be patient in taking revenge on an enemy, even if many days pass**
**Before the time comes when you have the power to slay him.**
**Learn from the baby birds who dwell on the cliffs of the rock;**
**They do not budge until they have grown feathers.**

גְּמוּלָה לְצַר הַנַּח, וְאִם אָרְכוּ יָמִים,
אֱלֵי עֵת אֲשֶׁר כֹּחַ לְהָרְגוֹ בְּךָ נִמְצָא.
לְמַד מִבְּנֵי עוֹף הַשְּׁכוּנִים בְּרֹאשׁ סֶלַע
אֲשֶׁר לֹא יְנוּעוּן עַד אֲשֶׁר יַעֲלוּ נוֹצָה.

## 66. In Their Cups

My son, do not turn to wine when it is seen in the cup.
Would you rather tarry over your cups and put an end to your wealth and property
And be hurt and have quarrels, even redness in the eyes?
Even many are moved to violence in their drunken state
And others there are who in their cups commit the deed of Cain!

בְּנִי, אַל תֵּט אֱלֵי יַיִן / בְּעֵת יִתֵּן בְּכוֹס עֵינוֹ!
הֲטוֹב אַחֵר עֲלֵי כוֹס שָׁם / רְכוּשׁ עָשִׁיר כְּמוֹ אַיִן
וְעַל פֶּצַע וּמִדְיָנִים / וְחַכְלִילוּת בְּתוֹךְ עַיִן?
וְכַמָּה יֵשׁ אֲשֶׁר הֵעִיר / בְּשִׁכְרוּתוֹ כְּלֵי זַיִן,
וְכַמָּה יֵשׁ אֲשֶׁר עָשָׂה / עֲלֵי כוֹס מַעֲשֵׂה קַיִן!

## 67. The Habitual Drunk

My son do not mix your drinks and vow to abstain from strong wine and intoxicating beverages;
It brings out the whore in a woman and leads to poverty and want for the man.
Do not drink and be led to anger against men and do not envy those who imbibe to intoxication.
Consider that the goblet will destroy your vigor and will make hell out of your life.
There are those who drink both evening and morning and end up with their houses disturbed and destroyed
And thereby get to be poor and lose their honor among men in the bargain.
For what good is it that your heart flies like a winged bird, like a buoyant angel or a swift camel?

I awakened him from his drunken state and reproved him when he vomited,—but he understood not nor did he know or remember.
And I pleaded with him and said, "Where is your wealth?" but he didn't care for that which he lost or sold.
He was laughed at among men but was not embarrassed, even in the gates,—and his mouth was closed even shut tight.

״בְּנִי, אַל תַּחְקֹר מִמְסָךְ, וְאַסֵּר / עֲלֵי נַפְשְׁךָ חֲמַת יַיִן וְשֵׁכָר,
מְיַפֶּה לַנְּקֵבָה אֶת זְנוּנִים / וּמֵבִיא רֵשׁ וְחֹסֶר כֹּל לְזָכָר.
וְאַל תִּשְׁתֶּה וְתִתְחַר בַּאֲנָשִׁים, / וְאַל תִּתְחַר בְּמִי שָׁתָה וְשָׁכַר!
חֲשֹׁב, כִּי תַאֲבִיד חֵילְךָ אֲשִׁישָׁה / וְתִתֵּן אֶת שְׁנוֹתֶיךָ לְנֵכָר.
וְכַמָּה הֶעֱרִיב עַל כּוֹס וְהִשְׁכִּים – / וּבַסּוֹף אָהֳלוֹ נִסַּח וְעָכַר,
וְלָקַח הֶעָנִי בִּמְחִיר, וְאָבַד / כְּבוֹדוֹ בֵּין בְּנֵי אָדָם בְּשָׁכָר.
וּמַה בֶּצַע בְּמַפְרִיחַ לְבָבְךָ / כְּעוֹף כָּנָף, כְּמַלְאָךְ קַל, כְּמוֹ כָר?״
הֱקִיצוֹתִיו וְהוֹכַחְתִּיו בְּקִיאוֹ – / וְלֹא הֵבִין וְלֹא יָדַע וְזָכַר,
וְרִיבוֹתִיו וְשַׂחְתִּי ״אֵי יְגִיעֲךָ?״ / וְלֹא שָׁת לֵב לְשֶׁאָבַד וּמָכַר.
וְשָׂחֲקוּ בוֹ בְּמַקְהֵלוֹת וְלֹא בוֹשׁ, / וּבַשַּׁעַר – וּפִיו סָתַם וְסָכַר.

## 68. War the Maiden

**War at the outset is like a beautiful maid**
**With whom every one wishes to flirt.**
**At the end it is like a despised hag**
**Bringing tears and sadness to whomever she meets.**

קְרָב דּוֹמֶה בְּרֹאשׁוֹ אֶל יְפֵיפָה / אֲשֶׁר כָּל אִישׁ לְשַׂחֶק בָּהּ יְאַוֶּה,
וְסוֹפוֹ כַּזְּקֵנָה הַמְּאוּסָה / אֲשֶׁר כָּל שׁוֹחֲרָהּ יִבְכֶּה וְיִדְוֶה.

## 69. The Gored Lion

**When you are depressed, make strong your heart**
**Even while standing at death's door.**
**There is light in the candle before 'tis put out**
**And in the gored lion, a roar.**

בְּעִתּוֹת עָצְבְּךָ חַזֵּק לְבָבְךָ / וְאִם תַּעֲמֹד עֲלֵי שַׁעַר הֲרֵגָה:
לְנֵר מָאוֹר בְּטֶרֶם הַדְּעִיכָה, / וְלִכְפִירִים מְדֻקָּרִים – שְׁאָגָה.

## 70. The Edge of his Pen

**Man's wisdom is in his writing**
**And all his good sense is at the edge of his pen;**
**With it a man may reach the rank**
**Which a scepter allows to a king.**

תְּבוּנַת אִישׁ בְּמִכְתָּבוֹ / וְכָל שִׂכְלוֹ בְּפִי עֵטוֹ,
וְיַגַּע אִישׁ בְּעֵט אֶל מַ־ / עֲלַת מֶלֶךְ בְּשַׁרְבִיטוֹ.

### 71. With Good Fortune

You may tread upon the desert heights with good fortune and find
Your needs fulfilled and load upon your land a moisture cloud.
But without good luck you may dwell in a garden by the Euphrates
And your waters will turn to salt and you will die of hunger!

דּוּשׁ בָּמֳתֵי מִדְבָּר בְּמַזָּל – וְתִמְצָא
שָׂבְעָךְ, וְתַטְרִיחַ עֲלֵי אַרְצְךָ עָב,
וּשְׁכֹן בְּלֹא מַזָּל בְּגַן עַל פְּרָת – יַמְ־
לִיחוּ לְךָ מֵימָיו וְתָמוּת בְּרָעָב!

# L.

# In Praise of Love and Beauty

### 72. You are Angry with Me

It is true that the gazelle is gathering roses in your garden.
I love him,—and for this reason you are angry with me.
And if you could see with your own eyes the object of my desire,
(You would become his alone and) none of your friends would find
you.

When he said: "Bring me down honey from your swarm of bees."
I replied: "Kiss me with your sweet tongue."
Whereupon he became angry and with ill-temper spoke: "Shall we
sin
Before the living God!" I replied: "Your sin be upon me, my lord!"

אֱמֶת, כִּי צְבִי לוֹקֵט וְרָדִים בְּגַנְּךָ / אֲהַבְתִּיו – לְכֵן עָלַי תְּשַׁלַּח חֲרוֹנְךָ.
וְלוּ תֶחֱזֶה אֵת שֶׁאֲהַבְתִּיו בְּעֵינְךָ, / אֲזַי שִׁחֲרוּךָ אוֹהֲבֶיךָ וְאֵינְךָ.
אֲשֶׁר שָׂח ״רְדֵה נָא לִי דְבַשׁ מִנְּחִילְךָ״ / עֲנִיתִיו ״תְּנָה לִי אֶת דְּבַשׁ מִלְּשׁוֹנְךָ״
וְקָצַף וְאָמַר לִי בְּזַעַף ״הֲנֶחֱטָא / לְאֵל חַי?״ עֲנִיתִיו ״בִּי, אֲדוֹנִי, עֲוֹנְךָ!״

## 73. I Have Shown You a Fawn

I have shown you a fawn in order to bring sorrow to your heart
By his eyes, even as you have brought grief to me.
The Lord who made your heart like cold snow to my entreaties
Has also placed within me flames of desire for you.

And the Lord has given you and your arrows excellence in power,
Greater even than the armed hosts and men of war:
The latter kill but a few with a thousand shafts
But you with one slay myriads!

אֲנִי אַרְאֲךָ עֹפֶר וְיָדִיב לְבָבְךָ / בְּעֵינָיו כְּעֵינֶיךָ לְבָבִי מְדִיבוֹת.
מְבֹרָךְ אֲשֶׁר שָׂם לִבְּךָ קַר כְּשֶׁלֶג / בְּקָרְאִי, וְשָׂם לָךְ תּוֹךְ לְבָבִי לְהָבוֹת,
וּבָרוּךְ אֲשֶׁר יֶתֶר שְׂאֵת שָׂת לְחִצָּךְ / וְלָךְ עַל בְּנֵי נֶשֶׁק וְאַנְשֵׁי קְרָבוֹת.
מְמִיתִים מְתֵי מִסְפָּר בְּחִצִּים רְבָבָה – / וְאַתָּה בְּחֵץ אֶחָד תְּמוֹתֵת רְבָבוֹת!

## 74. The Gazelle that Stutters

Where is the gazelle that stutters and where did go
The fawn perfumed with pure myrrh and frankincense?
The moon has covered up the light of the stars.
My love, arise and overlay the light of the moon!
He chirped with a tender voice and relied upon him
Who gave speech to turtle-doves and swallows when they
approached.
He wanted to say, "evil" but instead said to me, "touch!"
I drew near according to his word;
He desired to say, "stop" but uttered, "belly."
I hastened to it, fenced about with lilies.

אַיֵּה צְבִי עִלֵּג, וְאָנָה פָּנָה / עֹפֶר מְקֻטָּר מָר־דְּרוֹר וּלְבוֹנָה?
כִּסְּתָה לְבָנָה אֶת מְאוֹר כּוֹכָבִים – / דּוֹד יַעֲלֶה כִּסָּה מְאוֹר הַלְּבָנָה!
צִפְצֵף בְּלָשׁוֹן רַךְ וְהִשָּׁעֵן עַל / שָׂם פֶּה לְתוֹר וּלְסִיס בְּעֵת בֹּאָנָה.

בְּקֵשׁ לְדַבֵּר "רַע" וְאָמַר לִי "גַּע!"— / גַּשְׁתִּי אֲנִי כַּאֲשֶׁר לְשׁוֹנוֹ עָנָה.
חָפֵץ אֱמֹר "סוּרָה" וְאָמַר "סוּגָה"— / חַשְׁתִּי אֱלֵי סוּגָה בְּמוֹ שׁוֹשַׁנָּה.

## 75. How Shall I Repay my Friend

**How shall I repay my friend**
**For bringing me to grief?**
**If I exchange him for another**
**My glory will be turned to shame.**

**Behold I will reveal my secret**
**To him and place him in my confidence:**
**If he comes and stands before me**
**I will bow and kiss my hand!**

מַה זֶּה אֲשַׁלֵּם לְדוֹדִי / עַל כִּי יְפַלַּח כְּבֵדִי?
אִם אַחֲלִיפוֹ בְּאַחֵר – / אָמִיר בְּקָלוֹן כְּבוֹדִי,
הִנֵּה אֲגַלֶּה צְפוּנִי / לוֹ וַאֲבִיאוֹ בְּסוֹדִי:
אִם בָּא וְעָמַד לְנֶגְדִּי / אֶקֹּד וְאֶשַּׁק לְיָדִי!

## 76. Be Gentle

**Be gentle, for my heart is not like iron**
**And I am unable to bear the rage of my beloved.**
**Is my illness incurable even though you are a physician?**
**Can my pain be perpetual and you a charmer?**

**I will give you to drink wine and milk from my lips**
**And you will repay me in kind.**
**Stretch out your hand and place my heart therein**
**And do not allow strangers to touch me!**

לְאַט, כִּי אֵין כְּמוֹ בַרְזֶל לְבָבִי / וְלֹא אוּכַל נְשֹׂא קֶצֶף אֲהוּבִי.
הֲמַכָּתִי – וְאַתְּ רוֹפֵא – אֲנוּשָׁה? / וְאִם נֶצַח – וְאַתְּ לוֹחֵשׁ – כְּאֵבִי?
שְׁתֵה יַיִן וְחָלָב מִשְּׂפָתִי / וְתֵן תַּגְמוּל לְיֵינִי וַחֲלָבִי,
שְׁלַח יָדְךָ וְתֵן לִבִּי בְּכַפְּךָ / וְאַל זָרִים יְדֵיהֶם יִשְׁלְחוּ בִי!

## 77. All Young Lovers

My God, pray change the heart of the young dove who stole
My sleep that he may give back but a little of it to my eyelids.
My beloved, who came with solemn oath and gave to me
His hearts' love as a gift, without compulsion,
Has betrayed me. But then all young lovers are unfaithful.
And so do forgive him his sins, or failing that, punish me instead.

אֵלִי, הֲפָךְ נָא לְבַב גּוֹזָל אֲשֶׁר גָּזַל / נוּמִי – וְיָשִׁיב לְעַפְעַפַּי מְעַט שֵׁנָה.
אָהוּב אֲשֶׁר בָּא בְּאָלָתְךָ וְנָתַן לִי / אַהֲבַת לְבָבוֹ בְּלִי אוֹנֵס בְּמַתָּנָה –
בָּגַד וְכֵן כָּל צְבִי בוֹגֵד, וְעַתָּה אִם / תִּשָּׂא לְחֶטְאוֹ, וְאִם אַיִן – מְחֵנִי נָא!

## 78. One Heart Rejoined

The flame of love is kindled
Within me—how shall I contain it?
It is destroying me
For it waits in ambush close by.
It attacks me like the Sabeans
And burns with fierce anger
As it pierces my heart.

My tears that flow by day
Reveal my inmost secrets
What will ye say to my beloved?
"Tears do not prove me right."
How else can I be justified?

In my name speak to him
The words I have uttered:
"Do not be indifferent to me!"
Remove from my heart the injury
Made by the rupture of our love.

Comfort, comfort me,
For my insides are groaning,
Because of the pain that increases,
Even sleep is distant from me;
It eludes me and removes itself.

The hearts that were severed

Cried out to each other and embraced again.
They urged me as well
To hold him close,
To kiss and be reunited.
This poem, my love, is witness
(Like the words of a maiden singing.)
Respond to its lay of friendship
That two sections of one heart rejoined shall not again be sundered.

אֵשׁ אֲהָבִים נִשְּׂקָה / בִי – וְאֵיךְ אֶתְאַפָּקָה?

דִּמְּתַתְנִי אַהֲבָה,
כִּי לְיָדַי אֶרְבָּה.
נָפְלָה כִּנְפֹל שְׁבָא,
בְּחֲרִי אַף דָּלְקָה, / אֶת לְבָבִי בִתְּקָה.

יוֹם דְּמָעַי נִגְּרוּ
סוֹד לְבָבִי הֶעֱרוּ.
מַה לְּדוֹדִי תֹּאמְרוּ?
אֵין בְּדִמְעָה צְדָקָה / לִי – בַּמָּה אֶצְטַדָּקָה?
דַּבְּרוּ לוֹ עַל שְׁמִי
אֶת אֲרֶשֶׁת נָאֳמִי
״אַל דֳּמִי לָךְ, אַל דֳּמִי!״
מִדְוֵה לֵב רַחֲקָה / אַחֲוָה שֶׁנִּתְּקָה.

נַחֲמוּנִי, נַחֲמוּ,
כִּי קְרָבַי יֶהֱמוּ
עַל כְּאֵבִים עָצְמוּ,
וּשְׁנָתִי רָחֲקָה / נָדְדָה גַּם עָתְקָה.

הַלְּבָבוֹת נִתְּקוּ
יִזְעֲקוּ יִתְחַבְּקוּ,
וּלְבָבִי דָחֲקוּ
לַחֲבֹק – נִתְחַבְּקָה / נִדְבְּקָה נִתְנַשְּׁקָה!

שִׁיר אֲהָבַי מַעֲנֶה

. . . . . . . . .

שִׁיר יְדִידוּת תַּעֲנֶה

"יא שקין אעתנקא / רב לא יתפרקא".

## 79. One Chain of Your Neck

Beloved, will you rescue your lover captive in the pit?
Dispatch the fragrance of your garments to inform him thus!
Will you draw out your lips with waters of red tint
Or with the blood of fawns give scent to your cheeks?
Provide pleasure to your lover as reward for his ardor
And take my life and my soul as the price of your dowry!
If with your two eyes you break my heart,
But one chain of your neck will make it live again!

רַעְיָה, צְבִי מִבּוֹר שְׁבִי הַתְפַתְּחִי? / רֵיחַ בְּגָדַיִךְ לְבַשְּׂרוֹ שַׁלְּחִי!
הַבְמֵי אֲדָמִים תִּמְשְׁחִי שְׂפָתַיִכִי / אוֹ דַם עֳפָרִים תִּמְרְחִי עַל הַלְּחִי?
דּוֹדִים לְדוֹדֵךְ תַּגְמוּל אֲהָבָיו תְּנִי – / רוּחִי וְנִשְׁמָתִי מְקוֹם מָהֳרֵךְ קְחִי.
לֵב בִּשְׁתֵּי עֵינַיִכִי אִם תְּפַלְּחִי, / בְּאַחַד עֲנָק מִצַּוְּרוֹנַיִךְ יְחִי!

## 80. Be Merciful

For whom are my eyes like a spear sharpened with desire?
For you ever more ever more, support me then and be merciful!
With all my heart I love you,—while your heart is like a rock.
With all my eloquence I address you
And you do not respond.
Will you smite with lovely eyes your servant's heart and he not die
The selfsame day? Yet as God lives, his blood will be avenged.

לְמִי חִדְּדוּ עֵינֵי צְבָאִים חֲנִית, לְמִי?
לְאַט לָךְ לְאַט, סַמְּכִי לְבָבִי וְרַחֲמִי!
בְּכָל לֵב אֲהָבִים לָךְ – וְלִבֵּךְ כְּמוֹ צְרוֹר,
וְכָל פֶּה יְדַבֵּר בָּךְ – וְאַתְּ תִּתְּנִי דֳמִי.
הֲפִלַּחְתְּ לֵב עַבְדֵּךְ בְּעֵינֵי צְבִי וּמֵת
בְּיוֹמוֹ? דְּמֵי עַבְדֵּךְ – וְחֵי אֵל! – תְּשַׁלְּמִי.

## 81. You Take Lightly My Feelings

My love has kindled a fire between our flesh, how then
Will I be able to contain the rage which now consumes me?
I remember saying to her: "I would give my life for you"
While she in derision winked her eyes saying: "For whom?"
If you take lightly my feelings for you,—know that
The loveliest of women kiss their hands when mentioning my name!
Many have angered me and have come to regret it,—but you have provoked me and remain unrepentant.

הִיא שָׁלְחָה בֵּינוֹת לְחָמַי אֵשׁ, וְאֵיךְ / אוּכַל לְהָכִיל אֵשׁ תְּכַלֶּה לַחֲמִי?
אֶזְכֹּר בְּאָמְרִי לָהּ "בְּנַפְשִׁי אַתְּ" וְהִיא / קָרְצָה בְעֵינֶיהָ וְאָמְרָה לִי "בְּמִי?"
אִם אַתְּ הֲקִלֹּת אֶת הֱיוֹתִי לָךְ – וּבַת / עַיִשׁ לְיָד תִּשַּׁק בְּזָכְרָהּ אֶת שְׁמִי!
רַבַּת צְרָרוּנִי וְהִנַּחֲמוּ – וְאַתְּ / רַבַּת צְרַרְתִּנִי וְלֹא תִנָּחֲמִי!

## 82. Where Once You Walked

Like a wanderer I roamed upon a hill of frankincense
And pressed my cheeks upon the place where once you walked.
I was subjected to insults and upon my back they were
Like ploughmen of wide furrows, all because of you.

Indeed they have already surmised that no one
On God's earth is beautiful as you.
Why then do you with black paint encircle your eyes
And tint your lips with redness from the nut?

אָשׁוּט כְּהֵלֶךְ עֲלֵי גִבְעַת לְבוֹנָה וְאַדְבִּיק אֶת לְחָיַי אֱלֵי מִדְרַךְ הֲלִיכָיִכִי,
אֶשְׁמַע גְּדוּפָה, וְעַל גַּבִּי כְּמוֹ מַעֲנִית / חוֹרֵשׁ אֲרוּכָה לְמַעֲנֵךְ וְעָלָיִכִי.
אוּלָם כְּבָר שָׁעֲרוּ אִישִׁים אֲשֶׁר אֵין בְּתוֹךְ / אֶרֶץ אֱלֹהִים יְפֵיפִיָּה כְּמוֹתָיִכִי.
לָמָּה בְּפוּךְ תִּקְרְעִי עַיִן שְׁחוֹרָה וְעַל / מַה תִּצְבְּעִי בְאֱגוֹז אֹדֶם שְׂפָתָיִכִי?

### 83. The Jasmine

Behold the jasmine whose limbs are green
Like a topaz, even its leaves and sides
And its flowers are like white bdellium;
Its branches of the deepest red are
Like a pale looking young man holding
In his hands the blood of innocent folk.

רְאֵה יַאסְמִין אֲשֶׁר בַּדָּיו יְרֻקִּים / כְּמוֹ פִטְדָה וְעָלָיו וַאֲגַפָּיו,
וְצִצָּיו כַּבְּדֹלָחִים לְבָנִים / וּבָאֹדֶם מְאָדָּמִים סְעִפָּיו –
כְּמוֹ עֶלֶם לְבֶן פָּנִים וְשׁוֹפֵךְ / דְּמֵי אִישִׁים נְקִיֵּי כַף בְּכַפָּיו.

# M. Observations from Ben Qohelet

### 84. The Choice He Made

Man hastens to pursue the stubbornness of his heart and does not tarry
As if he never would have to come to judgment for the choice he made.
And how will he fare at the approach of his death and will he put it off.
For each morning turns to evening and each evening to tomorrow,
And every yesterday and day before which has already passed,—is named tomorrow!
Will he not fear on being told: "So and so is gone to the grave?"

אֱנוֹשׁ יָרוּץ וְתָר אַחַר / שְׁרִירוּת לֵב וְלֹא אֵחַר,
כְּאִלּוּ לֹא יְהִי בָא עוֹד / בְּמִשְׁפָּט עַל אֲשֶׁר בָּחַר.
וְאֵיכָה תַעֲמֹד מִבּוֹא / מְהוּמָתוֹ וְתִתְאַחַר?
וְכָל בֹּקֶר אֱלֵי עֶרֶב / וְכָל עֶרֶב אֱלֵי מָחָר,
וְכָל אֶתְמוֹל וְכָל שִׁלְשׁוֹם / כְּבָר הָיָה – שְׁמוֹ מָחָר!
הֲלֹא יִירָא בְּהֵאָמֵר: / פְּלוֹנִי אֶל שְׁאוֹל סָחַר?

## 85. The Ages of Man

The child at ages one or two crawls like a basilisk serpent,
And at the age of ten between his parents he jumps upon the ground like a kid among the male goats.
When he is twenty he is loved by others and himself loves to swagger and boast before the ladies
And to enjoy and take pride in his strength, his youth and beauty at the age of thirty.
At forty he becomes attached to the company of his old time friends
And is awakened from the sleep of infancy and youth by the whiteness of his head and beard at the age of fifty.
Even the terrors of time come upon man from all sides when he reaches sixty.
From sixty to seventy he groans from the pain of age and is seen among the holy ones.
Even time has caught the man of eighty in its snare and hidden trap.
As for the man of ninety his ways are confused and he knows not the harvest from the plowing time.
And the man of one hundred,—but who will reach one hundred?,—to him people will go for amazement.
But the one who dies,—is brother to the worm and the vermin, despised by his peers, polluted among men.
Yea I will compose words of lament wherewith to mourn from time to time for my heart and my flesh!

בְּשָׁנָה אוֹ שְׁנָתַיִם לְיֶלֶד / רְחִישָׁה יֵשׁ כְּצִפְעוֹנֵי נְחָשִׁים,
וּבֶן עֶשֶׂר יְקַפֵּץ בֵּין אֲבוֹתָיו / בְּאֶרֶץ כַּגְּדִי בֵינוֹת תְּיָשִׁים.
וּבֶן עֶשְׂרִים אֲהוּב לַלֵּב וְאוֹהֵב / לְהִתְפָּאֵר וּמִתְהַדֵּר לְנָשִׁים,
וְיִתְנָאֶה וְיִתְגָּאֶה בְכֹחוֹ / וְשַׁחֲרוּתוֹ וְהוֹדוֹ בֶּן שְׁלֹשִׁים.
וְיִתַּמֵּם וְיִתְחַבֵּר בְּבוֹאוֹ / בְּאַרְבָּעִים לְרֵעָיו הַיְשִׁישִׁים –
וְיִיקַץ מִשְּׁנַת יַלְדוּת וְשַׁחֲרוּת / בְּלִבּוּן רֹאשׁ וְזָקָן בֶּן חֲמִשִּׁים.
וּבַלְהוֹת הַזְּמָן עוֹבְרוֹת וְשָׁבוֹת / עֲלֵי אִישׁ עֵת אֲשֶׁר יָבוֹא בְשִׁשִּׁים.
וּמִשִּׁשִּׁים לְשִׁבְעִים נֶאֱנָח מִן / כְּאֵב זֹקֶן וְנִכְאֶה בֵין קְדוֹשִׁים.
וְיִלְכֹּד הַזְּמָן אֶת בֶּן שְׁמוֹנִים / בְּמַלְכֻּדְתּוֹ וּפֶחָיו הַיְקוּשִׁים,

וְיִתְעָרְבוּ לְבֶן תִּשְׁעִים דְּרָכָיו / וְלֹא יֵדַע קְצִירִים מֵחֲרִישִׁים.
וּבֶן מֵאָה – וּמִי יִגַּע לְמֵאָה? – / לְתֵמַהּ יֵלְכוּ אֵלָיו אֲנָשִׁים,
וּבֶן מָוֶת – אֲחִי תוֹלָע וְרִמָּה / מְאוּס אַחִים מְגֹאָל הַלְּבוּשִׁים.
הֲלֹא אַחְבִּיר דְּבַר נֶהִי לְקוֹנֵן / לְבָבִי בוֹ וְגוּפִי לְחֳדָשִׁים!

## 86. Without Using Words

Go forth and see, you who live in his home
While he dwells among the buried ones
And he will call you in the language of your heart
Even the discourse of your spirit without using words:
"On the morrow you will abandon my house even as I did.
And afterwards,—others will dwell therein! "

צְאֵה וּרְאֵה, אֲשֶׁר תִּשְׁכֹּן בְּבֵיתוֹ / וְהוּא שׁוֹכֵן בְּתוֹךְ בָּתֵּי קְבָרִים
וְיִקְרָא אוֹתְךָ בִּלְשׁוֹן לְבָבְךָ / וְשִׂיחַ רוּחֲךָ מֵאֵין דְּבָרִים:
לְמָחָר תַּעֲזֹב בֵּיתִי כְּמוֹתִי, / וְאַחַר – יִשְׁכְּנוּ אוֹתוֹ אֲחֵרִים!

## 87. Every Branch

You who love your days upon the earth,
Do you not know that you live in vain?
For from the beginning you are consigned to death
Even every branch to its root returns!

אוֹהֲבֵי יָמִים עַל גַּב אֶרֶץ, / הַיְדַעְתֶּם כִּי חַיֵּיכֶם שָׁוְא?
אַתֶּם מִשֹּׁרֶשׁ מָוֶת – כָּל / עָנָף יָשׁוּב אֶל שָׁרָשָׁיו!

## 88. When Death Comes

Will you have power when death comes and will it preserve you from the grave?
You will abide awhile and then the dignitaries will assemble as one man in your house.
You will then be washed and cleaned and anointed and spread upon the earth like a board.
Then you will be dressed in glorious shrouds and placed upon a bed like one who is awake.
And a cry will be heard in your room like the anguished voice of a woman in distress giving birth for the first time,

And someone will get up and lament over your loved ones as they bear you to the burial.
And many will stand by your grave as you are put into the dug out pit.
Then they will return home, their heads covered in mourning, their eyes like streams of tears and in their hearts a flame of sorrow.
They will then arise in the morning early to divide your possessions and their wailing will be turned into song.
Weep while you yet live and fear the terror of the day of your death, O my heart, and dread it!

הֲתִהְיֶה בָךְ בְּבוֹא מָוֶת גְבוּרָה / וְאִם מִיַּד שְׁאוֹל נַפְשְׁךָ שְׁמוּרָה?
מְעַט תֵּשֵׁב – וְיִקָּבְצוּ נְגִידִים / אֱלֵי בֵיתְךָ, כְּאִישׁ אֶחָד חֲבוּרָה,
וְתֵרָחֵץ וְתִנָּקֶה וְתוּסַךְ / וְתִמָּשֵׁךְ עֲלֵי אֶרֶץ כְּקוֹרָה
וְתִלָּבֵשׁ בְּכָל תַּכְרִיךְ מְפֹאָר / וְתִנָּתֵן עֲלֵי מִטָּה כְעוּרָה,
וְתִשָּׁמַע זְעָקָה בַּחֲדָרְךָ / וְקוֹל צָרָה כְּמַבְכִּירָה מְצֵרָה.
וְיָקוּם אִישׁ לְבַכּוֹת אוֹהֲבֶיךָ / בְּהוֹלִיכָם לְךָ אֶל הַקְּבוּרָה,
וְיָקוּמוּ עֲלֵי קִבְרְךָ הֲמוֹנִים / וְתִנָּתֵן בְּתוֹךְ שׁוּחָה חֲפוּרָה,
וְיָשׁוּבוּ חֲפוּיֵי רֹאשׁ וְעֵינָם / כְּמוֹ נַחַל וּבִלְבָבָם מְדוּרָה –
וְיַשְׁכִּימוּ לְחַלֵּק אֶת רְכוּשְׁךָ / וְיֵהָפֵךְ נְהִי פִיהֶם לְשִׁירָה.
בְּכֵה נַפְשְׁךָ בְּעוֹדְךָ חַי וְחִיל יוֹם / פְּקֻדָּתְךָ יְרָא, לְבִּי, וְגוּרָה!

## 89. I Am Old Enough

Since you are young you laugh at me
Seeing that I am old and gray.
Yes I am old enough to have seen carpenters
Make coffins and biers for young lads.

תְּשַׂחֵק בִּי בְּיַלְדוּתְךָ, לְמַעַן / רְאִיתַנִי אֲחִי זֹקֶן וְשֵׂיבָה:
אֲנִי זָקֵן וְרָאִיתִי חֲרָשִׁים / לְנַעַר יַעֲשׂוּ מִטָּה וְתֵבָה.

## 90. I Watch the Sky

I watch the sky and its stars
And look upon the earth and its creatures,
And I know that the fashioning of them,
Was a work of wisdom in its execution.

Behold the heavens above, like a tent
Sewn together with loops and hooks,
And the moon with its stars like a shepherd maiden
Sending her flock into pasture.

Like a sailing ship with its banners
Is the moon among the clouds.
And the cloud is like a young maid in her garden
Walking about and watering her myrtle shrubs.

And coverlet of dew is a girl shaking from
Her hair the drops of night upon the ground.
And men are like animals who go
To sleep,—their courtyards their mangers.

And all run from the fear of death
Like a dove whom the falcon pursues.
And their end is likened to a dish
Whose clay structure is broken into little pieces.

אֲצַפֶּה אֱלֵי שַׁחַק וְכוֹכָבָיו – / וְאַבִּיט בְּאֶרֶץ אֶת רְמָשֶׂיהָ,
וְאָבִין בְּלִבִּי כִּי יְצִירָתָם / יְצִירָה מְחָכְמָה בְּמַעְשֶׂיהָ.
רְאוּ אֶת שְׁמֵי מָרוֹם כְּמוֹ קֻבָּה / תְּפוּרִים בְּלוּלָאוֹת קְרָסֶיהָ,
וְסַהַר וְכוֹכָבָיו כְּמוֹ רוֹעָה / תְּשַׁלַּח בְּתוֹךְ אָחוּ כְּבָשֶׂיהָ,
כְּאִלּוּ לְבָנָה בֵּין נְשִׂיאֵי עָב / סְפִינָה מְהַלֶּכֶת בְּנִסֶּיהָ,
וְעָנָן כְּעַלְמָה עַל פְּנֵי גִנָּה / תְּהַלֵּךְ וְתַשְׁקֶה אֶת הֲדַסֶּיהָ,
וְעָב טַל כְּמוֹ נַעְרָה תְּנַעֵר מִן / שְׂעָרָהּ עֲלֵי אֶרֶץ רְסִיסֶיהָ,
וְשׁוֹכְנִים כְּמוֹ חַיָּה אֲשֶׁר נָטְתָה / לְלִינָה וְחַצְרוֹתָם אֲבוּסֶיהָ –
וְכֻלָּם יְנוּסוּן מֵחֲתַת מָוֶת / כְּיוֹנָה אֲשֶׁר הַנֵּץ יְנִיסֶהָ,
וְסוֹפָם לְהִדַּמּוֹת לְצַלַּחַת / אֲשֶׁר שִׁבְּרוּ כָתִית חֲרָסֶיהָ.

## 91. The Night in the Fortress

A mighty force I posted for the night in the fortress
Which sovereigns had long since destroyed.
We slept within it and by its side
Even as its owners slumbered below.

And to myself I said: "Where are the multitudes

And the nations who dwelt here before us?
And where those who built and laid waste;
The princes and paupers, the slaves and masters?

Where are the parents and those who mourn and where fathers
And sons and the bereaved and the bridegrooms?
Great nations follow one another
In the days and years that pass.

They were once neighbors upon the earth,
Even as now they lie within its bosom
Exchanging their palaces for the tomb;
For delightful gardens, the dust of earth.

Were they to raise their heads and come forth
They would make us lose our lives and property.
Indeed, O my soul, indeed like them will I be
On the morrow, myself and this huge force!

הֲלִינוֹתִי גְדוּד כָּבֵד בְּבִירָה / הֲרָסוּהָ יְמֵי קֶדֶם קְצִינִים
וְיָשְׁנוּ עֲלֵי גַבָּהּ וְצִדָּהּ – / וְתַחְתֵּינוּ בְעָלֶיהָ יְשֵׁנִים.
וְדִבַּרְתִּי לְלִבִּי: אֵי קְהָלִים / וְעַמִּים שָׁכְנוּ בָזֹאת לְפָנִים?
וְאֵי בוֹנִים וּמַחְרִיבִים וְשָׂרִים / וְדַלִּים וַעֲבָדִים וַאֲדוֹנִים
וּמוֹלִידִים וְשַׁכּוּלִים וְאָבוֹת / וּבָנִים וַאֲבֵלִים וַחֲתָנִים?
וְעַם רַב נוֹלְדוּ אַחַר אֲחֵרִים / בְּיָמִים אַחֲרֵי יָמִים וְשָׁנִים
וְהָיוּ עַל פְּנֵי אֶרֶץ שְׁכֵנִים – / וְהֵם הַיּוֹם בְּלֵב אֶרֶץ שְׁכוּנִים,
וְקֶבֶר חָלְפוּ מֵאַרְמְנוֹתָם / וְעָפָר – מֵחֲצֵרִים נַעֲמָנִים,
וְאִלּוּ הֶעֱלוּ רֹאשָׁם וְיָצְאוּ – / שְׁלָלוּנוּ נְפָשִׁים וַעֲדָנִים.
אֱמֶת, נַפְשִׁי, אֱמֶת כָּהֵם לְמָחָר / אֱהִי אָנִי וְאֵלֶּה הַהֲמוֹנִים!

## 92. A Scandal

Think what a scandal it is to be happy
When you are faced with sorrow from both sides:
You cried when you came into the world
And another will weep when you leave it.

שִׁית לִבְּךָ תָּבִין קְלוֹן שִׂמְחַת / לֵב בֵּין שְׁתֵּי בְכִיּוֹת לְךָ נִמְצֵאת:
תִּבְכֶּה בְּעֵת בּוֹאֲךָ אֱלֵי עוֹלָם / אַתָּה, וְאַחֵר יִבְכְּךָ עֵת צֵאת.

## 93. More Distant Than Yesterday

Man rushes toward the grave
Even as waters to the great ocean.
All living beings are destined to die
And the palace to become a ruin.

For man, nothing is more distant than yesterday
Nor as near as the day to come,
And both are equally remote from
The man concealed in the grave's depths.

מְרוּצַת אִישׁ אֱלֵי קֶבָה / וּמַיִם אֶל תְּהוֹם רַבָּה,
וְסוֹף כָּל חַי אֱלֵי מָוֶת / וְאַרְמוֹן לֶהְיוֹת חָרְבָּה.
וְאֵין רָחוֹק לְאִישׁ כִּתְמוֹל / וְלֹא קָרוֹב כְּמוֹ יוֹם בָּא,
וְזֶה וָזֶה רְחוֹקִים מִן / אֱנוֹשׁ בִּלְבַב שְׁאוֹל חֻבָּא!

## 94. We Are Surrounded

My friends, we are surrounded by a fence and by spheres that cannot be breached.
For behold we are like the yellow and the white in an egg and the world is the shell.
Do you think that there is escape for you on the evil day,—and how will you flee since there is no opening or exit?
And what can we do,—since God's works have preceded us, and what shall we deliberate when the matter has been resolved?

מְיֻדָּעַי, סְבָבַתְנוּ מְחִצָּה / וְגַלְגַּלִּים אֲשֶׁר אֵין בָּם פְּרִיצָה,
וְהִנֵּנוּ כְּמוֹ אֹדֶם וְלֹבֶן / בְּתוֹךְ בֵּיצָה וְהָעוֹלָם כְּבֵיצָה.
תְּדַמֶּה כִּי לְךָ מָנוֹס בְּיוֹם רַע — / וְאֵיךְ תָּנוּס וְאֵין פֶּתַח וּמוֹצָא?
וּמַה נִּפְעַל — וְקָדְמוּ מִפְעֲלֵי אֵל, / וּמַה נִּיעַץ — וְהָעֵצָה יְעוּצָה?

## 95. Man's Sojourn

Man's sojourn in the mother's womb is a life in cramped quarters until the time of exit.

And on the day of his going forth,—he comes into a distressing world and narrowly he escapes from trouble to trouble.
On the day when he returns,—it is to a scanty grave and to the anguish of recompense for sins.
Will he forever be handed over from one dread disease to another and from ruin to ruin?
For what is the value of man stricken with hardship in a world without a cure?

שְׁכִינַת אִישׁ בְּרֶחֶם אֵם – שְׁכִינָה / בְּמָקוֹם צַר אֱלֵי עֵת הַיְצִיאָה,
וְיוֹם צֵאתוֹ – לְעוֹלָם צַר יְהִי בָא / וְיֵצַר מִתְּלָאָה אֶל תְּלָאָה,
וְיוֹם יָשׁוּב – לְקֶבֶר צַר יְהִי שָׁב / וְאֶל צָרַת גְּמוּלָה עַל חֲטָאָה.
הֲלָעַד מֵחֳלִי צָרָה לְצָרָה / יְהִי נִמְסָר וּמִשּׁוֹאָה לְשׁוֹאָה?
וּמַה בֶּצַע לְאִישׁ חָלָה בְּצָרוֹת / בְּעוֹלָמָיו אֲשֶׁר אֵין בָּם רְפוּאָה?

# Notes

## NOTES TO INTRODUCTION

[1] Abraham Ibn Daud *Sefer ha-Qabbalah*, ed. G. Cohen (Philadelphia, 1967), pp. 75, 266, and 269ff.

[2] Cf. R. Dozy, *Histoire de l'Afrique et de l'Espagne intitulée al-Bayano'l-mogril*, (Leyden, 1848–51), Vol. I, pp. 86–8; and J. Schirmann, "Samuel Hannagid, the Man, the Soldier, the Politician," Jewish Social Studies, XIII (1951) p. 126.

[3] Cf. D. Yarden, *Divan Shmuel Hanagid (Jerusalem, 1966), pp. 237ff.*

[4] Cf. D. Yarden, *op cit.*, p. 66; and J. Schirmann, *Hebrew Poetry in Spain and Provence* (in Hebrew), (Jerusalem, 1959), Vol. 1, p. 124.

[5] Cf. Yarden, *op. cit.*, p. 283; and J. Schirmann, *op. cit.*, p. 160.

[6] Cf. Abraham Ibn Daud, *op. cit.*, p. 79.

[7] Cf. Yarden, *op. cit.*, p. 33; Schirmann, *op. cit.*, p. 111. Self-praise was a common conceit among both Arabic and Hebrew poets of this period. Moreover, Ibn Nagrela is less prone to this habit than was his younger contemporary the gifted philosopher-poet Solomon Ibn Gabirol, who once exclaimed "I am the one who before he was born had the understanding of a man of eighty." Cf. A. M. Habermann, *Toldot ha-Piyyut v'ha-Shira* (Ramat Gan, 1970), p. 172. Similar images are found in the works of the renowned 10th century Abbasid poet al-Mutanabbi, who states "If I have pride it is that of a prodigal man/ Who does not see anyone above him" or on another occasion "I am not noble because of my family; they are ennobled because of me." Cf. N. Ullah, *Islamic Literature* (New York, 1963), p. 59.

[8] Cf. A. Posnanski, *Schiloh* (Leipzig, 1904), pp. 105ff.; and J. Schirmann "Samuel Hannagid," p. 12.

[9] E. Garcia-Gomez, "Polemica religiosa entre Ibn Hazm e Ibn al-Nagrila," *Al-Andalus*, Vol. IV (1936), pp. 1–28; and J. Schirmann, "Samuel Hannagid," pp. 110–11.

[10] Cf. Judah b. Barzillai al-Barceloni, *Sefer ha-'Ittim*, ed. Schorr (Cracow, 1903), p. 267; and *Samuel Ibn Nagrela, Diwan*, ed. Habermann (Tel-Aviv, 1946), I, part 1, p. 98; and Abraham Ibn Daud, *op. cit.*, p. xlvii, nn. 12, 15, and p. 278.

[11] Cf. D. Yarden, *op. cit.*, p. 228; and J. Schirmann, "Hebrew Poetry . . . ," p. 147.

[12] Cf. Yarden, pp. 4ff.; and Schirmann, pp. 85ff.

[13] Cf. Yarden, pp. 16ff.; and Schirmann, pp. 94ff. Cf. also Y. Baer, *A History of the Jews in Christian Spain* (Philadelphia, 1961), Vol. I, p. 34.

[14] Cf. Yarden, *loc. cit.*, p. 14; and J. Schirmann, *op. cit.*, p. 92.

[15] Cf. Yarden, p. 26; and Schirmann, p. 102.

[16] Cf. Yarden, p. 3; and Schirmann, p. 78–9.

[17] Cf. Yarden, pp. 10–15 and 21; and Schirmann, pp. 89–93 and 110.

[18] Cf. Yarden, p. 20, note to line 59.

[19] Cf. J. Schirmann, "Samuel Hannagid. . . ," p. 122.

[20] D. Yarden, *op. cit.*, p. 62; and J. Schirmann, *Hebrew Poetry.. .* , p. 124.

[21] Modern scholars are skeptical of Ibn Daud's account of Samuel's meteoric rise to power as a result of his skill at letter writing and suggest that the road to the top was long and arduous. Cf. J. Schirmann, "Samuel Hannagid," p. 103; and Y. Baer, *op. cit.*, p. 33.

[22] Badis became king of Granada either in 1037 or 1038. Cf. E. Levi-Provencal, "Les 'Memoires' de 'Abd Allah, Dernier Roi Ziride de Grenade," *Al-Andalus*, III (1935), p. 245, n. 25; and Abraham Ibn Daud, *op. cit.*, p. 74, l.225.

[23] Cf. D. Yarden, *op. cit.*, p. 32; and J. Schirmann, *Hebrew Poetry. . .* , p. 110.

[24] Cf. J. Schirmann, *op. cit.*, p. 142; and S. Abramson, *R. Samuel Hannagid, Ben Mishle* (Tel-Aviv, 1948), p. 219.

[25] D. Yarden, *op. cit.*, p. 209; and J. Schirmann, *ibid.*, p. 83.

[26] Cf. Yarden, p. 31; and Schirmann, p. 109.

[27] Schirmann, "Samuel Hannagid," p. 104.

[28] Cf. *ibid.*, p. 105; and Abraham Ibn Daud, *op. cit.*, pp. 283, 285.

[29] Cf. *Encyclopedia of Islam* (Leiden, 1960), Vol. I, pp. 494–5; and J. Schirmann, "The Wars of Samuel Hannagid" (in Hebrew), *Zion*, Vol. I (1936), pp. 265–66.

[30] Cf. *Encyclopedia of Islam*, p. 491; and S. Baron, *a Social and Religious History of the Jews*, Vol. III, p. 130.

[31] Cf. J. Schirmann, "Samuel Hannagid," p. 113; and Abraham Ibn Daud, *op. cit.*, p. 74, l.234; and p. 136, n. 73.

[32] Cf. S. Baron, *op. cit.*, pp. 108–9; Y. Baer, *op. cit.*, p. 37; and S. D. Goitein, *A Mediterranean Society*, p. 79.

[33] S. D. Goitein, *op. cit.*, pp. 102, 111, 120, 126, 153–4; and Y. Baer, *ibid.*

[34] Cf. supra, n. 6.

[35] Cf. Abraham Ibn Daud, *op. cit.*, p. 80. This included such studies as physics, logic, mathematics, astronomy, ethics, metaphysics, and rhetoric as translated from Greek sources into Arabic and the way they were to be harmonized with traditional Jewish studies. Cf. *ibid.*, pp. xix and xx.

[36] Cf. J. Schirmann, "The Function of the Hebrew Poet in Medieval Spain," *Jewish Social Studies*, XVI (1954), pp. 235ff.

[37] Cf. supra, n. 6 and 34.

[38] Cf. Abraham Ibn Daud, *op. cit.*, pp. 84, 137, 237, and 274–5.

[39] Cf. Yarden, *op. cit.*, pp. 33–4; and J. Schirmann, *Hebrew Poetry. . .* , p. 111.

[40] Cf. S. Baron, *op. cit.*, Vol. VII, pp. 195–6.

[41] An evaluation of his poetry is discussed separately below.

[42] Cf. S. Baron, *op. cit.*, p. 238. His writings on the Talmud and his Responsa were also written to a large extent in Arabic, apparently the best known of the languages in his circle. Cf. M. Margalioth, *Hilkhot Hannagid* (Jerusalem, 1962), p. 25.

[43] Cf. Abraham Ibn Daud, *op. cit.*, p. 78.

[44] Cf. M. Margalioth, *op. cit.*, pp. 37ff.

[45] Cf. Yarden, *op. cit.*, pp. 265–6; and J. Schirmann, *Hebrew Poetry. . .* , p. 82.

[46] Cf. Yarden, p. 322; and Schirmann, p. 143.

[47] Cf. Yarden, p. 58; and Schirmann, p. 122.

[48] Cf. R. Dozy, *Histoire des Musulmans d'Espangne* (Leiden, 1932), Vol. III, pp. 19–20; and the English translation of the earlier 3rd edition of G. Stokes entitled *Spanish Islam* (London, 1913), pp. 608–9.

[49] R. Dozy, *loc. cit.*, p. 19; English version, p. 608.

[50] Cf. Y. Baer, *op. cit.*, p. 34.

[51] Cf. Yarden, *op. cit.*, p. 4; and Schirman, *loc. cit.*, p. 85.

[52] Cf. Y. Baer, *op. cit.*, pp. 35–6.

[53] Cf. Abraham Ibn Daud, *op. cit.*, pp. 74–5; and S. D. Goitein, *op. cit.*, p. 66.

[54] Abraham Ibn Daud, *op. cit.*, pp. 264 ff.

[55] Cf. Y. Baer, *op. cit.*, p. 35; and M. Margalioth, *op. cit.*, pp. 59–60.

[56] Cf. S. M. Stern, "Life of Shmuel ha-Nagid," *Zion*, XV (1950), p. 142, 1.15, and p. 144, 1.8; and Abraham Ibn Daud, *op. cit.*, p. 283.

[57] Cf. I, Abrahams, *Hebrew Ethical Wills* (Philadelphia, 1948), Part I, pp. 51 ff.

[58] On the Talmudic period, see J. Heinemann, *Prayer in the Period of the Tanna'im and the Amora'im* (in Hebrew), (Jerusalem 1966); and A. Mirsky, "The Origins of the Forms of Liturgical Poetry" (in Hebrew) *SRIHP*, VII (1948), pp. 1–129. On the anonymous

poets, see *idem*, "Gidrey ha-Piyyut shel ha-Payettanim Alumei ha-Shem" *Peraqim*, Vol. 1 (Jerusalem, 1967–8), pp. 111 ff. On the Palestinian, Babylonian and Persian schools, see A. M. Habermann, *Toldot* (Ramat Gan, 1970), pp. 26 ff and pp. 99 ff. On the North African and European development, see *ibid.*, pp. 227 ff; and *idem*, "Northern Europe and France", *World History of the Jewish People*, ed. C. Roth, Vol. II (Rutgers University Press, 1966), pp. 267 ff; and J. Schirmann, *Hebrew Poetry*. . . ; and *idem*, "Italy", *World History*. . . , pp. 249 ff. On Hebrew poetry in Greece and the Balkan states, see L. J. Weinberger, "Shirim Ḥadashim Mehatequfah ha-Bizantinit", *H.U.C.A.*, 1968, pp. 1–62 and 1972, pp. 1–39; and "A Note on Jewish Scholars and Scholarship in Byzantium," *Journal of the American Oriental Society*, 91.1 1971, pp. 142–4; and S. Bernstein, "Ha-Mahazor K'Minhag Kaffa Toldotav Vehitpatḥuto," S. K. *Mirsky, Jubilee Volume*, New York, 5718, pp. 451 ff.

[59] Cf. M. Kadushin, *Worship and Ethics* (Northwestern University Press, 1964), pp. 63 ff.

[60] Cf. A. Mirsky, *"The Origins* . . .," pp. 3–129.

[61] *Canticles Rabbah* 4:5.

[62] The term is derived from the Aramaic and in the liturgy is always introduced by the phrase, 'now let our Qedusha ascend unto Thee.'

[63] See his commentary to *Eccles*. 5:1.

[64] Cf. S. Spiegel, "On Medieval Hebrew Poetry" *The Jews* (Philadelphia, 1949), p. 548.

[65] J. Schirmann, "The Battle Between Behemot and Leviathan According to an Ancient Hebrew Piyyut," *The Israel Academy of Sciences and Humanities Proceedings* (Jerusalem, 1970), Vol. 4, No. 13, p. 336.

[66] Cf. J. Guttmann, *Philosophies of Judaism* (Holt, Rinehart and Winston, 1964), pp. 63, 76.

[67] See M. Zulay, *The Liturgical Poetry of Saadia Gaon and his School* (in Hebrew), (Schocken: Jerusalem, 1964), pp. 114 ff.

[68] Cf. A. M. Habermann, *Toldot*, pp. 265 ff.

[69] Cf. L. Finkelstein, *The Jews: Their History, Culture and Religion* (Harper and Row, 1960), 3rd Edition, p. 875.

[70] Cf. D. Yellin, "The Metrical Forms in the Poetry of Samuel Hannagid," *S.R.I.H.P.*, Vol. V, pp. 181–208.

[71] J. Schirmann, "Samuel Hannagid as Poet," *K'nesset*, Vol. 2 (1937), p. 395.

[72] Cf. *supra*, note 26.

[73] Cf. Yarden, *op. cit.*, p. 265; and Schirmann, *Hebrew Poetry . . . p. 82.*

[74] Yarden, p. 8; and Schirmann, p. 88.

[75] Cf. Schirmann, *loc. cit.*, p. 142; and S. Abramson, *R. Shmuel Hannagid, Ben Mishle* (Tel-Aviv, 1948), p. 295.

[76] Cf. Yarden, *op. cit.*, p. 24, lines 112–5, and Schirmann, *loc. cit.*, p. 100, lines 112–5.

[77] Cf. Leviticus 20:13; 18:22 and 18:27 and Sanhedrin 54b. Cf. also Schirmann "The Ephebe in Medieval Hebrew Poetry," *Sefarad* XV (Madrid-Barcelona, 1955) pp. 55–68; and N. Allony, "The Zevi (=Nasib) in the Hebrew Poetry in Spain," *Sefarad* XXIII, pp. 311–21.

[78] Cf. Schirmann, "Samuel Hannagid as Poet," p. 400.

[79] *Ibid.*, pp. 400–2.

[80] Cf. J. Schirmann, "The Function of the Hebrew Poet," pp. 241–3.

[81] Cf. J. Schirmann, "Samuel Hannagid as Poet," pp. 403–4.

[82] Cf. Abramson, *R. Shmuel Hannagid, Ben Qohelet* (Tel-Aviv, 1953), p. 9.

[83] *Ibid.*, p. 119.

[84] Cf. Abramson, *Ben Mishle*, p. 58.

[85] Cf. Yarden, *op. cit.*, p. 295.

[86] Cf. *ibid.*, p. 242.

[87] Cf. *ibid.*, p. 244.

[88] Cf. J. Schirmann, "The Function of the Hebrew Poet," pp. 244–5.

[89] Cf. Yarden, *op. cit.*, p. 228.

[90] Cf. *ibid.*, pp. 296–7.

[91] Cf. Abraham Ibn Daud, *op. cit.*, p. 286.

[92] Cf. Abramson, *Ben Mishle*, p. 184; and D. Pagis, *Secular Poetry and Poetic Theory, Moses Ibn Ezra and his Contemporaries* (in Hebrew), (Jerusalem, 1970), pp. 42 ff.

## NOTES TO THE POEMS

### 1. The Poet Leaves Cordova

S. p. 83; Y. p. 209.
The superscription of the poem reads: "He wrote this poem in his youth on leaving Cordova, [in 1013]."
*I have departed*, from Cordova.
*encircled with paint of night*, from lack of sleep. His friends think that he worries and cannot sleep because he wishes to increase his wealth.
*pure . . . . moon*, a play on the word *l'vanah* which means both, "pure" and "moon."
*with her wings*. i.e. the moon's.
*strengthening a tent-cloth*, i.e. making himself ready to attain full stature in life.
*I will sew . . . sail*, I will traverse desert and sea.
*Free men . . . them*. Lit. I will pierce the ears of free men even as mine are pierced to my familiars, Cf. Ex. 21:6.
*to you*. He addresses now the friend to whom the poem is dedicated, (Schirmann).
*threshold of the Temple*. Cf. Is. 54:12 and Bava Batra 75a.
*until the sun and moon are no more*. i.e. forever.

### 2. The Wanderer

S. p. 84; Y. p. 330.
*destined*, lit. 'it is written in God's book.'
*Cain*. Cf. Gen. 4:12
*Jonah*. Cf. Jonah 1:3.

### 3. The Battle of Alfuente

S. p. 85; Y. p. 4
The Arabic superscription to the poem reads as follows: "There then happened to him what is well-known with regard to Zuhair ruler of Almeria and the intervention of his vizier 'Ibn 'Abbas. Now when God rescued him he recited this poem with which he begins his letter. Therein he describes his relations with the two men mentioned above and what God, may He be blessed, ordained for their punishment. He called the poem, *Shira*. This great victory occurred on the morning of the sixth day of the week on the first of 'Elul in the year 4798 [August 4, 1038]."
*certain*, (Schirmann)
*haughty*. The reference is doubtlessly to 'Ibn 'Abbas whose arrogance according to R. Dozy, "almost amounted to insanity. 'Were all men my slaves' he declared in his verses, 'my soul would not be content. It would fain mount above the stars, and then would long to ascend yet higher'!" Cf. Dozy, *op. cit.* p. 23 and *Spanish Islam*, p. 611.
*The Rock for the distress*, i.e. 'God will help'. A play on the Hebrew words *ẓur* (Rock) and *zara* (distress). 'Rock', as a metaphor for God is based on a number of Scriptural

verses, cf. Deut. 32:4 and II Sam. 22:3.
redeemer. Cf. Ps. 144:10.
*recompense for Torah.* i.e. God rewards those like himself who are loyal to the Torah.
*the patriarchs covenant.* Cf. Deut. 7:12.
*eloquent,* lit. 'have a mouth'.
*A man of words.* i.e. skilled in the use of language.
*'Agag.* the reference is to the Slav Zuhair, prince of Almeria. Cf. Esther 3:1.
*shore of the sea.* Almeria was situated on the Mediterranean coast in southern Spain.
*'Abbas.* The pure-blooded Arab, 'Ibn 'Abbas, vizier of Almeria who according to Dozy, "hated the Berbers and despised the Jews." See Dozy, *ibid.*
*branch . . . pole,* i.e. the spies in Numbers 13:23, 32.
*not me alone . . . Lord's congregation.* Cf. Esther 3:6. The Nagid views these events as "a second Purim." The enemy is 'Agag who wishes to destroy "the Lord's congregation, remnant and offspring."
*my master,* i.e. the Berber King Ḥabbus of Granada.
*he died,* Ḥabbus.
*doom,* Ez. 7:7.
*a young lion.* A reference to Badis, elder son of Ḥabbus, who after the latter's death in June, 1038 succeeded him to the throne.
*my enemy wrote.* Again 'Ibn 'Abbas wrote the 'scandalous' letters, this time to Badis.
*without entreaty.* i.e. without expressing the proper amenities before a king.
*settlement in his place.* i.e. if you sacrifice Samuel peace will reign between us. After the death of Ḥabbus, Badis made every effort to renew the alliance between Granada and Almeria. It is likely that we have here a reference to the price for the renewal which for 'Ibn 'Abbas meant the removal of Samuel. Cf. Dozy, *op. cit.* p. 24 and English version p. 612 and cf. J. Schirmann, "The Wars of Samuel ha-Nagid" *loc. cit.* p. 271.
*'Amalek . . . 'Edom . . . sons of Q'turah.* i.e. the Slavs, Christian-Spanish mercenaries and Arabs respectively. According to the Rabbis Q'turah is another name for Hagar mother of Ishmael, cf. Gen. 25:4.
*Alfuente.* In Hebrew, 'Qiryat Ma'yan', fountain city.
*evil tidings,* i.e. the destruction of the two Temples on the 9th of 'Av.
*mountain . . . crossing.* The reference is to the mountains of the Sierra-Nevada which lie between Granada and Almeria. Dozy reports that since the bridge at Alfuente had been destroyed and the defiles were occupied by the Granadans, Zuhair's forces "were obliged to seek refuge in the mountains. Most of them were cut down by the Granadans . . . others were dashed to pieces at the feet of the savage precipices and among the latter was Zuhair." See Dozy, *op. cit.* p. 26 and English version p. 614.
*Even . . . opponent.* A play on the Hebrew words *Ẓur* (rock) and *Qum* (rise).
*prize.* Lit. 'first born' cf. Job 18:13.
*destruction of 'Amorah.* Cf. Deut. 29:22.
*the voice of the Almighty.* Cf. Ez. 1:24.
*bucklers as sieves,* from being pierced by the implements of war.
*blood . . . Temple court.* Cf. Ez. 43:20; 45:19 and Pesachim 65b.
*Young lions.* i.e. heroes in battle.
*knowledge of the "learned".* i.e. the so-called learned.
*awoke before the watches.* Cf. Ps. 119:148.
*Sisera . . . Barak and Deborah.* Cf. Judges 4:1ff.
*atone,* forfeit their lives instead of mine.
*son of 'Amram.* Moses.
*distress,* lit. 'the fire of war'.
*in the Machpelah,* at Hebron. According to a Rabbinic tradition, Adam and Eve, Abraham

and Sarah, Isaac and Rebeccah and Jacob and Leah are buried there. The Nagid requesting the patriarchs and Moses to pray for him is here following the practice of Jeremiah. Cf. Intro. to Lamen. Rabbah 24.
*take hold,* lit. 'hang on'.
*have mercy upon Joseph.* i.e. the Nagid's son who at that time was three years old.
*is this the reward for Torah.* Cf. Berachot 61b.
*'If thou passest . . . 'If you walk . . .*Cf. Is. 43:2. The reference is to a dream of the young Samuel wherein the Angels Michael and Gabriel promised to protect him. See poem #26.
*even stars.* The stars participated in the battle against Sisera, cf. Judges 4:20.
*humble scattered lamb.* i.e. Israel cf. Jer. 50:17.
*woman . . . anguish.* Cf. *ibid.* 4:31.
*Gerah.* One twentieth of a Shekel.
*Amalek was wiped out from Spain.* The rule of the Slavs in Almeria was now at an end (Schirmann).
'Agag . . . Samuel. Cf. I Sam. 15:33.
*the Logician.* Metaphor for Mordecai whose wisdom was highly praised, cf. Megillah 13b.
*'Amalek . . . evil.* Cf. Ex. 17:13.
*palace of marble* i.e. where the slain formerly lived.
*offspring of ostriches.* Micah 1:8.
*she-goat shall dance.* Cf. Is. 13:21.
*or the tenth,* of 'Av whereon the greater part of the Temple was destroyed by fire, cf. the opinion of R. Yoḥanan in Ta'anit 29a.
*nine and ninety.* i.e. the year 4799 since creation.
*salvation . . . light.* Similar terms are used in Esther 8:16.
*vizier.* 'Ibn 'Abbas.
*shore of rivers,* i.e. the River Genil and its tributaries.
*razor that is hired.* Cf. Is. 7:30, i.e. the mercenaries hired by Samuel.
*under saws.* Cf. II Sam. 12:31
*Even as I took hold of the Testimony,* i.e. the Torah, cf. Is. 8:16. Ibn Abbas died on September 24, 1038 at the hands of Badis and his courtiers. Cf. Dozy, *op. cit.* p. 29 and English version p. 616. This was the day of Simḥat Torah and the news of his death reached Samuel probably during the time while he was in the synagogue at prayer.
*father* i.e. Moses, cf. Deut. 33:11.
*children of song . . . incense.* i.e. the Levites from whom Samuel descended.
Zeresh . . . *Buyer with his Kikars.* i.e. Haman, cf. Esther 6:13 and 3:8–9.
*Men . . . 'Agorah.* i.e. Israel bringing the half-shekel, (cf. Ex 30:31) which is called 'Agorah (I Sam. 2:36), (Schirmann).
*Judgment of all vessels . . . break them.* i.e. instead of immersing you break them, cf. Lev. 11:32, 33 and Kelim 2.1.
*to slaughter . . . to guard.* This is based on Bava Qama 4.9.
*minister to all others.* i.e. that this *Shira* be a model for other poems.
*like the Tummin.* Cf. Ex. 28:15–30.
*Tehillim in number.* The *Shira* numbers 149 lines even as the number of Psalms, according to an earlier reckoning, was 149, cf. Berachot 9b.
*Nazarite . . . drink a cup,* even of wine which is normally forbidden.
*given leave . . . laughter.* Cf. Berachot 31a. Excessive laughter is forbidden in this world.
*children . . . Chosen House.* i.e. the children of Israel.
*Pumbeditha . . . Sura* The names of cities in Babylonia housing its most famous centers of Rabbinic studies.
*'Sister to the Happening,* i.e. a 'second Purim'.

4. Prayer Before A Battle

S. p. 93; Y. p. 15

The poem's Arabic superscription reads as follows: "When 'Ismail 'Ibn 'Abbad [son of 'Abbad b. Abu'l-Qasim Muhammad al Mu'tadid, ruler of Seville] stood in the way of the *ḥajib* 'Abu Munar ['Ibn Bakanna, Minister of Idris of Malaga, then ally of Granada] may God lift him up, [the Nagid] appeared against him with his armies on the eve of the fifth day of the week, the 13th day of Tishri in the year 4800 [4 October, 1039] and the battle began between them near the river Genil. Then spoke he [the Nagid] these stanzas and used them in place of the *minḥd* [afternoon] prayer on that day."

*angels . . . waters . . . flames* The reference is to Michael and Gabriel who promise protection to the Nagid through fire and water, cf. Poem #26 and Poem #3 above.

*for my son*. Joseph.

*and my Torah*. Cf. Poem #3 above where the poet also asks for God's help in behalf of his son and the Torah. Cf. Ḥagigah 16b: 'Recall his Torah but do not recall his deeds.'

5. Victory Over Seville

S. p. 94; Y. p. 16; B. p. 65

The Arabic superscription reads: "The defeat of 'Abbad's men occurred toward the evening of that day [i.e. the 13th day of Tishri 1039], and Ben 'Abbad was killed early Friday evening on the eve of Succot [October 5, 1039] and the Nagid sang the following song and called it *'T'hilla'* [A song of Praise].

*clothed with fringes*. i.e. the Jews who wear fringes on the four corners of their garments according to Numbers 15:38ff.

Ben 'Abbas. The men Samuel Ha-Nagid defeated at Alfuente in 1038. In celebration of the victory he wrote his *Shira*, cf. Poem #3 above.

*Ben 'Abbad*, Isma'il Ibn 'Abbad the commander of the armies of Seville against Granada.

*crown of royalty . . . commoner*. Ibn 'Abbad was the son of Seville's ruler Mu'tadid. 'Ibn 'Abbas, a pure blooded Arab was not of royal lineage.

*Berber*, lit. of the Philistines. This is the name commonly given in Hebrew sources to the Berbers. See Abraham Ibn Daud, *op. cit.* p. 40, 1. 143.

*my king*. Badis son of Ḥabbus, ruler of Granada.

*slew . . . slaughtered*. According to Dozy, Mu'tadid had a garden in his palace where the plants grew out of the skulls of his slain enemies with a label at the ear of each skull carrying the name of its former possessor. Cf. Dozy, *op. cit.*, p. 49 and English version p. 633.

*seized . . . cities*. A reference to his conquests in the region of Carmona east of Seville (Schirmann).

*stoned . . . living God*, i.e. spoke slanderously against the Jews of Seville.

*the Jewish community*, of Granada, lit. 'a city and mother in Israel' which the Sevillans planned to destroy and enslave.

*To take revenge*, for their defeated allies the men of Carmona.

*His spies* The spies of 'Ibn 'Abbas reported that the Granadans were in retreat but from the Nagid's report it would appear that they merely took up more advantageous positions. The battle was finally joined along the river Genil with the resultant rout of the Sevillans, but not before troops from Malaga came to the Nagid's rescue.

*hundreds upon thousands of hosts*. This is probably an exaggeration. Dozy reports that the death of a hundred of the enemy in the field of battle was considered in those days to be a great victory. Cf. Schirmann "Samuel Ha-Nagid. . . . " p. 120.

*the river's bank* i.e. the river Genil.

*When the brooks flowed over*. A reference to the battle of Moses against the Moabites according to Numbers 21:15. In the Aramaic Targum Yerushalmi, the above battle is described as follows: "When the children of Israel were crossing the river Arnon the Moabites hid in the caves by the river saying to themselves: When the children of Israel cross the river we will come forth (from hiding) and kill them. Whereupon the Master of the Universe motioned . . . to the mountains that their peaks approach each other and crush the heads of their warriors, and the rivers flowed over with the blood of the slain."

*the dead 'Agag,* i.e. Zuhair the Slav eunuch at the battle of Alfuente.

*Amalekites,* i.e. the forces of Zuhair.

*The commanders reluctant.* A reference to the leader of the forces of Malaga, Ibn Bakanna the ally of Granada, who at first refused to join in the battle against Seville (Schirmann).

*my voice with the name of God.* In a liturgical poem of R. Saadia Gaon published by M. Zulay it appears that the leaders of Israel knew how to utter the divine name YHWH and did so in times of severe crisis. This is probably what Samuel Ha-Nagid did here in the battle against Seville. See Zulay, *The Liturgical Poetry of Sa'adya Gaon and his School,* p. 22 and Y. p. 20.

*seventy angels,* lit. seventy banners. According to a statement in Pirqe d'R. Eliezer #24, angels representing the seventy nations stand about the divine throne holding aloft their banners.

*When they saw . . . close by.* When the men of Seville saw that men of Granada had not been routed in defeat as the spies of Ibn 'Abbad had reported earlier, they fled from fear and confusion.

*binding their hearts,* i.e. sealing off their wisdom (Yarden).

*To the king.* Badis of Granada.

*soles of feet . . . ground.* Having led a life of luxury (Schirmann).

*On the night of the sixth day.* i.e. the night between the fifth and sixth days of the week (Yarden).

*swarm of bees.* Cf. Deut. 1:44.

*exchanged their rooms etc.,* for the wild woods

*name,* the tetragrammaton which Samuel uttered at the start of the battle, see above.

*who took shoes for pledges.* A reference to the heavy taxes laid upon the Jews in Seville by their rulers (Schirmann).

*On the second day their judgment etc.* The battle began on the second day of the week in the year 1039 which was Yom Kippur. The poets' language: 'their judgment was declared' is taken from the Prayer Book for the High Holy Days when, according to Jewish tradition, man's destiny is decreed. The rout of the enemy occurred on the fifth day of the week.

*Abraham's son,* lit. the son of 'Etan. The latter is identified with Abraham in Bava Batra 15a.

*month of the Mighty Ones.* Heb. 'Etanim, i.e. the Patriarchs who were born in the month of Tishri according to Rosh Hashana 11a.

*Ninety nine years.* i.e. 4799 after the creation (Yarden).

*the uncircumcised.* i.e. the Christians (Yarden).

*the festival of the Harvest Gathering.* i.e. the Succot festival on the eve of 14 Tishri.

*the night of Abram.* A reference to Abram's victory over the five kings in Gen. 14:15.

*the night of Moses.* When there took place the slaying of the first born in Egypt. See Ex. 11:4.

*Joshua's afternoon,* when 'the sun stood still,' in his battle against the Amorites. See Joshua 10:12ff.

*when the burden . . . removed.* i.e. when Sennacherib's siege of Jerusalem was lifted. See II Kings 19:35.

*Dwellers in Tents* i.e. the children of Jacob, according to Gen. 25:27.

*Shofar and Atonement.* Rosh Hashanah when the Shofar (ram's horn) is sounded and Yom Kippur the Day of atonement.

*days of the Booth . . . pilgrims* i.e. through the eight days of Succot. This was one

of the three festivals when pilgrims went to Jerusalem to celebrate the feast in the Temple. The other two were Passover and Shavuot. See Ex. 23:14.
*some less scrupulous.* Some might be inclined to violate the Sabbath and festival laws in time of danger but not so the Nagid.
*armies freed . . . forbidden.* The Nagid here gives thanks that the battle ended before the Succot festival.
*booths . . . palm tree . . . willow . . . splendid tree . . . myrtle.* A description of the observance of the festival of Succot and the taking of the 'four kinds' of flora in the Holy Land. See Lev. 23:40–2.
*burnt offerings. Ibid.* 1:3–4.
*half-shekel.* Cf. Ex. 30:11–16.
*waters . . . waters.* This victory by the Genil's waters is the reward for the 'taking of the 4 kinds' (cf. Lev. 23:40–2) 'that grow upon the waters.'
*divide booty . . . alloted ruin.* God's justice is here meted out measure for measure.
recite the *Hallel* i.e. the Psalms 113–8 in praise of God recited in the synagogue on festivals.
*If you reward me . . . sins be forgiven?* Cf. Ta'anit 20b: 'R. Yannai said: "One should never stay in a place of danger and say, I shall be saved by a miracle, for it might be that no miracle will be performed for him, and even if one should be performed such performance would be charged against his merits" . . . the Biblical verse to prove it (is) "I am not worthy of all the mercies and of all the truth" (Gen. 32:11).'
*composed a Shirah,* in the year 1038 celebrating his victory at Alfuente.
*Tehilla.* lit. 'song of praise' in gratitude for his current triumph.
*Psalmist's praises.* Both *Shira* and *Tehilla* contain 149 lines. Earlier the number of Psalms consisted of 149 with Psalms currently numbered I and II combined. See B'rachot 9b.
*when . . . your sons will ask.* Cf. Ex. 13:14 and the Passover Haggadah.

### 6. The Poem in A Dream

S. p. 102; Y. p. 27.
The Arabic superscription to the poem reads as follows: "The regent of the kingdom [of Almeria] 'Abu J'affar 'Ibn 'Abi Musa supported the ambitions of 'Ibn 'Abbas and he succeeded in his activities even after the death of 'Ibn 'Abbas. One night while [the Nagid] was sleeping he saw himself in a dream reading the following stanzas."
*already perished,* at the battle of Alfuente in 1038.
*ruler.* i.e. 'Ibn 'Abi Musa, ally of 'Ibn 'Abbas.
*dill . . . threshed.* Cf. Is. 28:27.

### 7. On the Fall of 'Ibn 'Abi Musa

S. p. 103; Y. p. 27
The Arabic superscription to the poem reads: "The physician 'Abu Mudin slept near him and [the Nagid] awakened him and informed him what he saw in a dream. He never doubted the fall of 'Ibn 'Abi Musa [which is what he saw in his dream]. Indeed the latter was slain a few days later and he [the Nagid] spoke [the following] on being informed of his death. This was in the year 4800 (1040) and he called his poem *B'sorah* [the news]."
Yours. The reference is to God.
*Haman.* 'Ibn 'Abi Musa is compared to Haman, even as there are other references to the Book of Esther in the poem.
*bringer of good tidings.* The reference is to the messenger who brings to the Nagid the news of the death of 'Ibn 'Abi Musa.
*Ben 'Abbas.* Vizier of Almeria whom the Nagid defeated in the battle of Alfuente in 1038.
*The city.* i.e. Granada.

*excited and perplexed*. Cf. Esther 3:15. The fear of the slain 'Ibn 'Abi Musa's followers was so great that the city's inhabitants were amazed at this quick change in fortune (Schirmann).
*ropes about your heads*. A sign of mourning, cf. I Kings 20:31.
*Micah*, cf. Judges 17:4ff.
*The limit*, lit. to the neck. You have caused great distress. Cf. Is. 8:8.
*snare . . . net*. Cf. Ps. 91:3 and Job 18:8.
*Samson*, Judges 15:14.
*And he said:* i.e. the messenger. The question is rhetorical.
*Sabbath lesson*. The poet as head of the Jewish community ordered that this poem be read as part of the service of the synagogue on the Sabbath and that it be taught to the children in school.

8. The War with Yadair

S. p. 109; Y. p. 31
The poem's superscription as given by the Nagid's son Joseph read as follows: "The commander Yadair [Yazir, cousin of Badis and conspirator for the throne of Granada] attacked a place called Arjona in the summer of the year 4801 (1041). With him were Waṣil and Muwafaq, two well-known generals from the nobles of Al Andalus. They prevailed over Arjona and slew the commander of the city. They then marched from there to a place called Somontin and prevailed over most of their fortresses. Then [our] armies went forth to meet them and God's hand was against them [the followers of Yadair] and Waṣil and Muwafaq were slain. The Commander Yadair fled until he was barricaded in Cordova. But we carried him off from there and imprisoned him in the fortress Al Muñecar. And my lord, my father spoke telling what happened to him and how he participated in these events, praising God for granting him this great victory."
*evil words*. Lit. "The evil in your mouth."
*seraphs in a dream*. Cf. Poem #26.
*written in my book:* i.e. decreed for me in heaven.
*Tivni*. I Kings 16:21.
*Zimri*. Ibid. 16:10,15.
*the Egyptian*. Ex. 2:12.
*unjustly . . . childless*. This is the Nagid's proof that all of the above were destined for their fate.
*turban upon my head*. Cf. Ez. 24:23.
*canal*, cf. Poem #19.
*my enemies*, lit. ' 'Ashurites', cf. II. Sam. 2:9. This is the name the Nagid gives to the enemies of Granada in the revolt of Yadair, (Schirmann).
*this foe*. i.e. Yadair, cousin to King Badis of Granada. Cf. Dozy, *op. cit.* p. 618.
*fortified city*, i.e. Arjona.
*Two . . . viceroys*. i.e. Waṣil and Muwafaq.
*Zemari*. A Canaanite people, cf. Gen. 10:18.
*vanquished the city*, of Arjona.
*mountain fortresses*, in Somontin.
*ẓere . . . segol*. The names of Hebrew vowels having two horizontal and three points in a triangle respectively.
*'Og and Sihon*. Two Canaanites kings, cf. Deut. 1:4.
*rebels*. Possibly a hint to his friend of "the company of rebels" above.
*He said to me*. i.e. one of the men in the circle to whom the story is being told. The question is rhetorical.
*the David of my age*. Cf. Rosh Hashana 25b.
*Is Saul . . . prophets?* i.e. I am surprised to hear you say this. Cf. I. Sam. 10:11.
*Merari . . . Sitri*. All descendants of Levi whose heirs were the musicians in the Temple,

cf. Ex. 6:16, 22, 24.
*Yedutun.* Cf. Ps. 39:1.
*responsible . . . beholden.* Cf. Numbers Rabaah 19:33: "*Then sang Israel* (Num. 21:17). Israel reasoned thus: It is your (i.e. God's) duty to perform miracles for us, and our duty to bless and praise your name."
*on time,* lit. 'on my day', cf. Deut. 24:14, 15.

## 9. Lament for Zion; the War with Yadair II

S. p. 112; Y. p. 35
The superscription reads: "He, [the Nagid] may God help him, engaged in battle against Yadair from Arjona in the summer of 4801 (1041) and gained victory over him and over his two commanders Waṣil and Muwafaq at Somontin. He wrote a poem about it in addition to the poem I mention now."
*Ḥammat and Mepha'at.* Two Levitic cities, cf. Josh. 21:32 and I Chron. 6:64. The Nagid who was himself a Levite is filled with yearning for them (Schirmann).
*Siryon.* i.e. Lebanon, cf. Deut. 3:9.
*bring to Moriah.* In the Messianic age the nations will bring gifts to the Holy Temple on Mt. Moriah, cf. Ps. 68:30.
*'Ariel.* i.e. the area of the Temple altar, cf. Ez. 43:15.
*at home,* lit. "in Zion".
*They shall gaze upon the singing maidens . . . work.* At the time of the Messianic redemption the happiness of the moment will give the maidens of Israel added beauty (Schirmann).
*prince's daughter.* A metaphor for the 'house of Israel.' The 'nut garden' is a reference to Zion. The 'fawns' are the people engaged in planting and gathering lilies, i.e. in reclaiming the land of their ancestors, (Schirmann).
*roaring lions.* Metaphor for the powers who ruled in Zion at the time of the Nagid.
*She was ruined.* i.e. Zion.
*open flowers, the wreaths and the knobs.* These were ornaments in the Temple, cf. I Kings 6:18 and 7:29.
*foundation stone,* in the Temple, cf. Yoma 5:2.
*'Edom . . . Zion.* Cf. Lamen. 4:21, 22. 'Edom is here a metaphor for Israel's enemies.
*'Uz.* A chieftain of Edom, cf. Gen. 36:28 and Lamen. 4:21.
*hand . . . well known.* i.e. at the exodus from Egypt, cf. Ex. 6:6.
*Boẓrah. . . Teman.* The former was an Edomite city, cf. Gen. 36:33; the latter was a descendant of Esau, *ibid.* 36:11.
*full of your wide fury.* i.e. deserves to be punished.
*I thank You.* The Nagid now takes up the theme of Yadair's rebellion.
*rebel and king's kin.* Yadair, cousin to Badis of Granada.
*entered the fortress,* of Arjona.
*small . . . like locusts.* The image is designed to convey the height of the mountain upon which the fortress was situated.
*climbed to its tip.* The reference is to the fortress.
*that is broken in,* without much effort.
*Here . . . there.* The contrast between the victorious and the vanquished.
*two companions.* Waṣil and Muwafaq.
*escaped to a mighty potentate.* The 'potentate' is possibly 'Abu'l- Ḥazm Jahwar ibn Jahwar ruler of Cordova (1031–1043) or perhaps the Kady of Seville, cf. Schirmann, "The Wars of Samuel ha-Nagid" p. 275 and Dozy, *op. cit.* English version p. 618 and French p. 234.
*hastened to the pit . . . asp.* i.e. I risked my life.
*assembly rejoices.* The reference is to the Jewish congregations (Yarden).

10. On Lifting the Siege at Lorca

S. p. 117; Y. p. 41.

The Arabic superscription reads: "When it became known to those who were laying siege to the city of Lorca [in the year 1042] that the forces [of Granada] were approaching, they beat a hasty retreat while our forces hurried to Lorca and camped therein, and from there he wrote to me:'

*Adorned . . . red waters.* Letters sent in those days were both fragrant and attractive. Cf. Yarden, *ibid.*

*reaches the house of Joseph,* in Granada.

*slaying . . . crossing.* In their intense desire to get across the River Sangonera they apparently crushed one another to death.

*The fortified city,* of Lorca.

*the lobe to the liver.* Cf. Ex. 29:13.

*my song of praise.* Heb. *Tehilla.* Yarden suggests that this refers to the poem called *Tehilla* which the Nagid composed after his victory over 'Ibn 'Abbad in 1039. According to Schirmann it is the present poem which is to be recited by the assembly.

*emblem . . . hand.* Cf. Deut. 6:6–8.

*iron pen and lead.* Cf. Job 19:24.

11. The Death of Naja

S. p. 120; Y. p. 43

The superscription to the poem reads: "At the beginning of the year 4803 (1043) Naja the Slav went out from Ceuta to avenge the Slavs who fell in defeat at Alfuente. He made camp at Malaga and they conspired against him until they killed him suddenly [on February 5, 1043, cf. Dozy, *op. cit.* p. 37 and English version p. 623] Thereupon he [the Nagid] spoke [Yarden: 'sang'] the following and the (deed?) [Yarden: 'melody'] is well known.'

*O Mighty One of Jacob.* Metaphor for God, cf. Gen. 49:24.

*'Agag.* Metaphor for Slavs in general, cf. Poem #3. Here the reference is to Naja, minister to Malaga and conspirator for the caliphate after the death of Idris I, in 1039, see Dozy. *Ibid.*

*'Amalek,* who wished to destroy Israel, cf. Ex. 17:8–16.

*hand of God . . . throne. Ibid.* 17:16.

*his colleague's.* i.e. the Slav Zuhair who fell at Alfuente.

*The adder.* i.e. Naja.

*at the sea,* in the Mediterranean by Malaga.

*navy,* lit. 'waters'.

12. At Court

S. p. 142; A. p. 101.

*break an earthen jar . . . sherds?* Cf. Sanhedrin 52b.

13. The Monarch's Favors

S. p. 142; A. p. 219

14. Dread Your Great King

S. p. 141; A. p. 89

Y. Ratzabi notes the following parallel from Arabic sources: "One should be on guard before a king, for he becomes angry like a boy and is reconciled like a boy and wounds like a lion." Cf. his, "On the Sources of Ben Mishle and Ben Qohelet," *Tarbiẓ,* 25, p. 313.

*Your room or in the gates.* i.e. in private or in public.

15. He Promotes the Clowns

S. p. 141–2; A. p. 116

Y. Ratzabi gives the following parallel to the above from Arabic sources:

'The ruler has the qualities of a drunkard:
He appeases the one whom he should scold
And scolds the one he should appease." Cf. *op. cit.* p. 315.

16. A Letter on the Eve of the Battle of Lorca

S. p. 116; Y. p. 39.

The following is the superscription to the poem: "In the summer of the year 4802 (1042) 'Ibn 'Abi 'Amar ['Abd al-'Aziz, prince of Valencia during 1021–61] and Mujahid ['Abu 'l-Jaish Mujahid Muwafaq, ruler of Denia during 1009–1044] and the mighty men of the border countries and of the east and the Franks [Christian Spaniards from Catalonia] attacked the city of Lorca. It was decided to wage war against them. Thereupon the armies [of Granada] descended upon the city of Velez and made camp there for one night . . . The plan was to arise in the morning, march to Lorca and do battle against [the enemy] outside of the city. He [the Nagid] then wrote me from the camp at Velez during that night and described the existing situation and wrote for me a testament in the language of the Talmud. Its like is also to be found in the language of the Scriptures."

*roamed the world.* i.e. for my own pleasure (Schirmann).

*in waiting.* i.e. death.

*who asks,* according to Yarden's text which reads: *sho'el.*

*speak gently to him.* Cf. Bava Batra 9b.

17. A Writing Exercise

S. p. 119; Y. p. 34

The superscription to the poem as given by the Nagid's son Joseph reads as follows: "And he commanded me, may God honor him to copy one book in my youth promising to give me for each pamphlet one *batil* [name of a coin]. He then went out on one of the wars. When I sent him what I had copied, he wrote me the following:"

*carbuncle.* Cf. Ex. 28:17.

*in curtained ark.* i.e. preserved in curtained ark.

*pay and wages.* A reference to the *batil* mentioned above.

*liver . . . not . . . caul.* i.e. my affection is deep for you and not only on the surface.

*heirs.* i.e. my thoughts. In the time of the Nagid the heart was believed to be the seat of wisdom.

*revealed . . . concealed.* Cf. Prov. 27:5.

18. Take This Book

S. p. 124; Y. p. 66

The superscription to the poem written by the Nagid's son Joseph is as follows: "And he wrote with his own hand a number of select Arabic poems and sent them to me from his camp, having set out on a military campaign in Nisan, 4806 (March–April, 1046). He gave orders and commanded me that I read them in order thereby to improve my language and speak fluently in Arabic. With them he wrote to me the following:"

*Arabs.* lit. 'Qedar and 'Efah'. Cf. Gen. 25:13, 4. Both terms are metaphors for Arabs.

19. Advice to a Husband

S. p. 141; A. p. 117.

*regularly.* lit. 'with unceasing blows'.

20. In An Alcove

S. p. 160; Y. p. 283.
The Arabic superscription written by Joseph the Nagid's son reads as follows: "I planted a round area of pasture grass and surrounded it with a circular water-filled canal. Then I suggested that he [the Nagid] go out to the grassy area and rest thereon. He did so and rejoiced over it and said."
*heavens overarching the earth.* This is in keeping with the then current cosmology.
*rows.* i.e. columns in a scroll.
*Each patron.* A reference to the other notables who were invited to join father and son at the garden party (Schirmann).
*avoided the terebrinth and oak,* since they do not bear edible fruit.
*Which he sent to the drinker,* via the waters in the canal.
*bride's litter.* The drinks which were sent in vessels floating upon the waters were awaited like the carriage of the bride by the bridegroom.
*The latter.* i.e. the cupbearer who stood at a considerable distance from the guests awaited the return of the empty vessels via the canal waters which he then proceeded to refill with wine and send back to the party by the same route.
*One failing to witness* Cf. Mishna Sukka 5.1.

21. "Does Isaac Live?"

S. p. 106; Y. p. 237
The following is the poem's superscription: "The sickness [of his brother Isaac] grew worse and he [the Nagid] set out to go to him with the physician 'Abu Mudin. Whereupon he was met by a messenger while yet a short distance from home. This occurred on the fifth day of the week on the 25th day of 'Iyar in the aforementioned year [4801, 1041]. He died on [the evening of] that day and of him he [the Nagid] spoke:"
*may dust fill your mouth!* Cf. Bava Batra 16a. In the time of the Nagid it was a matter of form to curse the one who brought distressing news.
*great one . . . people.* Cf. Esther 10:3.

22. A Curtain of Stones

S. p. 106; Y. p. 242
The superscription reads: "He spoke in describing his entrance into his presence when he kissed him while he lay upon his bed."
*prince of death,* lit. 'first-born of death', cf. Job 18:13.
*cup.* i.e. 'your good fortune', Ps. 16:5. For the usage 'purse or cup' here, cf. 'Eruvin 65b: 'A man is known by three things: his purse, his cup and his temperament.'
*destined,* lit. 'has cast and poured out.'
*and in a little while I . . . drink.* At that time the Nagid was 48 years old (Schirmann).

23. I Carried him to his Grave

S. p. 107; Y. p. 242
The following is the superscription to the poem: "He spoke in describing the dressing [of his brother] in shrouds and his descent into the grave, may God have mercy upon him."
*brother and father.* i.e. the brother who was like a father.
*crushed in judgment.* Cf. Hosea 5:11.
*bear . . . cow . . . vile.* Cf. Is. 11:7–9.
*left side.* The rending of garments by mourners is based on II Samuel 13:31 and is made opposite the heart, cf. Mo'ed Qatan 22b.

*And they said*. The following line in Yarden's text is absent in Schirmann: "And they said: 'They have presented him there as a burnt offering;' (Said he) 'Would that they offered me for a sacrifice as well'."
*Lowered him*. With his own hands the Nagid buried his brother (Schirmann).
*this life*, lit. 'time'.
*after my brother* . . . i.e. after his death.

### 24. A Day Ago I Buried You

S. p. 107; Y. p. 244
The superscription over this elegy reads as follows: "And he visited his grave on the second day after he had buried him therein." The Nagid here follows an ancient Jewish custom of visiting the dead at the cemetery even during the *Shiv'a* (first seven days of mourning). See minor tractate, *S'mahot*, Chap. VIII, 1. quoted in Tur-Yoreh De'a, paragraph section 394.3.
*Lament?* Yarden's text then adds: "How do you sleep in your grave/Upon the dust in the fallen pit?"

### 25. Within the Earth They Have Locked You Up

S. p. 108; Y. p. 246.
The superscription reads: "He journeyed until he approached his burial place whereupon he stopped and said the following:"
*my release*. Lit. 'my change' i.e. my death.

### 26. The Promise

S. p. 78; Y. p. 3
*I remember*. This poem was probably written late in his life when he had already attained high status at court and needed its comforting words on days of 'distress and anguish' to remind him of the vision in his youth. Cf. B. Z. Dinur, *Israel in Exile* (in Hebrew), (Tel-Aviv, 1961), Vol. 1, Book 3, n. 5•, p. 216.
*Michael . . . Gabriel*. In the Book Bahir, a Qabbalistic document which appears in southern France toward the end of the 12th century, Michael is the 'prince of waters' and Gabriel the 'prince of fire,' (Yarden). The 'good tidings' of the two angels are based on Is. 43:2.
*chariot . . . environs*. i.e. in the vicinity of the divine throne. Cf. Ez. 1:1–28 and Mishna Ḥagigah 2.1.
*swords I see* i.e. of my enemies.

### 27. Will You Remember This Only?

S. p. 120; Y. p. 57.
The superscription to the poem reads as follows: "And he recited this (poem) on the way when passing through Jaén [in 1045]. There lay in ambush for him the lord Ben 'Abi Qura [the Berber 'Abu Nur 'ibn 'Abi Qorra, lord of Ronda during 1015 (5)–1053, ally of Mu'tadid of Seville and enemy of the Nagid] with all his armies, horsemen and foot-soldiers. My father fled, may God honor him, and entered into the great and deep river which is there [probably the Guadiara] and God preserved him there. He was saved from them, for the enemy did not intend to enter into the river after him. And he called the name of this poem, *T'ḥinna*."
*Samuel*. The poet addressing himself in the Spanish school used for the first time as here by the Nagid, (Schirmann).
*One . . . Cherubs*. Metaphor for God. Cf. Micah 6:6.
*Lips*. Lit. 'mouth'.

*On the day . . . kings pursued.* A reference to Ben 'Abi Qura and his followers.
*generosity.* Lit. 'hands'.
*light . . . nine months.* Cf. Niddah 30b for the statement that God lights a candle for the child while in the darkness of the mother's womb.
*cheese . . . milk.* Cf. Job 10:10.
*mouth . . . channels.* The child's mouth is closed while in the womb. His navel is open and he is fed thereby by his mother even as his excrement exits in this way. Cf. Niddah, loc. cit.
*your branches were moist.* An image of the young child.
*lands of the west.* i.e. the Maghreb.
*hands . . . shower* i.e. you were generous.
*so as to save a life from the pit.* The courtier's life was always in the balance and an improper word might bring about his downfall.
*heated passions.* Lit. 'battles like flames'.
*wells of rejoicing.* Cf. Is. 12:3.
*words.* Lit. 'a mouth'.
*And they will go.* i.e. God's deeds.
*Zoan . . . Lehabim.* Metaphors for Egypt and Africa respectively cf. Ps. 78:43 and Gen. 10:13 and the Targum Yerushalmi there.
*anxious.* Cf. Is. 66:5.
*broken cistern.* That holds no water, i.e. there is no substance to their argument.
*there are matters in my lines.* It is possible that the Nagid records here the opposition he encountered when he wished to include this *T'ḥinna* into the synagogue worship service together with his *Shira* and *T'hilla.*

## 28. The Mountain of Sand

S. p. 124; Y. p. 62
The poem's superscription reads as follows: "And when he set out to make war against Osuna and Morór he passed by a place where there was much sand, in the year 4806 [1046]. He had once before come by it in the days of his youth while fleeing from Cordova during a great battle. And (now) he spoke the following:"
*alone.* lit. 'with my cane'. Heb. *b'maqli.* Cf. Targum 'Onqelos to Gen. 32:11.
*tens of thousands.* This is certainly an exaggeration (Schirmann).

## 29. The Hour

S. p. 131; A. p. 16
*She said.* a common form of opening a poem in the days of the Nagid. See Abramson, p. 186.

## 30. At Age Sixty

S. p. 131; A. p. 64
*removes my perversity with its own.* The strange power of age sixty is able to remove from the poet 'crooked speech' and 'devious talk'. Cf. Prov. 4:24 (Schirmann).

## 31. In my Latter Days

S. p. 125; Y. p. 121
The superscription for the poem reads: "And he found,—may God honor him, his strength and body weakening from old age in the war that occurred in the summer of the year 4814 [1054] and thereupon recited this poem as one lamenting over himself."
*crocodile . . . mourn.* Cf. Micah 1:8.
*heavens . . . youth.* The poet compares the strength of his youth to the refreshing rain

and old age to the heavens which shut off the rain clouds. Cf. Job 37:11.
*I be in them.* i.e. the graves.
*within my skull.* i.e. only within my skull (Schirmann).
*the day of my fears.* i.e. the day of my death.
*my spirit live . . . (again).* At the resurrection of the dead (Yarden).
"*walk to the ancestors.*" Cf. Gen. 15:15 and I Chron. 17:11.
*that which is tied about me.* i.e. my shrouds.
*without requesting You to give me leave.* Cf. 'Abot 4:22: 'perforce you were created'.
*cause of all that befell me.* i.e. I was free to choose between good and evil.
*house . . . sons of men.* i.e. the graveyard.
*studies . . . investigations in the Torah.* The study of the Torah is 'equivalent' to all commands which 'a man enjoys their fruit in this life while the principle remains for him to all eternity'. Cf. Mishna Pe'ah 1.
*credits . . . transgressions.* Thus according to Yarden's text which reads: me'averai k'shurotai.
*when my lights will be gathered in.* i.e. when he will die. The 'lights' are the sun and moon, (cf. Is. 60:20) which shine for man on earth.

## 32. Rescue at Sea

Y. p. 261; S. p. 79
The following is the poem's superscription: "In his youth he once sailed the sea together with some merchants and there came upon them a beast called Al Ṭina by those knowledgeable in the sea and its life. They were persuaded that a ship has never escaped safely from her once she went out toward it. However, God rescued them from her mighty attack. Thereupon [the Nagid] recited this poem, describing what had happened in that situation and he called it *Todah* [thanksgiving]."
*By my soul etc.* The Nagid contrasts his faith in God with his fellow voyagers lack of it.
*Receive.* Heb. *v'qabbel* according to Yarden's reading.
*Ḥofni.* Cf. I Sam. 2:29ff.
*Zimri.* Numbers 25:1ff.
*'Onan.* Cf. Gen. 38:8.
*does not give birth nor is born.* Cf. *Piyyute Yannai*, Zulay ed. p. 131 and Qur'an 112:3–4 for a similar statement.
*'Qorha.* The name given to the monster, Al Ṭina mentioned in the superscription.
*thunder was a whisper.* i.e. compared to the noise the monster was making.
*Leviathan . . . tortuous serpent.* Cf. Is. 27:1.
*Tyre in the heart of the sea.* The monster was like the island cities of Tyre and Dumah, cf. Ez. 27:32. Cf. also Bar Bar Hana's account of a sea monster which is mistaken for an island in Bava Batra 73b.
*'Ashima.* A god made by the men of Hamath. Cf. II Kings 17:30.
*Jonah . . . spit out.* Cf. Jonah 2:1, 11.
*what . . . expect?* Lit. 'who am I'? i.e. I am not as righteous as the prophet Jonah.
*armies . . . sea.* Cf. Exodus 15:1, 4.
*she submerged.* i.e. Qorḥa.
*Lord rebuked her.* Cf. Ps. 106:9.
*plank of wood . . . pitch.* i.e. the boat.
*suspends them in space.* i.e. the cosmos. Cf. Job 26:7.
*I thank God.* The following lines contain six principles of faith for the Nagid (Schirmann). Cf. also Berachot 54b for the statement that among the four who are obligated to give thanks to God are those who go down to the sea in ships.
*hidden sins,* as well as for those that are manifest (Schirmann), cf. Eccles. 12:14.
*'Ayish and Kimah* - the Bear and Pleiades among the stars, cf. Job 38:31, 32.

33. Establish the Promise

S. p. 146; Y. p. 317
*Lord.* Schirmann thinks that the Nagid composed this as a private prayer for a specific occasion.
*children of Abraham.* lit. 'the children of the father of your multitudes'. Cf. Gen. 17:4, 5.
*'Edom.* Metaphor for the enemies of Israel.
*annul the covenant.* i.e. the pact that Israel's enemies have made in order to destroy her.

34. Answer Me

S. p. 146; Y. p. 319
*Build me up.* Israel is here addressing God. Yarden thinks that the work is an elegy for the Ninth Day of Av.
*heights of your sanctuary.* i.e. upon Zion's mount.
*seal . . . heart.* i.e. as a sign of your love. Cf. Cant. 8:6.
*cup of salvation.* Ps. 116:13.
*nearly a thousand years.* i.e. since the destruction of the Temple in the year 70.

35. Arise, Awake

S. p. 146; Y. p. 318.
*evil queen.* A reference to 'Edom which holds Israel in exile. Cf. Berachot 61b.
*Sarah.* Wife of Abraham, here a metaphor for Israel.
*fawn of S'nir.* A designation for Israel according to Canticles 4:8. At the time of her redemption Israel will descend like a bride from the top of S'nir and Ḥermon.

36. Day of Redemption

S. p. 147; Y. p. 318
*Shake yourself free.* Cf. Is. 52:2. These words are addressed to Israel.
*anguish.* Heb. *ẓir.* This is Yarden's reading which together with the Hebrew *ẓori* (healing) forms a play on words. Schirmann reads *ẓilech* 'your darkness', a metaphor for the exile.
*tossed about . . . reeling.* Metaphor for Israel. Cf. Is. 51:21 and 54:11.
*visible . . . foretold.* The reference is to the redeemer (of Israel) as described by Balaam (Schirmann). Cf. Num. 24:17.
*'rebellious people'.* Cf. Is. 30:9.

37. He Who Stretched Out the Heavens

S. p. 143; Y. p. 322
The poem is called *S'licha* [penitential piyyut] and was recited in the synagogue rituals of Greece, Allepo and Germany on the nights of the month of 'Elul, the Day of Atonement or on Rosh Hashana eve.
*like a tent.* Cf. Is. 40:22.
*glitter of amber.* Heb. *ḥashmal.* God dwells in the center of the chariot-throne 'surrounded by fire and flame'. Cf. Ezekiel 1:1–28.
*no one exits or enters.* i.e. 'no one has access to him'.
*Forgive.* Heb. *s'lach.* This term designates the poem as a *S'licha.*
*God is greatly etc.* Ps. 99:8.
*cloud . . . garment . . . mist.* Cf. Job 38:9.
*light.* Heb. *'nogah'.* Cf. Ezekiel 1:4, 27.
*He who measured.* At the time of creation (Schirmann).
*homer,* Heb. *'b'ḥomer*—a unit of measure (Yarden) cf. Lev. 27:16.

*Who . . . span*, Heb. 'u-mad shaḥaq b'zeret' (Yarden) cf. Is. 40:12.
*waters . . . 'omer*. Heb. 'v'ha-mayim b''omer' (Yarden). CF. Ex. 16:18.
*with his stars*. Heb. 'b'kochavov.' The lines of stars upon the 'skin' of the heavens evoke an image of a leopard's stripes.
*lights . . . green and black*. Cf. Rashi to Ez. 1:14.
*fire rages*. This is possibly a reference to the *hashmal* surrounded by fire mentioned earlier (Schirmann).
*each consumes his neighbor*. The Nagid is here discussing the esoteric doctrines of the *Ma'ase Merkabah*, the description of the chariot-throne in Ezekiel 1:1–28. Speculations concerning this subject-matter were to be transmitted only to those who were worthy and only to one person at a time. Cf. Mishna Ḥagiga 2.1.
*treasured people*. Metaphor for 'Israel'. Cf. Ex. 19:5 and Ps. 135:4.
*look . . . trembles . . . pillars*. Cf. Job 9:6.
*channels . . . water*. Cf. II Sam. 22:16.
*offences . . . forgiveness*. The notion that God's forgiveness is equal to man's sins is found in the Nagid's *Ben Qohelet* #270 as well as in Saadia Gaon and the Arabic poet 'Abu Nuwas (Yarden).
*Send honor*. The change is from third to second person but the subject is the same.
*white . . . red*. Cf. Is. 1:18.
*bill of divorcement*. Cf. Is. 50:1 and Jer. 3:8.
*Betroth her*. Cf. Hosea 2:22.

38. Street Scene

S. p. 133; A. p. 119
*street of butchers*. This is a revealing description of the marketplace, perhaps in Granada, with its separate streets for butchers, fish peddlers and bakers. The Nagid here stresses the unity of all life which ultimately is reduced to 'death and birth, sleeping and waking, sitting and standing.'
*next to it* i.e. the street of the butchers.
*as numerous as the fish of the sea*. The image is one of prosperity (Schirmann).
*their mystery*. This is the 'mystery of the world' which he develops in the following lines and mentions again at the end of the poem. For the Nagid it is the unity of all life forms, from the plant of the 'bakers' through the fish and cattle to man.
*God gave them as food for you*. Since the days of Noah. Cf. Gen. Rabbah 36.6.
*temperament*. Heb. *ruach*.
*know that this is all there is to man* i.e. that which he shares in common with all living creatures.

39. A Study Group in the Synagogue

S. p. 147; Y. p. 228
The Arabic superscription reads: "Upon entering [a house of study] he composed [a poem] about a group of men he heard studying the Talmud and making many errors. He then described them along with their teacher."
*destiny be cruel*. lit. 'will time exalt itself against.'
*Rabbi*. Judah ha-Nasi, redactor of the Mishna. d. after 200.
*Rava*. Babylonian 'Amora of the fourth generation. Among other things he is known for his discussions with 'Abaye. Rava died in 352.
*Mephiboshet*. In Rabbinic literature he is known as an expert in *Halacha* (law). See Berachot 4a.
*Rav Hai Gaon*. He was regarded as the leading Talmudist in his age. When he died in 1038 the Nagid composed elegies in his memory.
*Ziva*. II Sam. 16:1.

*fringes*. Num. 15:37ff.
*Hoshanah Rabbah*. Known as 'the day of the willow.' It is the seventh day of the Sukkot festival when the beating of the willow-sprigs takes place.
*ass . . . oxen*. Metaphors for the study group.
*Talmud*. Heb. 'Bava' refers to any of the three sections: Qama, Meẓi'ah or Batra.
*and I whither shall I go?* Cf. Gen. 37:30.
*Hillel . . . Shammai . . . 'Aqiva*. They are noted authorities frequently cited in the Talmud. For a similar image in Moses Ibn Ezra see Pagis, *op. cit.* p. 304.
*difficulty . . . response*, i.e. the teacher wanted to give the impression that his students understood the texts they were studying (Yarden).
*morning prayers*. lit. '100 blessings'. Cf. M'nachot 43b: "a person is obligated to recite 100 blessings each day".
*And not a woman*. This is one of the blessings that a man recites each morning. Cf. *ibid*.
*testifies . . . woman*. In the Nagid's time women, generally, were not scholars.

## 40. On Parting From Friends

S. p. 149; Y. p. 218
*A pair of evils*, i.e. my silence and my weeping. See below.
*Since you do not look at me*. The poet refrains from sending messengers or letters to his friend not in anger but from envy since they and not he are 'favored by your gaze.' On the theme of parting from friends see also the 11th century Cordovan poet Ibn Zaydun writing to his beloved Wallada in N. Ullah, *Islamic Literature* p. 68.

## 41. Leave the Hidden Things

S. p. 157; Y. p. 279
*leave the hidden things*. Cf. Ḥagigah 13a: "Thus it is written in Ben Siraḥ's book: 'Do not investigate that which is incomprehensible to you and that which is hidden from you do not search out'."
*'alamot*. Cf. Ps. 46:1.
*rule of Qohelet*. i.e. "no one has power over the day of death", cf. Eccles. 8:8. The Nagid here moves from the theme of *carpe diem* (sieze the day, i.e. eat, drink, and be merry for tomorrow you die) to that of *memento mori* (remember your death and therefore repent). Cf. Pagis, *op. cit.* p. 259.

## 42. A Place for Festivities

S. p. 158; Y. p. 280
The poem's superscription reads as follows: "And he recited the poem in which he boasts [of his achievements] and in it he tells of wine (drinking) describing it with consummate skill."
*I prepared a place*. i.e. I invited all the above mentioned to the festivities in my home.
*companionship and life are sisters*. Cf. Ta'anit 23a: "either a companion of death."
*wise*. Heb. "arumin' (Yarden).
*rain . . . hidden plants*. Rain like wine has the power to bring forth that which is hidden. Cf. 'Eruvin 65a: "When wine enters, secrets emerge," (Yarden).
*world's light*. Metaphor for wine.
*brothers-in-law*. i.e. 'Onan and Shelah. Cf. Gen. 38:6–9.
*It was like . . . old man*. i.e. the wine.
*lightning . . . sometimes fails*, But not so the wine. See above Yarden's comment and the citation from 'Eruvin 65a.
*into their bodies*, lit. upon their bodies.
*unable to look upon the heavens*, since their eyes were unaccustomed to the light.

*they go into hiding.* i.e. their intelligence and knowledge (Schirmann).
*wine,* lit. 'depressed'.
*sledge hammer of Ya'el,* The latter slew Sisera at the battle on the Plain of Esdraelon. Cf. Judges 4:21.
*"Give heed to my words . . . "* Here begins the boast referred to in the superscription.
*Q'hot.* son of Levi. Cf. Gen. 46:11.
*M'rari. Ibid.*
*When the nations are assembled,* at the resurrection of the dead.
*Levites . . . priests.* This is Yarden's interpretation. Schirmann reads "Arabs" and "Christian monks" instead of "Levites" and "priests".
*as if laden with guilt.* Therefore they do not speak (Schirmann).

### 43. A Ransom

S. p. 168; Y. p. 305
*Ransom.* i.e. I am willing to sacrifice my life for him (Schirmann).
*young lad.* Heb. 'opher.
*'ud.* The Arabic name for a string instrument in use at that time, cf. S. p. 165, no. 11, l. 4.
*"Drink . . . lips!"* i.e. "Kiss me!"
*wine.* lit. 'blood of grapes' according to Deut. 32:15.
*colors of gold.* lit. 'waters of gold'.

### 44. The Face of Darkness Flees

S. p. 165; Y. p. 295
*Come at dawn.* The drinking parties were often held in the stillness of dawn before the rising of the sun (Schirmann). The Nagid's enemy, the poet 'Ibn 'Abi 'Amar (see above Poem #16) and his circle apparently engaged in similar practices as may be seen from the following: "Turn the cups of wine/ For the night breeze blows/ And the stars arrest their motion/ Soon the dawn will offer it's white camphor/ And the night will withdraw its dark amber." Cf. N. Ullah, *Islamic Literature,* p. 72.
*black man . . . maiden.* On the beauty of young men-slaves many of whom were Negro see, Moses Ibn Ezra, *Shiray ha-Ḥol,* ed. H. Brody vol. 1 (Berlin, 1935) #249.
*hand . . . attire.* Cf. Ps. 45:14.

### 45. Look at the Morning Light

S. p. 165; Y. p. 286
*The call . . . sleep.* According to Yarden this is the friend's reply.
*Who will . . . death.* 'Her lyrics arouse my desire and give me renewed life, even as in the same instant she destroys me by her failure to respond to my entreaties' (Schirmann).

### 46. Gamblers

S. p. 163; Y. p. 290
*subdues . . . them.* This is according to Yarden's reading. Schirmann: 'It rules over heads that have fallen.'
*passing the cup.* In lieu of this reading from Schirmann there is a lacuna in Yarden's text.

### 47. Captured Without A Net

S. p. 167; Y. p. 288
*young lad.* Heb. 'Ẓ'vi'.
*Though waters . . . fires.* Cf. Canticles 8:7.

*My desire . . . flame.* Cf. Jer. 20:9.
*hands . . . gold.* Cf. Canticles 5:14. Schirmann suggests that the love for the cup bearer here is the preparatory stage for the later themes of spiritual love in the Hebrew poetry of the 13th century. Cf. Pagis, *op. cit.* p. 274. On Arabic models of this genre see the Nagid's contemporary Ibn Hazm, *Le Collier du Pigeon,* p. 28.

48. Her Translucent Glass

S. p. 167; Y. p. 290
*fire . . . hail.* Cf. Ex. 9:24.
*threads of scarlet.* Cf. Canticles 4:3.
*palate . . . wine. Ibid.* 7:10, i.e. her kisses are sweet (Schirmann).
*blood of her victims.* Cf. Prov. 7:27. It refers to those who have fallen captive to her beauty.
*half crimson.* The blood from her fingertips has dripped down to cover half of her hand. On this familiar theme see the Umayyad poet, the Caliph Yazid ben Mu'awiya in N. Ullah, *Islamic Literature,* p. 39 and the Andalusians Ibn Quzman and Ibn Sahl, *ibid.* pp. 74–76.

49. Cold Days Have Come

S. p. 167; Y. p. 285
*cold days . . . new wine.* In the time of the Nagid it was customary to give parties at the beginning of winter for the purpose of tasting the new wine (Schirmann).
*do . . . intends.* i.e. to invite them to the party.
*They say:* The poet records the conversation at the party.

50. Pluck the Roses

S. p. 166; Y. p. 285
*young turtle-doves . . . land.* Cf. Canticles 2:12.
*blossoms . . . swallows,* a familiar theme of the period, cf. Pagis, *op. cit.* p. 263.

51. Garments of the King's Daughters

S. p. 166; Y. p. 294
*time is evenly divided,* i.e. in the spring.
*garments . . . king's daughters.* Cf. Ps. 45:14.

52. Among the Spikenard

S. p. 163; Y. p. 287
*bread . . . wine.* Cf. Eccles. 9:7.
*dance . . . gazelle.* Cf. Cant. 2:8, 9.
*mouth . . . filled.* Cf. Ps. 126:2.
*works . . . favor.* Cf. Eccles. 9:7.

53. Left Alone

S. p. 165; Y. p. 294
*drinks . . . heart.* Cf. Eccles. 9:7.
*Pen minus the ink.* A metaphor for the small bow used to play the 'ud.

54. Take a Cup

S. p. 164; Y. p. 284
*young gazelle.* i.e. the boy cup bearer.

*healing balm.* i.e. wine.
*heart.* Heb. *lev.* This is a pivotal word in the poem around which are built such terms as, 'tender hearted', 'sick at heart' and 'men (lit. hearts) will attend him', (Schirmann).
*cup . . . portion.* Ps. 16:5.

55. Drive Away Grief

S. p. 164; Y. p. 291
*happy.* Lit. 'pour happy wine'.
*five things.* The eighth century Persian poet 'Abu Nuwas in his Diwan (Ahlwardt ed. Poem #71 p. 40) speaks of four things that drive away sorrow: water, wine, a garden, and a beautiful face. Cf. Yarden, *ibid.* p. 292.
*a poet.* Heb. *shar.* This is Yarden's reading. Schirmann reads, *shir,* a poem.

56. Among the Ruins

S. p. 162; Y. p. 288
*Light wine.* Lit. 'golden waters'.
*light . . . dark.* The poem is a study in contrasts between light and dark, the storm and the calm, the ruins and the threat of destruction and the warm company of friends drinking happily. The theme of drinking to such an extent that you know not how to distinguish etc. is probably based on Megilla 7b where on Purim one should continue to imbibe until he know not the difference between Haman and Mordecai.

57. A Fire I See

S. p. 162; Y. p. 289
*Grapes.* Heb. 'eshkol.
*children of 'Eshkol.* i.e. merchants. Cf. Gen. 14:13. The Canaanites descended from 'Eshkol. The poet in a play on words is using the term, 'Children of 'Eshkol' in lieu of 'Canaanites' to signify 'merchants' after Proverbs 31:24.
*fire . . . consumed.* Cf. Ex. 3:2. The image of the 'burning bush' is probably intentional and is designed to convey the notion that even as Israel is redeemed from slavery as a result of the words that issue from the flaming bush so too are the 'oppressed' aided by the 'fire' in their cups of wine.

58. Let This be the Reward

S. p. 161; Y. p. 286.
*upon him lie.* i.e. upon God; its origin probably lies in the early 'honorific sacrifice' characterized by the formula *do ut des,* ('I give that you may give').
*a time for God.* Cf. Pesachim 68b.
*music with your jugs.* i.e. from the sound of pouring wine.
song . . . *wine . . . friend.* This is clearly related to the familiar phrase, 'wine, woman and song' in both the English and German, see S. *ibid.* The theme is *carpe diem.*

59. Today

S. p. 138; A. p. 157
*today.* i.e. at the time of my need (Abramson).

60. When You Are Poor

S. p. 138.
*a lion's back.* i.e. place yourself in danger. It is possible that the above may have influenced a similar statement by the 12th century Joseph Ibn Zabara. See Abramson, *Ben Mishle,*

p. 372. The Rabbis made every effort to discourage people from becoming public charges. Cf. Shabbat 118a.

61. Because of His Wealth

S. p. 138; A. p. 62.
*the rich man's friends.* Cf. Prov. 14:20.

62. My Son

S. p. 138; A. p. 60.
*experiment by drinking deadly drugs.* This is comparable to taking 'women into your confidence'. A familiar conceit in both Hebrew and Arabic literature of this period. Cf. Abramson, *Ben Mishle,* p. 373, note to #215.

63. Beware of the Poet

S. 139; A. p. 184
*He will incite you.* The poet's rhetoric is suspect. Exaggeration and the use of lies was not only 'permitted' the Andalusian poets but was accepted as a standard form. Cf. Pagis, *op. cit.* pp. 42, 46–51.

64. Woman

S. p. 141; A. p. 210
*Her face . . . highways.* A familiar conceit of the period. Cf. al-Mutanabbi's observation: 'Those who have experienced women know that outwardly they are brightness but inwardly, darkness!' See. N. Ullah, *Islamic Literature,* p. 58.

65. The Baby Birds

S. f. 139; A. p. 84.

66. In Their Cups

S. p. 140; A. p. 73.
*it is seen in the cup.* i.e. when it sparkles in the cup. Cf. Prov. 23:31.
*tarry. Ibid.* 23:30.
*hurt . . . quarrels. Ibid.* 23:29.
*deed of Cain.* i.e. to murder. Although the Nagid makes a distinction between the 'social' drinker and the habitual drunk (see note to following poem) he nevertheless shows considerable ambivalence on the subject which S. Abramson sees as part of his humanity. Cf. A. p. 371.

67. The Habitual Drunk

*My son.* The reference here is not to the Nagid's son but to one who drinks excessively (Schirmann).
*awakened him.* i.e. the drunkard. Apparently the Nagid makes a distinction between the habitual drunk whose habit leads him to poverty and loss of status and the 'social' drinker.

68. War the Maiden

S. p. 142; A. p. 295

69. The Gored Lion

S. p. 139; A. p. 58

70. The Edge of His Pen

S. p. 141; A. p. 340
*With it . . . king.* The reference here is to the art of Arabic calligraphy which was a highly prized skill in the author's day. According to Abraham Ibn Daud, Ibn Nagrela's rise in the Granadan court was due to his writing skill and on the strength of this Judah Ibn Tibbon in his Testament recommends it to his son. Cf. A. p. 433.

71. With Good Fortune

S. p. 137; A. p. 98
*load . . . moisture.* Cf. Job 37:11
*Euphrates.* The river whose waters are sweet.

72. You are Angry with Me

S. p. 154; Y. p. 297
*gazelle.* Metaphor for the beloved. Heb. *ẓ'vi.* Cf. Cant. 2:9 where both the Hebrew terms *ẓ'vi* and *'opher* are used as similes for the beloved.
*is gathering . . . garden.* The poet is telling his friend that he will now have to share his love with the 'gazelle'.
*When he said.* i.e. the 'gazelle'.
*"Kiss me . . . tongue"* Lit. 'give me the honey from your tongue'.
*sin be upon me.* Cf. I Sam. 25:24.

73. I Have Shown You A Fawn

S. p. 155; Y. p. 301
*fawn.* Metaphor for the young lad, the object of the poet's love.
*bring sorrow to your heart.* The poet hopes that his friend will also fall captive to the charms of the "fawn."
*brought grief to me.* The friend has not reciprocated the love of the poet.
*The Lord.* Lit. 'Blessed is He'. In spite of his disappointment the poet gives thanks to God and accepts his grief with benevolence (Schirmann).
*with one.* lit. 'with one arrow'. The term is a metaphor for the gaze of his eye.
*slay.* i.e. make sick with love for you.

74. The Gazelle That Stutters

S. p. 156; Y. p. 296
*gazelle that stutters.* These were the ornately dressed cupbearers, who by stuttering were able to draw attention to themselves. The Arabs would frequently train young maids for this purpose whom they would dress in boy's clothing and have them serve at their parties. The Nagid here is following in this tradition (Schirmann).
*gazelle . . . fawn.* Metaphors for the cup bearers.
*the moon.* i.e. the cup bearer.
*relied upon him.* Cf. Jer. 8:7.
*"evil" . . . "touch"* The former in Hebrew is *'ra"* while the latter is *'ga"*.
*"stop".* Heb. *'surah'*.
*"belly".* Heb. *'sugah'*. The stuttering cup-bearer confused the Hebrew letter 'resh' with the 'gimel'.
*fenced . . . lilies.* Cf. Cant. 7:3.

75. How Shall I Repay my Friend

S. p. 156; Y. p. 309
*to grief?* The poet is unhappy because his love for the "friend" is unrequited.
*glory . . . shame.* Cf. Hosea 4:7.
*kiss my hand.* This act will reveal my love for him.

76. Be Gentle

S. p. 155; Y. p. 299
*physician . . . charmer?* though you have the power to cure me (Yarden).
*drink . . . from my lips.* i.e. kiss you.

77. All Young Lovers

S. p. 155; Y. p. 301
*young dove.* Metaphor for the beloved.
*young lovers,* lit. 'gazelle'.
*are unfaithful.* On this familiar theme of the period see Pagis, *op. cit.* p. 270.
*punish me instead,* lit. 'blot me out.' Cf. Ex. 32:32.

78. One Heart Rejoined

S. p. 153; Y. p. 314
*Sabeans.* Cf. Job 1:15, and Rashi *ad loc.* who says that the reference is to the kingdom of the Queen of Sheba. According to Rabbinic tradition Job was said to have lived during her reign. Cf. Bava Batra 15b. Here, the term is used to designate robbers in the wilderness, (Yarden).
*my inmost secrets.* Lit. 'the secrets of my heart'.
*The hearts that were severed.* The friends of the poet tell him about lovers who were reunited after a separation and urge him to do likewise.
[*Like the . . . singing*]. This is Schirmann's suggested reading for this missing line in the one surviving manuscript of this poem.
*That two sections . . . sundered.* In the manuscript this last line is written in the Arabic.

79. One Chain of Your Neck

S. p. 153; Y. p. 297
*captive in the pit.* A metaphor for the love he bears for the 'beloved'.
*inform him thus.* i.e. that you will favor him.
*blood of fawns.* The 'fawn' here is a metaphor for the young men who have fallen in love with the 'beloved'. The 'blood of fawns' is used to designate their sorrow after having been rejected by the 'beloved'.
*one chain of your neck.* Cf. Cant. 4:9.

80. Be Merciful

S. p. 152; Y. p. 308
*his blood.* Cf. 'the blood of fawns' above.

81. You Take Lightly My Feelings

S. p. 152; Y. p. 306
*"For whom?"* i.e. she did not take me seriously.
*loveliest of women,* lit. 'the daughters of stars.' Cf. Job 38:32.
*kiss their hands.* i.e. to symbolize their deep longing for me, see above poem #75.

82. Where Once You Walked

S. p. 151–2; Y. p. 299
*hill of frankincense.* The landscape of lovers. Cf. Cant. 4:6, 14.
*insults . . . furrows.* The friends of the poet mock him because he is so helplessly in love. Cf. Ps. 129:3.
*black paint . . . redness.* You are beautiful enough without them (Yarden).

83. The Jasmine

S. p. 151; Y. p. 278
The superscription reads: "And he said, may God glorify him, upon (seeing) a flower called jasmine the following three stanzas."
*young man . . . blood.* The reference is to the the young "gazelle" who captures the hearts of men with his beauty even as does the jasmine.

84. The Choice he Made

S. p. 130; A. p. 23
*death.* lit. 'destruction'. Cf. I Sam. 5:11.
*is named tomorrow.* i.e. one cannot expect tomorrow to be any different than the days that have passed (Abramson).

85. The Ages of Man

S. p. 131; A. p. 33
The theme of the poem is 'The Ages of Man'. It appears first in Hebrew literature in the statement of R. Judah ben Temah in 'Abot 5.21. It occurs also in later Rabbinic literature (Qohelet Rabbah, Chap. 1), in Hebrew poetry (Abraham Ibn Ezra, Davidson, Thesaurus, Letter Bet. #853) and in world literature (Shakespeare, As You Like it, Act II, Scene 7).
*is seen among the holy ones.* Abramson suggests the Heb. reading *nir'eh* (is seen). Schirmann's reading is *nich'eh* (is depressed).
*for amazement.* i.e. to wonder at him.

86. Without Using Words

S. p. 134; A. p. 126
*others will dwell therein!"* The above possibly influended a similar statement by the 13th century Judah Al-Harizi. See Abramson, *Ben Qohelet,* p. 254.

87. Every Branch

S. p. 133; A. p. 9
*love your days,* i.e., 'who chase after the vanities of the times' (Schirmann). In line with this, it is noteworthy that Abramson mentions an alternate reading, *'ohve ḥayyim'* (you who love life). See his *Ben Qohelet,* p. 176.
*from the beginning you are consigned to death.* Lit. 'you are from death's root'.

88. When Death Comes

S. p. 136; A. p. 50
*as one man.* Cf. Judges 20:11
*Weep while you yet live.* Since you will be quickly forgotten after your death (Abramson).

89. I Am Old Enough

S. p. 135; A. p. 155
Yes, *I am old enough, etc.* Cf. Sanhedrin 52a.

90. I Watch the Sky

S. p. 136; A. p. 11
*heavens . . . hooks.* The image is taken from Ex. 26:4–6. The poet follows here the Biblical cosmology which viewed the earth as a flat disc overlaid by the heavens in the form of an inverted bowl.
*their courtyards, their mangers.* i.e. the former is to men what the latter is to animals.

91. The Night in the Fortress

S. p. 132; A. p. 50
*slumbered below,* in their graves.
*the bereaved and the bridegrooms.* Cf. Shabbat 114a (end). The theme is *ubi sunt.* It was frequently used by the Andalusians. Cf. Pagis, *op. cit.* pp. 107 and 231.

92. A Scandal

S. p. 130; A. p. 152
Y. Ratzabi gives a parallel to the above from Arabic sources:
When your mother gave birth to you, you cried
While around you people rejoiced
Be proficient in (good) works so that when they weep
On the day of your death, you may rejoice.
Cf. Ratzabi, *op. cit.* p. 307.

93. More Distant Than Yesterday

S. p. 135; A. p. 102.
*the grave.* The Hebrew *qubbah* refers to a building with a cupola. It is likely that here the reference is to a grave with a covering sepulchre.

94. We are Surrounded

S. p. 129–30; Y. p. 329; A. p. 97.
*surrounded by a fence.* In *Ben Qohelet* #38 the poet speaks of the earth as man's prison house, since wherever he runs the heavens are always above him. It is likely that the same image is intended here.
*spheres.* i.e. the spheres of the heavens.
*cannot be breached,* because of the 'fence' which keeps man on earth.
*yellow . . . white . . .* egg. Cf. Niddah 31a. The poet here continues the image of man locked up in his world.
*God's works . . . preceded us.* And there is no changing them.

95. Man's Sojourn

S. p. 130; A. p. 143
*in a world,* lit. 'in his worlds'. Abramson thinks that it refers to 'the seven worlds which a person sees in his lifetime'. Cf. Eccles. Rabbah Chap. 1, (beginning). Schirmann states that the reference is to this world.

# Bibliography

*Tannaitic, Amoraic, and Anonymous Rabbinic Sources*

*Abot de R. Nathan.* Edited by S. Schechter. Vienna, 1887.

*Babylonische Talmud.* Edited by Lazarus Goldschmidt. 9 Vols. Leipzig, Berlin and The Hague, 1906–1935.

*Bereschit Rabbah.* Edited by J. Theodor and C. Albeck. Berlin, 1903–1931.

*Mekilta de-Rabbi Ishmael.* Edited by J. Z. Lauterbach. 3 Vols. Philadelphia, 1933–1935.

*Midrash Debarim Rabbah.* Edited by S. Liebermann. Jerusalem, 1940.

*Midrash Echah Rabbati.* Edited by S. Buber. Vilna, 1899.

*Midrash Haggadol. Genesis.* Edited by M. Margulies. Jerusalem, 1947. *Exodus.* Edited by M. Margulies. Jerusalem, 1956. *Leviticus.* Edited by E. N. Rabinowitz, New York, 1932. *Numbers.* Edited by S. Fisch. 2 Vols. London and Jerusalem, 1957–63.

*Midrash Rabbah.* 2 Vols. Vilna, 1878. Facsimile edition: New York, 1952.

______ Edited by C. Albeck. 7 Vols. Jerusalem, 1952–1959.

*The Passover Haggadah.* Edited and translated by N. Glatzer. New York, 1953.

*Pesiqta de R. Kahana.* Edited by S. Buber. Luck, 1868.

______ Edited by B. Mandelbaum. 2 Vols. New York, 1962.

*Sifra-de-Bay Rab.* Edited by I. H. Weiss. Vienna, 1862. Facsimile edition: New York, 1946.

*Tosefta.* Edited by M. S. Zuckermandel. Jerusalem, 1938.

______ *Zera'im and Moed.* Edited by S. Lieberman. 2 Vols. New York, 1955–62.

II

GAONIC AND POST-GAONIC AND GENERAL WORKS:
TEXTS AND SECONDARY SOURCES

Altmann, A., "Shire Q'dusha B'Sifrut ha-Hekhalot ha-Q'dumah," *Melilah II*, Manchester (1945).

Azriel, R. Abraham b. R., *Sefer 'Arugat Habosem*, 4 volumes, Ed. E. E. Urbach (Jerusalem), 1939–63.

Abel, A., "Spain: Internal Division," in G. E. von Grunbaum, *Unity and Variety in Muslim Civilization*. Chicago, 1955.

Ashtor, E., *Qorot ha-Yehudim bi-Sefarad ha-Muslimit.* Vol. I Jerusalem (1960).

Assaf, S., "New Documents for the History of the Jews in Palestine and Egypt," A review of Gottheil-Worrell's *Fragments from the Cairo Genizah in the Freer Collection*, Zion (O.S.), II (1927–28), 111–22.

______ *Tequfat ha-Geonim we-Sifrutah.* Ed., M. Margalioth. Jerusalem, 1955.

Baer, F. T., *A History of the Jews in Christian Spain*, I, Philadelphia, 1961.

______, "The Political Situation of the Spanish Jews in the Age of Jehuda Halevi" (in Hebrew), *Zion*, I (1935–36).

Bargebuhr, F. B., "The Alhambra Palace of the Eleventh Century," *Journal of the Warburg and Courtauld Institutes*, XIX (1956).

Baron, S. W., *A Social and Religious History of the Jews*, 8 vols. and Index vol., Philadelphia, 1952–60.

Ben Iehuda, E., *Thesaurus Totius Hebraitatis.* 17 vols. Jerusalem, 1948–1959.

Ben-Sasson, H. H., "Exile and Redemption Through the Eyes of the Spanish Exiles" (in Hebrew), *I. F. Baer Jublee Volume.* Jerusalem, 1960.

Benjamin of Tudela, *Itinerary.* Translated by M. N. Adler. London, 1907.

Bernstein, S., *'Al Naharot Sefarad.* Tel Aviv, 1956.

Bloch, A., "Zur altarabischen Spruchdichtung", *Westöstliche Abhandlugen.* Wiesbaden, 1953, 181–224.

Brody and Wiener, *Mibchar ha-Shirah ha-Ivrit* (Leipzig, 1922).
Brockelmann, C., *History of the Islamic Peoples.* Translated by J. Carmichael and M. Perlmann. New York, 1944.
Cantera, F. and Millas, J. M., *Las Inscripciones Hebraicas de España.* Madrid, 1956.
Caskel, W., *Das Schicksal in der altarabischen Poesie.* Leipzig, 1926.
Castro, A., *The Structure of Spanish History.* Princeton, 1954.
Davidson, I., *Thesaurus of Medieval Hebrew Poetry.* 4 vols. New York, 1924–33.
Dinur, B. Z., *Israel ba-Gola.* 2nd edition. 6 vols. Tel Aviv, 1961–68.
Dozy, R., *Histoire des Musulmans d'Espagne.* New Edition. Edited by E. Levi-Provencal. 3 vols. Leiden. 1932.
———, English translation of the earlier 3rd edition by G. Stokes under the title *Spanish Islam.* London, 1913.
———, *Recherches sur l'Histoire et la Littérature de L'Espagne pendant le Moyen Age.* 3rd edition. 2 vols. Leiden, 1881.
Elbogen, I., *Der juedische Gottesdienst* (Frankford, 1931).
Even-Shmuel, J., *Midreshay Geulah.* 2nd Edition. Jerusalem, 1954.
Garcia Gomez, E., "Polemica Religiosa entre Ibn Hazm e Ibn Nagrela," *Al-Andalus,* IV (1936–39).
Gibb, H.A.R. and Kramers, J. N., eds., *Shorter Encyclopedia of Islam.* Leiden, 1953.
Ginzberg, L., *A Commentary on the Palestinian Talmud* (in Hebrew). 4 vols. New York, 1941–61.
———, *Genizah Studies* (in Hebrew). 2 vols. New York, 1928–29.
———, *Geonica.* 2 vols. New York, 1909.
———, *The Legends of the Jews.* 7 vols. Philadelphia, 1909–38.
Goitein, S. D., "Jewish Community Organization in the Light of the Cairo Geniza Documents" (in Hebrew), *Zion,* XXVI (1960–61).
———, *Jewish Education in Muslim Countries* (in Hebrew). Jerusalem, 1962.
———, "From the Mediterranean to India," *Speculum,* XXIX (1954).
———, "Who Was the First Nagid? " (in Hebrew), *Zion,* XXVII (1961–62).
———, *A Mediterranean Society,* California, 1967, Vol. 1.
Goldziher, I., "Bemerkungen zur arabischen Trauerpoesi", *WZKM,* Bk. 16 (1902) 307–339.
Graetz, H., *Geschichte der Juden.* 11 vols. Leipzig, 1897–1911.
Grunebaum, G. E. von, *Medieval Islam.* 2nd edition. Chicago, 1953.
———, *Kritik und Dichtkunst.* Studien zur arabischen Literaturgeschichte. Wiesbaden, 1955.
———,*A Tenth-Century Document of Arab Literary Theory and Criticism,* (Chicago 1950)
Habermann, A. M., "Yehosef bar Samuel ha-Nagid," *Tesoro de los Judios Sefardies,* IV (1901).
———, *Toldot ha-Piyyut v'ha-Shirah* (Ramat Gan, 1970).
Halkin, A. S., "Judeo-Arabic Literature," *The Jews: Their History, Culture and Religion.* 2 vols. Edited by L. Finkelstein. New York, 1949.
———, "The Judeo-Islamic Age," *Great Ages and Ideas of the Jewish People.* Edited by L. W. Schwarz. New York, 1956.
Hanagid, Divan Shmuel, *Ben Tehilim,* ed. Dov Yarden (Jerusalem, 1966).
al-Ḥarizi, Judah *Taḥkemoni.* Edited by Y. Toporowsky. Tel-Aviv, 1952.
Harkavy, A. A., "Le-Toledot R. Samuel ha-Nagid," *Meassef.* Edited by L. Rabinowicz. St. Petersburg, 1902.
———, *Zikron la-Rishonim.* 6 vols. St. Petersburg and Berlin, 1879–1903.
*Hebrew, Ethical Wills.* 2 vols. Edited and translated by I. Abrahams. Philadelphia, 1926.
Heinemann, J., *Prayer in the Period of the Tanna'im and the Amoraim* (in Hebrew) (Jerusalem, 1966) 2nd edition.
Ibn Daud, Abraham, *Sefer ha-Qabbalah,* ed. G. Cohen (Philadelphia, 1967).

Ibn Ezra, Moses, *Collected Liturgical Poems* (in Hebrew). Edited by S. Bernstein, Tel Aviv, 1957.

———, *Kitab al-Mudhadarat w'al-Mudhakarat.* Translated into Hebrew under the title *Shirat Israel,* by B. Z. Halper. Leipzig, 1923–24.

———, *Shiray ha-Hol.* Edited by H. Brody. 2 vols. Berlin-Jerusalem, 1935–41.

Ibn Gabirol, Solomon, *Shiray Solomon b. Judah Ibn Gabirol.* Edited by H. N. Bialik and I. H. Ravnitzky. 3 vols. Berlin and Tel Aviv, 1923/24–31/32.

Ibn H'azm al-Andalusi, *Le Collier du Pigeon (T'awq al-H'amama)* ed. by L. Bercher, Alger, 1949.

Ibn al-Khatib, Muhammad, *Histoire de l'Espagne Musulmane. Extraite du Kitab A'mal al-A'lam.* Edited by E. Levi-Provencal. Rabat, 1934.

Ibn Nagrela, Samuel, *Diwan.* Edited by D. S. Sassoon. London, 1934.

Ibn Shahin, *Ḥibbur Yafeh me-ha-Yeshu'ah.* Edited by H. Z. Hirschberg, Jerusalem, 1954.

Ibn Verga, Solomon, *Shebet Yehuda.* Edited by A. Shohet and Y. Baer, Jerusalem, 1946–47.

Jellinek, A., *Bet-ha-Midrash.* 2nd Edition. 6 Vols. Jerusalem, 1938.

*Josippon.* Edited by H. Hominer. Jerusalem, 1956.

Judah b. Barzillai al-Barceloni, *Commentar zum Sepher Jeẓira* (in Hebrew). Edited by S. J. Halberstamm. Berlin, 1885.

Judah ha-Levi, *Diwan.* Edited by H. Brody. 4 Vols. Berlin. 1901–30.

Kahle, Paul, *Masoreten des Westens* II (Stutgart, 1930).

———, *The Cairo Geniza.* 2nd Edition. (Oxford, 1959).

Kasowski, C. F., *Thesaurus Talmudis.* 16 Vols. (Jerusalem, 1954–66).

Kaufman, Y., *Golah we-Nekar.* 2 Vols. Tel Aviv, 1929–32.

Klar, B., *Mehqarim we-'Iyyunim.* (Jerusalem, 1954).

Klein, S., *Toldot ha-Yishuv ha-Yehudi B'Eretz Yisroel.* (Tel-Aviv 1935).

Levi della Vida, G., "La Traduzione Araba della Storie di Orosio," *Al-Andalus.* XIX, (1954).

———, "The Bronze Era in 'Moslem' Spain," *JAOS* LXIII (1943).

Levi-Provencal, E., *La Civilisation Arabe en Espagne, Vue Générale.* 3rd Edition. (Paris, 1961).

———,*Historire de l'Espagne Musulmane.* 3 Vols. Paris, 1950–53.

———, "Les 'Mémoires' de 'Abd Allah, Dernier Roi Ziride de Grenade," *Al-Andalus,* III (1953); IV (1936–39).

Levy, R., *The Social Structure of Islam.* (Cambridge, 1957).

Lewin, B. M., *Otzar ha-Geonim.* 13 Vols. (Haifa-Jerusalem, 1928–43).

Lichtenstädter, I., "Das Nasib der altarabischen Qaside," *Islamica,* Bd. 5, (1932), 17–66.

Lieberman, S., *Greek and Hellenism in Jewish Palestine* (in Hebrew). (Jerusalem, 1962).

———, *Hayerushalmi Kiphshuto.* (Jerusalem, 1934).

Luzzato, S. D., *Bet ha-Oṣar.* 3 Vols. Lemberg, Premysl, 1847–49.

———, *Mavo L'Maḥzor B'net Roma.* Edited by E. D. Goldschmidt (Jerusalem, 1965).

Mahdi, M., *Ibn Khaldun's Philosophy of History.* (Chicago, 1957).

Maimonides, Moses, *Epistle to Yemen,* Edited by A. S. Halkin, New York, 952.

———, Mishneh Torah. 5 Vols. (New York, 1947).

Mann, J., *The Bible as Read and Preached in the Old Synagogue.* Cincinnati, 1940).

———, *The Jews in Egypt and Palestine Under the Fatimid Caliphs.* 2 Vols. (Oxford, 1920–22).

——— "The Response of the Babylonian Geonim as a Source of Jewish History," JQR, NS VII–XI (1916–22).

———, *Texts and Studies in Jewish History and Literature.* 2 Vols. (Cincinnati and Philadelphia, 1931–35).

Margalioth, *Hilkhot Hannagid.* Jerusalem, 1962.

———, "Mo'adim we-Ṣomoth be-Eres Israel U-be-Babel bi-Tequfat ha-Geonim," Aresheth, 1943–44.

———, The Differences Between Babylonian and Palestinian Jews (in Hebrew). Jerusalem, 1938.
Mehren, A. F., *Die Rhetorik der Araber*. Kopenhagen-Wien, 1853.
Mirsky, A., "The Origins of the Forms of Liturgical Poetry" (in Hebrew), *Studies of the Research Institute for Hebrew Poetry in Jerusalem*, VII (1958).
Mommsen, T. H., *Medieval and Renaissance Studies*. Edited by E. F. Rice, Jr., Ithaca, 1959.
Munk, S., *Mélanges de Philosophie Juive et Arabe*. Paris, 1859.
Nahmanides, Moses, *Sefer ha-Geulah*. Edited by I. M. Aronson. Jerusalem, 1958.
Neubauer, A., *Medieval Jewish Chronicles*. 2 Vols. Oxford 1887–95.
Nicholson, R. A., *A Literary History of the Arabs*. Cambridge, 1956.
Nykl, A. R., *Hispano-Arabic Poetry*. Baltimore, 1946.
Obermann, J., *Studies in Islam and Judaism. The Arabic Original of Ibn Shahin's Book of Comfort*. New Haven, 1933.
Pagis, Dan, *Secular Poetry and Poetic Theory: Moses Ibn Ezra and His Contemporaries*, Jerusalem, 1970.
Pérès, H., *La Poésie Andalouse en Arabe Classique* 2nd ed., Paris, 1953.
Perlmann, M., "Eleventh Century Authors on the Jews of Granada," *PAAJR*, XVIII (1949).
Posnanski, A., *Schiloh*. Leipzig, 1904.
al-Qirqisani, Ya'qub, *Kitab al-Anwar wal-Maraqib*. Edited by L. Nemoy. 5 Vols. New York, 1936–43.
Ratzabi, I., "On the Sources of 'Ben Mishle' and 'Ben Qohelet' " (in Hebrew), *Tarbiẓ*, Vol. 25 (1956) pp. 301–322).
———, "The Translation of Lamentations by R. Saadya Gaon" (in Hebrew), *Tarbiẓ*, XII (1941–42).
Ringgren, H., *Studies in Arabian Fatalism*. Uppsala-Wiesbaden, 1955.
Rosenthal, E.I.J., *Political Thought in Medieval Islam*. Cambridge, 1958.
Saadiah b. Joseph al-Fayyumi, *The Book of Beliefs and Opinions*, (New Haven, 1948).
———, *Siddur R. Saadja Gaon*. Edited by I. Davidson et. al. Jerusalem, 1941.
Sassoon, S. D., *Ohel David*. 2 Vols. Oxford, 1932.
Schechter, S., *Aspects of Rabbinic Theology*. New York, 1961.
Schirmann, J., "The Function of the Hebrew Poet in Medieval Spain," *Jewish Social Studies*, XVI (1954).
———, "Poets Contemporary with Moses ibn Ezra and Jehuda Hallevi" (in Hebrew), *Studies of the Research Institute for Hebrew Poetry*, II (1936), IV (1938), VI (1945).
———, "Qinot 'al ha-Gezerot be-Ereṣ Israel, Africa, Sefarad etc., "*Kobez al Jad*, III (XIII) (1939).
———, "Samuel Hannagid, The Man, The Soldier, The Politician," *Jewish Social Studies*, XIII (1051).
———, *Ha-Shirah ha-Ibrit bi-Sefared u-bi-Provence*. 2 Vols. Jerusalem and Tel Aviv, 1954–56.
———, "The Wars of Samuel Ha-Nagid" (in Hebrew), *Zion*, I.
———, "Hebrew Liturgical Poetry and Christian Hymnology", *J.Q.R.* Vol. XLIV (October, 1953) 123-161.
———, "L'amour spirituel dans la poésie hébraïque du moyen âge," *Les Lettres Romanes*, XV (1961), pp. 315–325.
———, "The Ephebe in Medieval Hebrew Poetry", *Sefarad*, XV (1955) pp. 55–68.
———, "Samuel Hannagid as Poet" (in Hebrew), *K'nesset*, Vol. 2 (1937) pp. 393–416.
———, *New Hebrew Poems from the Geniza*. (Jerusalem, 1965).
*Seder R. Amram ha-Shalem*. Edited by L. Frumkin. 2 Vols. Jerusalem, 1912.
Silver, A. H., *A History of Messianic Speculation in Israel*. (New York, 1927).
Spiegel, S., "On Medieval Hebrew Poetry," *The Jews, Their History, Culture and Religion*. Edited by L. Finkelstein, 2 Vols. New York, 1949.

Steinscheider, M., *Die Arabische Literatur der Juden*. Frankfurt A. M., 1902.
———, *Die Hebraeischen Uebersezungen des Mittelalters*. Berlin, 1893.
———, "An Introduction to the Arabic Literature of the Jews," *JQR*, XI (1899).
———, *Polemische and Apologetische Literatur in Arabischen Sprache*. Leipzie, 1877.
Ullah, N., *Islamic Literature* (New York, 1963).
Waxman, M., *A History of Jewish Literature* (New York, 1960) Vol. 1.
Weinberger, L. J., "Shirim Ḥadashim Mehatequfah ha-Bizantinit," *Hebrew Union College Annual*, 1968 and 1972.
———, "A Note on Jewish Scholars and Scholarship in Byzantium," *Journal of the American Oriental Society*, 91.1 (1971).
Weiss, J. F., "Tarbut Ḥaṣranit we-Shirah Ḥaṣranit," *World Congress of Jewish Studies*, Vol. 1 (Jerusalem, 1947).
Wertheimer, S. A., *Battay Midrashot*. 2 Vols. Jerusalem 1950–53.
Zulay, M., "Lashon ha-Payettanim" Moznayim, Vol. 16 (Tel Aviv, 1943), 217-223)
———, "Iyyune Lashon B'Piyyute Yannai" *SHIRP* Vol. 6 (Jerusalem, 1945), pp. 161–248.
———, *Piyyute Yannai* (Berlin, 1938).
———, *Ha-Askolah Ha-Paytanit Shel Rav Sa'adya Gaon* (Jerusalem, 1964).
Zunz, L., *Die Synagogale Poesie des Mittelalters*. 2nd edition. Edited by A. Freimann. Frankfurt, A. M., 1920.
———, *Literaturgeschichte der synagogalen Poesie* (Berlin, 1965).

## Abbreviations

A. *R. Shmuel Hannagid, Ben Mishle*, ed. S. Abramson (Tel-Aviv, 1948)

A. *R. Shmuel Hannagid, Ben Qohelet*, ed. S. Abramson (Tel-Aviv, 1953)

B. *Mibchar ha-Shirah ha-Ibrit*, ed. Brody and Wiener (Leipzig, 1922)

S. Ch. Schirmann, *Ha-Shirah ha-Ibrit bi-Sefarad u-bi-Provence*, 2 Vols. (Jerusalem and Tel-Aviv), 1954–6.

Y. *Divan Shmuel Hanagid, Ben Tehilim*, ed. D. Yarden (Jerusalem, 1966)

SRIHP. *Studies of the Research Institute for Hebrew Poetry*, 7 Vols. (Berlin-Jerusalem, 1933–58)